Alexander Vance

Romantic Episodes of Chivalric and Mediaeval France

Alexander Vance

Romantic Episodes of Chivalric and Mediaeval France

ISBN/EAN: 9783337048228

Printed in Europe, USA, Canada, Australia, Japan

Cover: Foto ©ninafisch / pixelio.de

More available books at **www.hansebooks.com**

PREFACE.

WING to a refidence of many years abroad, as well in the capital as provinces of France, it was my fortune to come by, one way or another, a fomewhat unufual amount of old-world, pleafant, rare, and curious Gallic lore. And fhould there be any little felicity obfervable in the method by which fuch acquirement is now being fubmitted to the reader, it may fafely be traced to an anfwering familiarity with the poets and writers of an age more emphatically known as *The Elizabethian*: one ftill retaining much in common, not only in its outer but inner life, with the faft receding "days of chivalry;" and

hence, as on various other grounds, *the latest and only English* to which any *earlier* or contemporary standard classic could, to be done any sort of justice to, be brought down to.

I had originally intended to have prefixed to the work, sketches, more or less succinct, of the various authors therein abstracted from. But coming to reflect upon the number of excellent biographical dictionaries and lives about, most of which are, or, at any rate, *should be*, on the shelf of all pretending to the education of an English gentleman or lady, I gave the idea up.

The few pages of *Montaigne*, little as they may have of "episode," philosophically viewed, have so much of "romantic" about them, that, however out of *place*, out of *keeping* I am willing to believe they will hardly seem, at least to the more gentle and meditative reader.

CONTENTS.

		PAGE
Preface.		iii
Ordinance of Duels, with the Ceremonies enjoined in all cafes of Mortal Combat.	Favyn — Le Théâtre d'Honneur et de la Chevalerie	1
Ceremonies attendant on the Degradation of a Knight.	Favyn — Le Théâtre d'Honneur et de la Chevalerie	18
Glimpfe at the Life of a Gallant of the Court of Henri IV.	Mémoires du Marefchal de Baffompierre	24
The final Combat between Damp Abbot and the Lord de Saintré.	Hiftoire de Jehan de Saintré.	44
Death of the Count de Buren	Brantôme — Hommes Illuftres	65
A grand, and a fublime Apoftrophe	Fabliaux ou Contes du xiie et xiiie Siècles	71
A very quaint, curious and pleafant Parallel.	Brantôme — Hommes Illuftres	73
The Vow of the Heron.	St. Pelaye, Mémoires fur l'ancienne Chevalerie.	75

		PAGE
The piteous Death, through too long a Concealment of his Attachment, of a Gentleman of Dauphiny.	*L'Héptameron*	87
Pauline and her Lover, renouncing the World, betake themſelves to a Monaſtic Life.	*L'Héptameron*	95
The Prologue to the Chronicles of Froiſſart.	*Froiſſart*	107
The Death, and Dying Inſtructions of Charles V. of France.	*Froiſſart*	111
An Account of Two or Three Remarkable Duels.	*Brantôme*	117
A ſomewhat naïve Account of the Duke de Sully's Courtſhip.	*Mémoires de Sully*	133
The Birth of Henry the Fourth	*Hardouin de Perefixe*	137
The Death of Henry the Fourth	*Mémoires de Sully*	142
Bons Mots and Anecdotes of Henry the Fourth.	*Various Sources*	177
The Story of Patient Grizzel.	*Fabliaux ou Contes du xiie et xiiie Siècles*	211
The Life of Mary, Queen of Scots.	*Brantôme*	229
Selections from the Knight of the Tower, his Book, for the Inſtruction of his Daughters.	*Le Livre du Chevalier de La Tour Landry*	272

    And firſt, the Prologue 272
    The Firſt Chapter 277
    Of Two Knights who loved Two Sisters . . 278
    Here is ſhown, how all Women ought to Faſt . 280
    Here it is ſhown, how all Women ought to be Courteous 281
    How they ought to carry themſelves, without twiſting their heads right or left 283
    It is here told of her whom the Chevalier de La Tour dropped, through her too much Lightness . . 283

	PAGE
Of her who eat the Eels	286
Of Abstinence	287
How perilous it is to meddle with Men of the World; and of the Lady who undertook to cross-question the Marshal de Clermont	287
Of those who delight to go on Pilgrimages and to Tournaments.	289
Of the Lady who took a Quarter of a Day to Dress Herself.	292
Here speaks of Discovering the Matters of One's Lord	293
Of the Olden Customs	295

A Lament, or Lilt; written by Richard Cœur de Lion, in his Captivity.	*Histoire littéraire des Troubadours*.	299
Bayard meets with his First Love.	*Berville, Histoire de Bayard*.	301
Title and Introduction to Perceforest.	*Perceforest*	310
Introduction		311
A Royal Airing in the Sixteenth Century.	*Brantôme*.	318
An Unadmirable Crichton	*Mémoires de Sully*	320
Marriage, alias the Farce or Interlude of Adam, the Hunchback of Arras.	*Fabliaux ou Contes du xiie et xiiie Siècle*	323
The Crusades, alias the Controversy between the Knight of the Cross and the Uncrossed Knight.	*Fabliaux au Contes du xii^c et xiiie Siècle*	327
The seventh, eighth, tenth, eleventh, twelfth, and thirteenth chapters of the Sixth Book of the Memoirs of De Commines.	*Philipe de Commines*.	334

CHAPTER 7.—How King Louis, by a distemper, lost the use of his senses and his speech; alternately re-

	PAGE
covering and relapfing; and of how he carried himfelf in his chateau of Pleffis les Tours	334

CHAPTER 8.—How the King fent from Tours for one known as the Holy man of Calabria, thinking he would cure him; and of the unheard-of things which the said King did, during his malady, for the retention of his power 347

CHAPTER 9.—[Omitted] 351

CHAPTER 10.—How the King carried himfelf, as well toward his neighbours, as his fubjects, during his malady; and of all was fent to him, from divers quarters, for his recovery 352

CHAPTER 11.—How King Louis, on his deathbed, had his fon, Charles, fent for; of the ordinances and injunctions with which he charged, as well him as others 355

CHAPTER 12.—A comparifon of all the miferies and fufferings undergone of King Louis, with thofe which he inflicted on many others; with a continuation of all he did, and had done to him, up to the time of his end 358

CHAPTER 13.—A diverfion on all the miferies of the ftate of man; more efpecially of princes; as fhown in those who lived in the times of the author; and firftly of King Louis 370

Conclufion of the Author 375

A pleafant Tale of Louis XI. . *Brantôme* . . 378

Selections from Montaigne 381

 That to philofophife, is to learn to die . . 381

 Apology for Raymond de la Sebonde . . . 403

NOTES 441

ROMANTIC EPISODES

OF

CHIVALRIC & MEDIÆVAL FRANCE.

ORDINANCE OF DUELS; WITH THE CEREMONIES ENJOINED IN ALL CASES OF MORTAL COMBAT.

[The following ordinances comprife the fifteen concluding paragraphs of a body of enactments, drawn up in the year 1306, by Philip the Fair, of France. The firſt five are omitted, as no longer offering any fort of intereſt to other than the profeſſional antiquary.]

VI. And firſt, the king-at-arms, or herald, ought to come on horſeback to the barrier of the liſts, and there cry once, before the appellant arrives. Next, a ſecond time, when both the appellant and the defendant ſhall be entered, and have ſignified their preſence to the judge. And thirdly, when they have withdrawn, the final oaths taken, in the forms to be after given. And to begin; with a loud voice he is to cry, "Hear, hear,

"hear; lords, knights, squires, with men of all degrees, what our sovereign lord, the king of France, commands and forbids, on pain of loss, of life and goods!

"That none come armed; wear dagger, sword, or other implement whatever; saving alway the guardians of the field, with such as, by license of the king, are specially permitted.

"Farther, the king, our lord, commands you, and forbids; that any, of what condition soever, shall, during the battle, be on his horse; under the penalty, the gentlemen, of forfeiting the same; the common people, their ear. Farther, the counsellors and allies accompanying the champions to the field are likewise on arriving to dismount, and send their horses away, equally subject to the same penalty.

"Farther, the king, our lord, commands, and enjoins on every person, be his condition what it may, that he seat himself either upon a slope, or bank; or on the grass, so that all may equally see the fight; on pain of the loss of a finger.

"Farther, the king, our lord, commands, and forbids, that any speak, spit, make sign, cry, start, or other signal whatsoever, on pain of loss of life and goods."

VII. Item; and in accordance with old established custom of this our realm of France; the appellant ought to be the first to present himself upon the field: the said appellant before the hour of twelve; and the defendant before the time of noon. And should either be wanting at the said hours, he is to be held and judged for recreant; and condemned as such; should so be, that the mercy of the judge be not extended to him, &c. . . .

VIII. And to the constable, marshals, or marshal, who shall be there present, the said appellant shall say, or cause to be said by his counsellors; and in like manner, after, to the judge, when he shall be mounted, and in the field, the following words. And to begin with, at the entry to the field. "Right honourable, "my lord, the constable;" or, "Sir, the marshal of "the field; I am So and so;" or, "See So and so "before you, as him who is delegated by our lord, the "king; equipped and horsed as befits a gentleman "who has come prepared to encounter such and such "another gentleman, in such and such a quarrel; for "a false, an injurious, a malicious traitor and murderer, "as he is. And of this, I take to witness, our Lord, "our Lady, and my lord St. George, the good knight "—that this day am I come, as commanded was, and "duty is, to make as much in your presence good. "Farther, I demand at your hands, and as is meet, "my just partition of the field, the sun, and wind, as "of all other claims, or advantages, necessary, equit-

"able, or defirable in fuch cafes;" protefting that, this duty done, on his part, he would, with the help of God, our Lady, and my lord St. George, the good knight, do his.

And in addition to what is here rehearfed; it is enjoined, that he be at liberty to fight either on foot, or on horfe, as he prefers; as alfo either more or lefs fully armed, whether for offence or defence. That is to fay, that he fhall be permitted either to pick up, or to throw away, any part of his arms or armour, in the courfe of the fight; as he may deem for his advantage; that is, always fuppofing that God may give to him the time and opportunity.

Item. That fhould his opponent take with him into the field other weapons than thofe allowed by the conftitution of France, he be deprived of them; nor are any other to be permitted to him in their place.

Item. That if his adverfary fhall have brought upon him weapons prepared either by crookednefs, fpell, charm, incantation, lot, or other devilifh contrivance or inftigation, and by which it is evidently feen that the chances of the other were prejudiced, either before or during the battle—or fo as that, even after he had gotten the better, ftill his honour was not fully cleared—that then this hellifh and treacherous adverfary be punifhed as an enemy to God and man, traitor or murderer, according as the circumftances might be. And farther, it is ordered that on the faid arms, be they charmed, or be they not, the said adversary is to swear.

Item. He ought to demand and protest that, if by the setting of the sun it had not been the will of God that he should have discomfited and destroyed his adversary, (which, with the permission of God, he purposes to do,) that so much daylight may be awarded to him on another day as had been consumed on that one, either with the preliminaries, or through other unavoidable delay : such being the ancient right and custom of our realm. Otherwise he might say, that a full day had not been given to him, which we ought to, and do grant to him.

Item. That in case his adversary have not put in his presence at the appointed hour, and by the king assigned, the said adversary shall not be permitted to enter, but held by the other for guilty; and as such censured and condemned. And this, his demand, it is to be at our option to allow or disallow at our discretion. However, if it was without our permission, command, or connivance that the delay occurred, judgment is to proceed.

Item. He ought and has perfect right to demand, that he may carry with him into the field so much bread, wine, or other victual as would suffice for one whole day, as likewise provision for his horse, with all other necessaries befitting such a case; that is, if so be, he may care to have them. And all these protestations and demands, whether general or particular, he should see conceded by special instrument, as by us willed. Farther, we permit that the defendant and appellant can conform alike, and after any regulations drawn up by the defendant; always supposing that, by mutual consent, they are not later departed from. We also will and appoint, that they may engage on horse or foot; and either armed at his discretion, with any kind of weapon, saving only such as shall have been prepared or tempered by any sort of machination, divination, charm, chance, or other devilish incantation or contrivance, forbidden as well by the laws of God, as of holy church, to all good men.

IX. Item. We will and ordain that all lists for trial by battle shall be of one hundred and twenty paces round; that is to say, forty wide by eighty long. And this, all judges are required to see attended to, and that the same be kept in the necessary repair.

Item. We will and appoint, that the stool and tent of the appellant, let his rank be what it may, be at our right hand, or at that of the judge; and those of the defendant on the left.

Item. As soon as each of them shall have rehearsed either for himself, or by his counsellors, the aforesaid protestations and requests, or ever they enter the field, they are to lower their vizors. Then making through them the sign of the cross, they are to come to the foot of the ſtand, where their judge or the king, if preſent, is to cauſe them to open their vizors again. He will then ſay, "Right excellent and moſt puiſſant prince, and "our ſovereign lord : I, So and ſo, to your preſence "am come, as to that of my rightful lord and judge, "at day and hour appointed, to do my duty upon So "and ſo, for the murder or treaſon by him committed. "And of this am I ſatisfied, that God will be on my "ſide, and aſſuredly with me in the fight." Should, however, the judge only be preſent, he will ſimply ſay, "My much redoubted lord, etc." And when he will have ſaid all this, or, as nearly as he can, words to the like effect, his counſellors are to hand to him an indenture couched in the ſaid form ; and which again, with his own hand, he is to preſent to the marſhal, who is to take it. This over, we give him leave to return to his tent. And ſhould it have been found that he was unable to retain the words well and in order, then we conſent that his counſellors rehearſe them for him.

Item. Theſe ceremonies over, the king-at-arms, or the herald, ought to mount upon the rail of the barrier and make his ſecond cry, with the five prohibitions, in the form and order following :—

Item. First is to come the appellant, all on foot, from his tent, in all his harneſs and his frock, or tunic over all. Next he is to be led by the wardens of the field, and ſurrounded by his counſel, to the front of the ſcaffold erected at the middle of the lifts, where our majefty may be, or another in our abfence. Then is the faid appellant to fall upon his knees before a chair and table, both richly covered, and on which latter is to be the image of our true Saviour and God—Jefus Chrift upon the Crofs, refting on a handfome cufhion, with the miffal. And on the right hand of the altar, a prieft, or religious, is to be feated, who is to fay to him as follows: "Sir Knight," or "Lord," or "Squire" of fuch a place; "fee before you here the "indubitable image of our Saviour and true God, Jefus "Chrift, who for our fakes was willing to die and give "His ever precious body for our fouls. Cry you "mercy now to Him, and crave you Him, that this "day He may come to your aid and be on your fide, "according as right and juftice may be with you, for "He alone is Judge. Revolve you well the oath "which you are now about to take, for affuredly "in bitter peril are your life, your body, and your "foul."

Thefe words over, the marfhal is to take the appellant by both his hands, his gauntlets on, and placing his right hand upon the crucifix and his left upon the *Te igitur*, he is to require him to repeat as follows after him: "I, So and fo, appellant, fwear upon this remem-"brance of our Lord God, Jefus Chrift, as upon the "holy evangelifts who here are, and by the faith of "a true Chriftian; and by the baptifm which I hold

" of God, that I have holy, good, and juſt quarrel, and
" every right to challenge the defendant, So and ſo, for
" a falſe and accurſed traitor, or murderer, or perjurer,
" (as the caſe might be), and who has no better or other
" than a feigned and deſperate cauſe to defend. And this
" will I this day ſhow, my body to his, with the help
" of God, our Lady, and of my lord St. George, the
" good knight." This oath taken, the appellant riſes
and returns to his tent, his counſellors about him, and
conducted by the guards as before.

XI. And next upon this, the guards of the field are
to proceed to the tent of the defendant, whom they are
to lead before the altar, there to take the oath as under;
his counſellors being with him, and he at all points
armed, and in all reſpects received, as was the other.
And as ſoon as he ſhall have been exhorted by the
prieſt, the marſhal ſhall take his two hands, the gauntlets
on, and reſting them as he had done the appellant's, then
addreſs him, " You, So and ſo," or, " Lord of ſuch a
" place," ſay after me : " I, So and ſo, the defendant,
" ſwear upon this remembrance of the paſſion of our
" Lord God, Jeſus Chriſt ; and on the holy evangeliſts,
" here before me ; and on the faith of a Chriſtian ;
" and by that baptiſm which I hold of God; that I
" both have, and firmly believe that I have, for certain,
" ſufficient, holy, and juſt quarrel; and every right to
" defend myſelf in this wager of battle, againſt So and

"so, who fiendishly and maliciously has accused me, like a perjurer and mischievous contriver as he is, to have branded me such. And as much will I this day bring home to him, my body to his, with the help of God, our Lady, and of my lord St. George, the good knight." This oath taken, the said defendant rises up, and returns to his tent, in like manner as had done the appellant.

Item. After this second oath, the two are to advance; the one following the other; who, to be short, are to swear as under.

XII. Item. At the third oath, the guards are to separate themselves into two equal divisions, and of which one is to proceed to the tent of the appellant, and the other to that of the defendant, and thence to lead them before the judge, as is the custom, their counsellors around them. Each side to come two and two, and step for step. And as soon as they shall be on their knees, before the cross and the *Te igitur*, the marshal is to take the right hand of each, and, drawing off their gauntlets, place them upon either arm of the cross. And as soon as they are in this position, the priest, who is to be in waiting, is to come forward, and put them in remembrance of the passion of our Lord God, Jesus Christ; the certain perdition, soul and body, of him, whichever of the two it were was in the wrong; of all the terrible oaths which they as well had taken, as were about to take; how the fuccour of God could only ftand with one, with him who had the right; and, laftly, counfel them, rather to throw themfelves upon the mercy of their natural and their earthly prince, than to expofe themfelves unto the wrath of God in heaven above, or yet the vengeance of the enemy in hell. And for the following oath, we ordain it to be the laft of the three, by reafon of the deadly, mortal, and inextinguifhable hatred which is between the two; and only when thus confronting one another face to face, and either clafping other by the hand.

Then fhall the marfhal finally require of the defendant, "You, So and fo, as appellant, are you prepared "to fwear?" and then add, "If you will even yet "repent, and, confeffing, difburden your confcience, as "becomes a good Chriftian, we extend to you our "mercy;" (or, our judge, before whom he is, will do fo); "prefcribing and requiring penalty, reparation, in-"demnity; or, otherwife proceeding as we find fit." If he repents, we defire that they each be led back to their tents, and that neither ftir therefrom till our farther command be known, or that of the judge before whom they are. But if the appellant be willing to fwear, and fay "Yes," then the marfhal is to put the fame to the defendant. And if he too perfifts, then is he to turn to the appellant, and bid him to fay after him, "I, So and fo, appellant, fwear, on the true image "of the paffion of our Lord God, Jefus Chrift, and on

"the holy evangelists, now here present; and by the
"baptism which, as a Christian man, I hold; and by
"the true God; by all the highest joys of paradise, and
"which I all renounce, and for the direst pains of hell;
"by my soul, upon my life, and on my honour; that I
"have holy, good, and just quarrel to fight with this
"treacherous and accursed traitor, murderer, perjurer,
"and liar, So and so, whom I now behold before me.
"And for the truth of this, I appeal to God, as to my
"true judge, our Lady, and my lord St. George, that
"good knight. And that all I do is done in loyalty,
"and in obedience to the oaths by me taken; I farther
"swear, that I neither bear about me, nor on my horse,
"writings, herbs, stones, charms, amulets, divinations,
"characters, or other devilish contrivance, or sorcery;
"that, in no other art do I place my confidence, or
"look for help, than in the Grace of God, a rightful
"cause, my proper person, my harness, and my horse.
"In testimony whereto, I now kiss this true cross, the
"holy evangelists, and am silent."

After this oath has been taken, the said marshal is to draw near to the defendant, whom he is to require to swear after a similar manner. And when the defendant shall have kissed the crucifix and the *Te igitur*, still farther to discover on which side the truth lies, he is to take both parties by the right hand; and when he has warned them, he is to desire the appellant first to repeat after him, and looking his adversary steadily in the face : " O thou, whofe right hand I now hold, " know, by all the vows I now take, the caufe for " which I have accufed you is a right caufe. Where- " fore had I juft and rightful ground to challenge you, " and this day will I finifh you. Your caufe is " naughty ; nor have you any right to fight in fuch a " one, or to oppofe yourfelf to me. You know it well. " And in truth of this, I call to witnefs God, my lord " St. George, the true knight ; counterfeit, traitor, " murderer, perjurer, and liar, as you are ! "

This done, the marfhal fhall fay to the defendant, that he repeat after him, and addreffing himfelf to the defendant : " O thou, whom I now hold by the right hand, know, " by all the oaths that I have fworn, the caufe upon " which you have challenged me is falfe and bafelefs. " Wherefore I have juft and good right to defend " myfelf in it, and to oppofe myfelf to you this day. " Your caufe is faulty, and no occafion had you to have " defied me, or reafon have you to fight me ; and well " you know it. Wherefore, and of fuch, I call God, " our Lady, my lord St. George, the good knight, to " witnefs ; evil and falfe one that you are."

And as foon as the faid oath fhall have been admi-niftered, and defiancy exchanged, they are to kifs the crucifix anew ; and then, at the fame moment, each is to rife and return to his tent, there to prepare to do his duty. They gone, the prieft is to take up the crucifix, with the *Te igitur*, as the table on which they ftood, and remove the whole out of the courfe, and then withdraw entirely himfelf. And then, as foon as the courfe is clear, the king-at-arms, or the herald, is to make the laft of the three cries, in the form which follows :—

XIV. Item. As foon as the king-at-arms, or the herald, fhall have cried, "Let all be feated, nor another "word fpoken!" and admonifhed the champions to be ready to fulfil their duties, then, at the commandment of the marfhal, is the faid king-at-arms to proceed to the middle of the lifts, and there cry three times— "Do your duties!" And as foon as they hear thefe words, both combatants are to iffue out of their tents, and, with the aid of their chairs or ftools, get upon their chargers, which are to be in waiting, and take their refpective arms wherewith they propofe to defend themfelves; their counfellors being ftill with them. Then, as foon as they are ready, the tents are to be on the inftant ftruck, and the whole thrown over the rails.

XV. When the whole has arrived at this ftage, the marfhal, who is to be on a fcaffold, facing the middle of the courfe, and carrying the gage in his hand, is to cry three times, "Let them go!" and at the third time, he is to caft down the glove. Then is it for each either to mount upon his horfe or to remain on foot, exactly as he pleafes. And on the inftant, the counfellors on either fide are to be gone, leaving with each a bottle of wine and a loaf wrapped up in a cloth. Then is it for each to look to himſelf, for need will he have.

XVI. Item. We will and ordain, that the wager of battle is not to be final, ſaving on one of two conditions. That is to ſay, firſtly, when one of the two parties confeſſes his fault, and has ſurrendered. And, ſecondly, when either ſhall have forced the other out of the field, alive or dead. But whether living or dead, the body is equally to be given up by the judge to the marſhal, who is either to retain it, or let juſtice take its courſe, at his or our good pleaſure. But ſhould, however, the breath be ſtill in him; we deſire that he be delivered to the heralds, and kings-at-arms, by whom he is to be ſtripped of his armour. His points are to be cut, and his armour is to be broken and ſcattered in pieces about the place; and he himſelf laid upon his back, and on the ground. And ſhould he even, contrary, be dead, he is ſtill to be ſtripped and left there, till our final word be taken, and pleaſure known, whether it be for pardon, or that judgment proceed to extremity. In any caſe, the hoſtages of the conquered party are to be held till ſuch time as full compenſation ſhall have been made to the other ſide; and the remainder property of the ſaid conquered is to be confiſcated to his prince.

XVII. Item. We will and ordain, that the conqueror retire from the lifts honourably, efcorted, and with the fame formalities with which he entered; that is, fuppofing him not to be prevented upon fufficient grounds, as lofs of blood, difablement, or other hindrance of his perfon. And in his right hand he is to carry the weapon wherewith he had defpatched his opponent. Farther, his hoftages and pledges are at once to be releafed and remitted to him. And for the vindication of the faid quarrel never is he again to be called upon to defend himfelf, let what will come to light; nor is any juftice or other to interrogate him, or in any way moleft him, faving always with his own allowance.

Item. We will and ordain, that his horfe, caparifoned as he ftands, as well as the arms which he brought with him into the field, whether foughten with or difpenfed with, become, as cuftom is, the perquifite of the conftable, marfhal, or marfhals of the field, who are to take them there and then.

And now, to end, we make our prayer to God, that He will guard the right to him who has it, and that all good Chriftian men will well bethink them or ever they commit themfelves to fuch ordeal or extremity. For affuredly of all the perils into which a man can fall, that of the wager of battle is the moft fearful to be thought on, and many is the noble man who has found his reckoning to be out therein, had he right or had he wrong, through too much confidence in his prowefs, his

cunning, or his ſtrength ; or blinded and led on by
paſſion, or overweening felf-fufficiency. Others again,
either out of fear, or encouragement of the world, refuſe
peace, or reaſonable compromiſe or conceſſion ; and for
which, as for old ſins, they bear about on them, and to
their dying day, an anſwerable penance, having diſre-
garded and made light of the juſt judgments, warnings,
and offerings of God. Finally, to end the matter, let
him that is wronged nor can any juſtice find from man,
feek it of God. Should, however, the cafe be ſuch,
that, as of an overruling neceſſity, he is compelled to imperil himſelf in ſuch a ſtrife, and his cauſe be righteous,
certes let him do it. But let it be in ſoberneſs and in
lowlineſs ; diveſted of all heat, and pride, and paſſion,
and then ſhall not any power on earth have maſtery on
him, for God, our Lord Jeſus Chriſt, that day will be
with him in the fight, his fupporter, his right arm and
his ſhield. — *Favyn : Le Théâtre d'Honneur et de la
Chevalerie.*

CEREMONIES ATTENDANT UPON THE DEGRADATION OF A KNIGHT.

THE juſtices deſignate this ceremony *ex-auctorare*; that is to ſay, *inſignia militaria detrahere*, which, in our language, anſwers to the word *degrade*; inaſmuch as ſuch proceeding takes place by degrees; the arms and honours of him who is to be deſtituted being ſtripped from him, and annulled ſucceſſively, one after the other. Among ourſelves, the oldeſt ceremonies on record, attendant upon the degradation of a knight or gentleman, were theſe :—

As ſoon as, by commandment of the king, the indictment had been drawn up againſt the priſoner charged with the felony, the ſaid indictment was laid before a counſel compoſed of the eldeſt, moſt venerable, and experienced knights of the court; aſſembled to the number of ſome five and twenty, or thirty; who condemned the accuſed to loſe his life, according to the information before them, and nature of the profecution; treafon or felony; at the fame time prefcribing that, previoufly to the fentence of the said execution and death being carried out, the faid criminal be degraded from his nobility. And this is the way in which it was done.

And, firft, two fcaffolds were erected in a fair and open fpace, fecurely fenced in with pofts and bars. One of them was covered overhead, and handfomely hung about with tapeftries, and otherwife provided with chairs, tables, and all becoming requirements for the ufe of the knights-judges and of their officers. The other was to be both lower, and bare, and pitiful, for the reception of the condemned knight, the kings-at-arms, heralds, and purfuivants. And, farther, at each end of this fcaffold, were to be ftools, or low benches, in number fufficient, or long enough, for twelve priefts to fit at ; and in the midft of it, the condemned knight was to be ftanding, armed at all points; his fhield, bearing all his devices and emblazonings, in front of him ; and hanging from a ftake driven into the ground, alongfide of the fcaffold. And after that the charge and fentence of the condemned knight had been read, in a clear, audible voice by one of the heralds, or kings-at-arms, incontinent the priefts began to fing, diftinctly and harmonioufly, the vigils and the fervice of the dead, from the *Placebo* to the *Miferere mei, Deus*. And at the clofe of each Pfalm, as after the *Requiem æternam*, the priests made a pause and were silent. And with the first of the said pauses, the kings or heralds-at-arms began to divest and degrade the condemned knight, commencing with the crest or bunch upon his helmet; and at the interval between each stanza, the herald, holding aloft each piece as taken from the condemned knight, proclaimed, with a high voice: "See here the crest, or helmet, of So and so;" (naming him by his name, surname, lordship, or other quality), "knight, attached and convicted of felony, "treachery, murder, incendiarism, &c.," according as the case might happen; ",and for this cause con-"demned to such and such a death and ignominy." Similarly, holding up, piecemeal, to the view of all, he was used to announce of the armour, joint by joint, belt, sword, his gilded spurs and gauntlets; naming each at successive pauses in or between the Psalms. And when it came to the shield, which was ordinarily swinging from a stake alongside the stand, one of the pursuivants used to turn it round, back foremost, as upside down as well; and then announce at the top of his voice: "This was the shield, and this is the scutcheon "of the traitor, the perfidious and disloyal knight, whom "now you see before you all." Then, taking up a hammer, he was to smash it into three pieces; and as soon as the last Psalm in the offices of the dead had been sung, the priests got up from their seats, and closing in a ring round the condemned knight, placed their hands upon his head, and in this pofition they proceeded to fing the 109th Pfalm of David, commencing with the words, *Deus, laudem meam ne tacueris*, in the which Pfalm are fulminated the imprecations and maledictions againft the traitor Judas, with all his fellows and his like. And fimilarly, as the fquire who was about to be conftituted of the moft honourable order of knighthood, on the evening precedent to the day of his inftallation, was wafhed and bathed, and, farther, bound to pafs the night in watching and in prayer, fo as to be both qualified and worthy, body and foul alike, to receive fo great an honour; in like manner, the pfalm of imprecation ended, a purfuivant-at-arms was to take and place a brazen veffel, filled with tepid water, upon the head of the condemned knight. On this, the king-at-arms demanded three times, and in an articulate voice, the name, furname, quality, and condition of the deftituted knight. To which, when the purfuivant had refponded, equally three times, to the faid demand, the king or herald-at-arms told him, "He deceived himfelf; for that he "whom he had afked about was other, a man of "honour; that this man was a traitor, a deceiver, a "murderer, a perjurer, and a liar." And in order to fatisfy all thofe prefent that what he fpoke was truth, he then turned to the knights-judges; the prefident of whom, through the prothonotary, attefted, that by the majority of the votes of thofe then fitting, he of whom it was in agitation, and whom the purfuivant had named three times, had been adjudged to be unfit any longer to be held a knight; and, for his vices and mifdeeds, banifhed from all fuch honourable company, degraded of his nobility, and condemned to fuch and fuch a punifhment and death. This affirmation finifhed, the king, or herald-at-arms, upfet the bafon of water upon the head of the degraded knight.

This laft act over, the knights-judges came down from their ftand, decorated and covered with their mourning hoods and robes, and in this equipment proceeded to the neareft chapel. The degraded knight was at the fame time taken down from his fcaffold, but neither by ladder nor ftairs, nor in the manner in which he had gone up; for he was let down by a rope paffed under his arms. And as foon as he had been lowered he was laid upon his back, and on a bier, or hearfe, covered itfelf with a funeral cloth, and over all were thrown the grave cloths of the dead. And in all this folemnity he was carried to the church, where the knights were already in waiting. And as foon as he was entered, the priefts commenced the ufual fupplications, with the fervice for the dead, over the condemned man, and who, as foon as it was over, was there and then committed to the juftice of the Court Royal, or to the prefident of that of High Jurifdiction, to be executed as condemnation was. However, when the king at any time extended his grace to the condemned, he was moftly either banifhed for a feafon, or for ever, from the realm.

After the execution, the king-at-arms proclaimed publicly, and fo that all might be advifed, the children and defcendants of the dead knight to be deftituted of their nobility; ignoble, henceforth, peafants, unworthy as incapable of bearing arms; forbidding them ever to be prefent at, or take part in field, tilt, tournament, fiege, court, camp, or other affembly whatfoever, where kings, princes, nobles, lords, or gentlemen were wont to haunt, under penalty of being purfued and chaftifed, naked, with rods, as attainted, and for villains as they were.—*Favyn: Le Théâtre d'Honneur et de la Chevalerie.*

GLIMPSE AT THE LIFE OF A GALLANT OF THE COURT OF HENRI IV.

GOING one day to fee M. the Conftable, who had ever been partial to me, and ever fhown it, he told me that on the morrow he was intending to give me a dinner, and on no account was I to fail to come. Accordingly I went. There were alfo invited, MM. d'Efpernon, de Roquelaure, Zamet, and a councillor named La Cave. As foon as we were all affembled he ordered the doors to be clofed, faying, that he would have nothing to break in on the harmony, or interrupt the fatisfaction which he hoped to find in the company of such valued friends. Nor would he have any one about the place fave only thofe of his houfehold, with Mons. du Tillet, Girard, and Ranchin, his doctor, who had a table laid for them in his dreffing room, in order to be at hand as foon as dinner was over.

And when we had all done ample juftice to his good
cheer, and gotten up from table, he made us fit down
befide him, firft ordering everybody out, and defiring
Ranchin to keep the door and deny the entry to all
alike. We neither knew, nor had we even fo much
as a fufpicion of what he was intending to do or fay.
At length, when all was arranged to his fancy, he
began : "Gentlemen, it is now fometime fince I had de-
" termined to get you all together; you are my neareft,
" beft, and deareft friends, and from whom nothing has
" ever been referved a fecret, fat it light or fat it heavy
" at my heart; to break to you the matter which you
" now fhall hear. Of all the many and memorable graces,
" mercies and favours which, in the courfe of a long
" and profperous life, I have received at the hands of
" God, I need fcarcely tell you. How He had caufed me
" to be born the fon of a great and an illuftrious father :
" how He has led me by the hand in all my walkings
" by the way, and to the fummit of the higheft
" honours, offices, and dignities. Not but that mid all
" thefe fweets He had found good to mingle bitter; to
" try me with fore and grievous croffes and perplexities.
" And of them all, praife to his grace, none was I
" better enabled to undergo, or with greater patience, or
" to furmount with greater courage and magnanimity,
" than the difafters which befel my houfe towards the
" end of the life of King Charles, and during the
" reign of Henry III. And much as they put my

"endurance to the proof, I can thank my God, I and
"mine came scathless from them all. In my time I
"have had many and sad afflictions: as the loss of my
"late son, d'Auffemont, and the death of my wife,
"who left me with two little children of tender age upon
"my hands. The marriages of my two eldest daughters
"were not, as it has proved, all that I could have
"wished, notwithstanding I had done all which was in
"my power to provide parties for them, suitable as well
"to them as to myself. But in return, God has favoured
"and blessed me with a son, begotten when well on
"in life, who is in every way to my mind, and bids fair
"to carry down the honours and succession of my house.
"And if He has given me this, so has He, as well, a
"daughter nobly born; and for whom, as she has now
"arrived at marriageable years, I have been looking
"about for some one to match her with, as well to her
"inclination as my own. All my thought has been, to
"find a husband for her in whom her affections, as
"my own beside, might centre. And albeit I could
"have the choice of every prince in France, I have not
"so much looked to see her lodged in eminence as in
"contentment; and in such a manner as that she should
"live for the residue of my, as all her days, in quiet,
"joy and satisfaction. And out of the esteem that I
"have ever had for the house, person, fortune, and
"other advantages of M. de Baffompierre, whom you
"all see, I have determined to make to him, who

" least expects it, the offer of a hand which the highest
" and noblest of the land have aspired to. And this
" I wished to do in the presence of you all; his, as
" my, most special and dearest friends. And I now tell
" you, M. de Baffompierre," addressing himself to me,
" that having, as long as I knew you, loved you as my
" own child, I now intend to convince you of the
" sincerity of such a protestation, by making you so
" indeed, in marrying you to my daughter. In doing
" so, I doubt not but what she will be happy with you;
" knowing, as I do, your naturally excellent disposition;
" and flattering myself that you will feel honoured, as
" happy too, in marrying the daughter and grand-
" daughter of the Constable, and of the house of
" Montmorency; and that I as well would be happy,
" for the remainder of my days, could I see you both
" so, and finding your happiness in one another. As
" settlement, I will give with her one hundred thousand
" ecus down, on her marriage; and she will have fifty
" thousand as well, on my brother's decease. And now,
" should there be nothing interposing, or that I have
" not thought of, I will give orders at once to Girard,
" whom you see, to treat with your people, or your
" mother, if she is near, of the articles and other
" conventions necessary."

By the time that he had finished his harangue, the
tears were fairly standing in his eyes for joy. Whilst
as for me, I was so confounded at this unexpected

stroke of fortune, in every way so bewitching to me, that I could not so much as think of any words whatsoever, let alone such as would be worthy of such an occasion, wherewith to reply. At last I said, "that the "thoughts of an honour so great and undreamt of, as "that which his goodness had just disclosed to me a "prospect of, had so completely deprived me of utter- "ance, that I was literally incapable of anything, save "of wondering at the fortune which was happening to "me. That as such a compliment, and an elevation, "were so much above, not only my wildest aspirations, "but my merits; it was only to be acknowledged by "the most respectful services, and most dutiful submis- "sion. That my life would be too short to requite "them, and all that I could offer was a heart which "would be the continual slave of his every wish. "That he did not so much give a husband to Made- "moiselle, his daughter, as a creature by whom she "would ever be adored as a princess and honoured as "a queen. That he had not so much selected a son- "in-law, as a faithful servant for his house, and all "whose conduct should be regulated so as how soonest "to anticipate his lightest wish. And that if amid all "the visions of beatitude which he had opened up to "me, I could be reasonable enough to see anywhere "a cloud upon the scene, it would be this — that "Mademoiselle de Montmorency would scarcely be "able to bring herself, but with a sigh, to forego her "claims to the dignity of princefs, which unqueftionably it was hers to command, contenting herfelf with that of fimple lady. And that fooner would I die, and caft to the winds the honour which M. the Conftable was deftining to me, than caufe to fo fublime a lady fo much as a fhadow of difappointment or vexation."

Having finifhed, and I had been feated on a chair clofe to him, I fell upon my knee, and feizing his hand, kiffed it; on which he caught me in his arms, and held me locked for fome time. Prefently, recovering, he faid to me, "Let not that diftrefs you. Before fpeaking to you, I had taken the precaution to found my daughter; and as I find her in all things, fo did I more efpecially in this, the willing gratifier of the wifhes of her father." Hearing this, MM. d'Efpernon and de Roquelaure at once began to commend the choice that M. the Conftable had made in me; and faying much more in my favour than, I fear, was ftrictly true; as likewise did Zamet, La Cave, du Tillet, Girard; all of whom embraced me, extolling at once the difcernment of the Conftable, and my good fortune as well. M. the Conftable then told them that it was not defirable, for the prefent, to broach the matter; and that it muft remain a fecret till he gave them leave to refer to it; inasmuch as he was not juft then in the good graces of the king, on account of his refufing to allow M. de Montmorency to marry his daughter,

Mademoifelle de Verneuil. They all promifed to keep it quiet, as did I as well. He then told me to come and fee him in the evening, as Madame d'Engoulême, his fifter-in-law, was to be with him; and he would openly fpeak with me before her, as his daughter, of the refolution which he had taken refpecting us both. This I did. And feeing me, taking me to her, he faid to me, "My fon, fee a wife whom I have long been rearing "for you, falute her." And I did fo, kiffing her. Then he fpoke to her and Madame d'Engoulême, who expreffed herfelf in every way fatisfied with the choice which her brother had made for her niece.

On the next day, my mother begged of Madame, the Princefs de Conté, to accompany her to Madame d'Engoulême's, who, on feeing her, faid, "We two fhall "foon be the mothers of our young efpoufed. I know "not, Madame, are you or I the happier, at this "moment, of the two." From thence fhe went to fee M. the Conftable, who told her that the matter was not yet to be difclofed, but that the families might meet and arrange about the articles and indentures: which they did.* * *

And now the report of my intended marriage began to be the theme of every tongue. And the king, out of compliment, went the next day to wait on Madame d'Engoulême, having firft feen the Conftable in the forenoon, and to whom he had given the frankeft of receptions. He told her, on entering, "that he had "come, as my particular friend, to fee Mademoifelle, her niece, and to rejoice with them both at the thoughts of feeing her fo foon and happily difpofed of;" at the fame time recurring with much kindnefs to me. Well, that very evening M. de Bouillon arrived at court; and no fooner had the king begun to found him about the affair of his poft, than he told him, that it was that very account which had brought him to his Majefty. I paid my refpects to him, as did I to the others who were prefent; but I forgot to wait on him the next day, which, I confefs, I ought to have done. Even had he not been the nephew of the Conftable, it was a refpect owing to him; and at all this he was naturally nettled. And, befides, he had all his life been emulous of M. d'Efpernon, through whofe machinations, as he fancied, the match had been made up. And fo the next evening, as he was goffiping with the king, who, on the preceding one, had feen Mademoifelle de Montmorency at the queen's, and whom he had found, as, indeed, had everyone, divine, he faid to him, "he could not conceal his "aftonifhment, how his Majefty had ever come to "allow fuch a woman to marry in the quarter which "he did, feeing that M. the Prince was as yet un- "provided with a fuitable match; that it was not "defirable to allow him to connect himfelf out of "France; whilft that in it, no one now remained for "him, but her and Mademoifelle du Mayne, whom

"he could marry; that no one who sincerely had his
"Majesty's interests at heart would ever counsel him
"to allow the Prince to be united to the latter, seeing
"that the dregs of the Ligue were still too formidable
"to permit of their being headed, or stirred by such a
"chief; whilst Mademoiselle de Montmorency would
"only bring with her alliances already his own, M.
"the Prince being the nephew of M. the Constable."
And so ended, begging his Majesty most humbly to
weigh the advice which he had given to him, and make
his own reflections on it. The king told him that he
would, and then went to bed.

The next day the queen began to rehearse the
grand ballet which she intended to have danced at the
coming Lent. This was on a 16 of January, 1609. She
would allow no one to be present. However, the king
went in to see them practising, taking only with him
M. Le Grand, and Montespan, his captain of the guard.
Seizing the opportunity, the said Le Grand, whose
manner it ever was to make the most of all novelties,
and particularly of Mademoiselle de Montmorency,
who, truly, was worthy of all his admiration, then first
infused into the mind of the king, unhappily, but
too easily kindled with such fuel, an attachment
which has since led him into such lamentable and inextricable troubles and extravagances. And, un-
luckily, the same night he was overtaken with an
attack of the gout, whilst, to make matters worse, so

was the Conſtable, which prevented him from proceeding to Chantilly, there to celebrate our marriage, as had been intended.

All this time, I was perfectly ſenſible of how ill-diſpoſed M. de Bouillon was towards me; for he had ſaid to M. de Roquelaure, who repeated it to me afterwards, " that M. de Baſſompierre was wanting to get
" his poſt of firſt gentleman of the chamber, yet he
" never had had the courteſy to mention the matter to
" him; that he alſo wanted to marry his niece; nor
" had he ever alluded to that either; but that he
" would ſee his papers in the fire or ever he ſhould
" have either his place or his niece." And to make good his threat, he began at once to put his irons in the fire, by propoſing to M. the Prince, his marriage with Mademoiſelle de Montmorency; telling him " that
" here was an alliance which would connect him with
" all the greateſt houſes in France; that the relations
" of a perſon of his quality muſt neceſſarily become his
" creatures; and that on that account, of itſelf, he
" ſhould proſecute ſuch a match, even in preference to
" one of higher pretenſions as to rank; that if he let
" that chance ſlip, he would have to remain ſingle all
" his life, seeing the king would never allow him to
" chooſe out of France; whilſt in it, there remained
" no one ſave Mademoiſelle du Mayne, and to her the
" king would never liſten." And ſo effectually did he work him, that at laſt he conſented that he ſhould go

to M. the Conſtable and propoſe the matter to him, whom, however, I had warned, how M. de Bouillon was ſworn to upſet and ruin all. But M. the Conſtable told me " not to be alarmed; that, let what " party would be preſſed upon him, he would refuſe it, " intimating that he was too well aware of the malice " of M. de Bouillon to allow him to have any ſort of " aſcendancy over him." And ſo, when he came to him, he received him ruffledly enough, telling him, " his daughter was no longer to be had; a huſband " had been found for her already; that he had, as it " was, the honour to be grand-uncle to M. the Prince, " and that this was quite ſufficient for him."

Whenever the king had the gout it was our cuſtom, M. Le Grand to ſit up with him on one night, Grammont another, and me the third, and ſo on in rotation. And during the night we uſed to read to him out of *Aſtrée*, which was then all the vogue, or elſe talk or otherwiſe divert him, in the intervals of reſt, when awake and tortured with his feet. It was cuſtomary alſo for the princeſſes to come and ſee him; and of them all, Madame d'Engoulême was more in his intimacy than any other. With her he was under no ſort of reſtraint. And whenever Madame d'Engoulême turned to any of us, he would entertain her niece, telling her, " that he would love her as his own daughter; " that ſhe ſhould live at the Louvre during the year " that I was to fill the office of firſt gentleman of the "bedchamber, and that he bid her to tell him frankly, "would the match be to her liking? And if it were "not, that he would manage to get her out of it, "and marry her to M. the Prince, his own nephew, "if she pleased." She told him, "that the match had "been of her father's making, and his whole heart was "set upon it; she believed that she both could and "would be happy with me." He subsequently confessed to me, that it was this admission of the lady's which determined him to break all, fearful that she might be too fond of me if it proceeded. The night following on when this had passed, it was M. de Grammont who sat up with him; nor had he a moment of peace or rest, for love and gout are two things, either of which singly, let alone when together, are wondrous apt to keep a man wakeful. On the morning after, he sent for me, towards 8 o'clock, by a page-in-waiting. And as soon as I had got to him he asked me, how it came that I had failed to be in attendance on him during the night past. I told him, it had been M. de Grammont's turn, and that mine came next. He then told me that he had never closed an eye, and how often he had been thinking of me. Then he bid me to kneel on a cushion by the side of his bed, and next went on to say how he wished me well, and was intending to marry me. I, who was expecting nothing less than what was coming, plumped out, "Had it not been for the Constable's gout, I had "been married already." "Nay, nay," said he, "but I was thinking of marrying you to Mademoiselle d'Aumalle; and under such conditions I would have been willing to revive the duchy of Aumalle in your favour." On hearing this, I said, "Surely to goodness, Sir, you do not want me to have two wives?" When I had said this, with a deep sigh, he began again, "Bassompierre, I want to say a word to you as to a friend. Not only am I in love with Mademoiselle de Montmorency, but miserably and hopelessly gone and lost with her. If you marry her, and she returns your affection, I shall hate you. If she returns mine, you will hate me. I beseech you, let not this be the means of destroying our present excellent understanding: of my own nature, I both like you and love you. I am resolved to marry her to my own nephew, the Prince de Condé, and to keep her about my family. To see her will be at once the consolation and support of an old age which already is creeping fast upon me. I will give along with her to my nephew, who is young, and cares a hundred thousand times more for the chase than he does for the ladies, a hundred thousand ecus to regale himself with. And I will not look for any other return from her than simple respect and affection, nor making any other sort of pretension."

And as he told me all this, I reflected that, should I in my answer say, I would not give her up, it would

only be a useless indiscretion, seeing he was all-powerful, and his will was law in such a matter. So, making up my mind to cede the point with as good a grace as I was able, I said to him, " Sir, I have long and ardently
" longed for one thing, and which at length has come,
" though at a time and in a form that least had I ex-
" pected. And that was, that by some signal instance,
" I might be enabled to show to your Majesty, the depth
" of the submission and attachment which I have for
" him, and how faithfully I am prepared to serve him.
" And certes, Sir, long had I sought, ere I had found a
" more convincing opportunity than this—to abandon,
" without a sigh or a prayer, so illustrious an alliance,
" so perfect a mistress, and so dearly loved by me;
" since by this pure and frank retirement and resigna-
" tion which I make, in some degree I contribute to
" your Majesty's satisfaction. Yes, Sir, I give up all my
" hopes of happiness, and for ever, and have only now
" to pray, that this new attachment of your Majesty's
" may be as fruitful to you of felicity, as it would be of
" misery to me ; did not the recollection of all your
" Majesty's content therein outweigh in the balance
" as well the memory of all the past with me, as the
" hope of all that was yet to come." Finding me thus ready to meet him in his every wish, he caught me in his arms, and literally wept with emotion, assuring me,
" that he would make my fortune, as though I were
" one of his own natural sons ; that he would love me

"even more dearly than before; and, happen what would, he would never fail me;" adding, "he was well aware of all the worth of my friendship, as of the sacrifice which I had made." On this, some of the lords and princes coming in, he bid me rise; first saying, he would marry me to his cousin, d'Aumalle. But I told him plainly that, "though it was perfectly in his power to unmarry me, marry me elsewhere, that, he never should." And so our dialogue ended.

Leaving him, I proceeded to dine with M. d'Espernon, and to whom I related what had passed with the king in the morning. To which he answered, "It is but a passing fancy of the king's: it will go as it came, and as has many another. Do not be making yourself uneasy. M. the Prince will not be long in divining the real cause of all this sudden attention on his Majesty's part; and consequently will waive the honours intended to him." And that such would be the end of it, he succeeded in persuading me; simply, I suppose, because I wished it; and from that time I said not another word to anyone.

It is certain that, under heaven, a lovelier creature than Mademoiselle de Montmorency existed not; nor yet of a grace more exquisite, or one coming nearer to perfection; so, little wonder is it that my heart was all on fire about her. But as it was attachment which necessarily would have to end in matrimony, I am afraid it must be confessed, that I hardly was sensible of, or regretted the loss as I should.

It happened one day after dinner that the king was

playing at dice, as was his cuftom, at a table which had been rolled to the fide of his bed; and in the courfe of the evening in came Madame d'Engoulême, with her niece, whom he had on purpofe fent for, and with whom he was long in deep talk, at the other fide of the bed. All this while, I kept my eyes riveted on her; fhe knowing nothing of what paffed between myfelf and the king; nor could I ever have credited that fhe was to be won upon fo eafily. Having fpoken a moment with the aunt, he turned again to the niece: and on Madame d'Engoulême rifing to leave, Mademoifelle de Montmorency, at léaft as it feemed to me, flightly fhrugged her fhoulders as fhe looked at me, as much as to fay, You fee what he has been telling me! It is no untruth when I fay, that this little movement, to me fo full of meaning, had like to have fplit my heart in twain. I could ftand it no longer. So feigning to find my nofe bleeding, I hurried away through the chambers and the lobbies. At the back ftairs, the valets-de-chambre brought me my coat and hat. My ftakes I left all lying about; and Beringhen kept them for me; and M. d'Efpernon's carriage ftanding at the door, I made the coachman take me home. I there found my valet-de-chambre, with whom I mounted to my room, forbidding him to allow to anyone that I was within. And there I remained for two days, tormenting myfelf as one poffeffed; nor did I once either eat or drink or fleep. It was only thought that I had gone to the country, as I often made fuch excurfions. At last, my valet, fancying that I would either die, starve, or run out of my senses, went and told M. de Praslin, who came, and the same evening carried me to the court, who were all in astonishment to find me so changed in two short days; so emaciated, pale, and altered, that hardly was I longer recognisable. Two days after this, M. the Prince having openly declared his intention to marry Mademoiselle de Montmorency, meeting me, said, " M. de Bassompierre, I have to ask " you to come to my hotel this evening, and thence to " accompany me to Madame d'Engoulême's, where I " am to pay my respects to Mademoiselle de Montmo- " rency." I made him a most profound reverence, but never a step did I go. However, not to be idle, and in some degree to console myself for my loss, I amused myself by coming to terms with three ladies, whom I had been forced to abandon as long as the marriage was in view. One of them was d'Entragues, whom I managed to meet at Madame de Sentenay's. The other two, I came across by accident, so that I was soon fairly launched again upon the world.

About the year 1609 my mother retired to Lorraine. M. the Prince at length married his mistress; and on the morning, as I was with the king, he came to me and said, as he had done to a number present, " M. de Bassompierre, I have to beg that you will " come here this afternoon, so as to accompany me to " my wedding." The king, who had observed him addressing me, asked me, " What he had been say-

"ing?" "Something, Sir," said I, "that I won't do."
"And what?" said he. "He wants me," I rejoined,
"to be present at his wedding. Is he not considerable
"enough but what he can go by himself? Can't he
"get married without me? Your Majesty may take
"my word for it, if he is to have no one but me to wait
"on him, he will have but a scanty following." To
this he said: "It was his wish that I should go."
On which I said to him, "that I most humbly must
"beseech him not to put such a command on me; for
"go I would not. That his Majesty should be satisfied
"with the submission which I had already shown, in re-
"linquishing, at his instance, my own undoubted rights;
"with having ravished from me, as he had, my wife
"and my content; without compelling me to be ex-
"hibited in this way; as it were led in triumph at a
"rival's heels." On hearing me, the king, who was
the kindest and most forbearing of mortals, only said,
"I see well, Bassompierre, that you are in a huff; I
"am perfectly certain that you will think better of it,
"and go, when you reflect that it is my nephew, and
"the first prince of the blood who has asked you."
And with this he left me, and looking for MM. de
Praslin and de Termes, told them "to follow and dine
"with me, and insist on my going, seeing it was my
"duty to do so, and that I was bound as well by the
"commonest courtesy." I did so at last, on their remonstrance; but it was with so ill a grace that I only
joined the princesses at the front of my own door, as

they passed, conducting the bride to the Louvre. * * * The ceremony was performed in the gallery of the Louvre; and, out of sheer mischief, the king kept leaning on me the whole time. So that I was necessarily as close as well could be to both the prince and Mademoiselle. Two days later, I fell sick of a tertian ague; and after that I had had four violent returns; one morning, and I had just been taking medicine, a Gascon gentleman, named Noé, came to me in bed, and told me, " that he wanted to fight with me, as soon as I " was up and well." I told him, " that I was always " well when matters of that sort had to be attended " to." And up I got on the spot, my physick in my stomach, and went to the rendezvous which we had agreed on, at Bisseftre, in a thick fog, and with two feet of snow upon the ground. And scarcely had we reached the place, before two Gascon gentlemen, with one named Le Fay, came about us, to arrest us. On seeing them, he said to me, " To another time." But I called to him, to get on his horse; which he did: but so dense was the fog, that it was only by hallooing that we could, either of us, make out where the other was. And as I was making up to him, Carbon, who was determined to separate us, took Noé's horse in the flank, and fairly bore him to the ground. It was awful risky for us all; and I had well nigh killed La Graulas, mistaking him for Noé.

At length I went to Gentilly, no longer able to endure my medicine. But scarcely was I there, till

Regny, La Feuillade, with fome others came, and carried me back, ill as I was, to the court. And as there was a ballet to be danced by all the younger people, at the arfenal, and at which the king, queen, princes and princeffes were to be prefent, I did not hefitate to go, feeing I was invited, even in the wretched ftate I was. I remained there all the night, and part of the next day; and by which I was fo weakened, that I almoft thought it would have coft me my life. Nor did I ever once get out of my bed, faving only on *Mardi-gras* ; and that was to go to the arfenal, to fee the running at the ring, for the jewel which Mademoifelle de Montmorency was to give. I did not take any part myfelf, being too feeble to fit my horfe. So the king made me to come alongfide of him, to help him to entertain the lady. I did my part well enough ; but there was fome difputing about a favour which he overlooked, and which Dandelot, without his obferving, gave to M. le Grand, who wore it in his cap, as he ran ; and which I called the king's attention to.

The ballet of the queen was danced on the firft Sunday in Lent, and was as well the fineft as the laft that fhe ever got up. After it, the king went to Fontainebleau, and I remained in Paris; where an affair fell out which brought me into fome little fcandal. . . .

Mémoires du Marefchal de Baffompierre.

THE FINAL COMBAT BETWEEN DAMP ABBOT AND THE LORD DE SAINTRÉ.

LL this while [that is, during the wreſtling of Saintré with the Abbot], the two Squires that Saintré had retained about him had like to die with grief and ſpite, thus to ſee Madame and Damp Abbot twitting and laughing at the Lord de Saintré, than whom, in all the realm of France, there lived not, that day, a gallanter gentleman or a nobler knight. So, as he was coming away, they ſaid to him, " Our lord, it will be more than human " in you, if you forbear to revenge this day's brutality."

But he only ſaid to them, " My friends, do not be " diſtreſſing yourſelves. Keep quiet; never fear, I'll " put all this to rights."

Then the Lord de Saintré, who had now for ever extinguiſhed in his breaſt all love or hope of Madame, indignant at ſuch treatment from one whom he had ſo paſſionately loved and faithfully ſerved, feigning to take it all in good part, carried himſelf as though he had not in any way taken his defeat to heart. So, good-humouredly, and as if half talking to himſelf, he ſaid to Madame, " Alas, Madame, it is a thouſand pities " ſuch a man as my Lord Abbot, of ſuch a build and " ſtrength, ſhould never have been brought up to " the noble ſcience of arms. Such a man ſhould have " been defending the marches of our Lord the King. " I much queſtion if there are above one or two men " in all this realm who would dare to meet him in an " open field."

Then Damp Abbot, on hearing ſo handſome a tribute to his prowefs, ſcarcely now knowing whether he was on his head or his heels, turned another great ſummerſault, to the no ſmall entertainment of Madame and the remainder of the company. Then he ſent for wine and cherries to refreſh them all. And while all theſe fine Olympics were going on, word was ſuddenly brought to the priors, and other more venerable eccleſiaſtics of the convent, all about the wreſtling, and the taunting of Madame and of Damp Abbot. And as they had long been ſufficiently ſcandalized with Damp Abbot's courſe of life, which they well knew to be not only ſuch as it were unbecoming a churchman to lead, but as it would but ill become any other man to lead, they came to the concluſion, there and then, that two of their body ſhould be deputed to Damp Abbot on the part of the convent, and who were to expoſtulate with him as follows :—" Right reverend father in God, and our

" very honoured Lord, the priors and adminiſtrators
" of your convent, *unâ voce dicentes*, with their moſt
" humble and beſeeming duties, accredit us to you,
" inſtructing us to appriſe you how they have heard
" with pleaſure, that on more than one occaſion you
" have entertained our ever-to-be-redoubted Lady, as
" well at dinners as at ſuppers, as on other occaſions;
" for all which, ſeeing that ſhe is at once our Lady
" and our Foundreſs, the convent cannot ſufficiently
" expreſs its obligation to you; and this the more, that
" it has been the means of procuring for our poor houſe
" the honour of the preſence of ſuch a Lord as the
" Lord de Saintré, of whom common rumour ſpeaks ſo
" loudly, and whom we believe to ſtand moſt highly
" with our Lord the King. But ſeeing that, owing to
" ſome provocation on your part, this Lord was, as it
" were, compelled to wreſtle with you; and not only
" that, but thrown ſeveral times, and after ridiculed by
" you; conduct but ill becoming any prelate or any
" churchman, under what reſerve ſoever, but, leaſt
" of all, openly, being a thing forbidden by our rules
" and ſtatutes: for all this, our convent is exceedingly
" diſturbed and diſtreſſed, and ſo we have to pray and
" beſeech of you, that you will endeavour, in ſome way
" or other, to accommodate matters, and that, before
" he leaves, all cauſes of jealouſy may be removed, as
" well from yourſelf as the convent, in our perſons.
" And we have to let you know that if any miſchief,

"or misunderstanding whatsoever comes of it, to the
"damage either of us or of our house, we shall not
"hold you excused, but will, on the contrary, lay all
"the responsibility to your door. And for this you
"will be pleased to pardon us all."

Damp Abbot, having heard all this sermon, and the remonstrance of his convent, replied to them, "Priors,
"return to your brethren, and tell them that all I did
"was out of pure frolic and gaiety of heart. Say,
"they are not to be uneasy, for, before he goes, I will
"have made it all right."

And after all this embassy from the convent had been received and dismissed, wine and cherries began walking round again, and every one was merry and jolly to their hearts' content. And when they all had drunk, Damp Abbot took the Lord de Saintré by the hand, and drawing him aside, said to him: "My Lord de
"Saintré, once, with God's permission, I had the ho-
"nour of seeing you in my poor hotel, which, if you
"would deign to accept of it, shall be yours. And
"this I had long wished for, so much had I heard
"of you. And now, as a favour, I have to ask you if
"you would again, with Madame, confer a like honour
"on me, and dine with me quietly to-morrow. You
"will not refuse me, I know: and, indeed, it is a
"gratification I shall not readily forget." To which the Lord de Saintré answered; "My Lord Abbot, for your
"first dinner, and the hearty cheer and reception I

"then met with, as fincerely as I can, I thank you.
" And for your fecond offer of a dinner to-morrow, I
" do no lefs cheerfully alfo thank you; and which
" nothing lefs than fome affairs to be attended to in the
" good town, and which it would never do to neglect,
" could poffibly prevent my accepting."

" Alas," faid Damp Abbot, " I am forry for this.
" Sir, if I did anything, out of mere thoughtleffnefs and
" frolic to annoy you, I humbly entreat I may be for-
" given. Sir, I have one of the beft and handfomeft
" mules in the kingdom, let who will have the fecond;
" I have as noble a falcon, whether for the water, or
" the wing, as any man alive; and I have three thou-
" fand écus. Sir, befides the king and the pope, there
" is not the man in Chriftendom, fave yourfelf, to
" whom I would part with one of them. As humbly
" as I can, I afk, entreat, and implore that, which you
" pleafe, of my three offers, you will deign to accept at
" my hands; and that you will pardon me, and we may
" part good friends."

Having heard him to the end, the Lord de Saintré faid,
" My Lord Abbot, as for the mule, it is not exactly
" the kind of thing which it is my manner to mount.
" Your three thoufand écus, were I in any fort of want
" of them, believe me, I would not hefitate one fingle
" half-fecond to take them from you. As regards
" your beautiful falcon, it is otherwife. It fhall be
" accepted, out of a refpect to you. I will not, how-

" ever, deprive you of it ; ufe it for my fake, and
" fhould anybody, at any time, ever happen to afk it
" from you, you have only to tell them, that it is the
" Lord de Saintré's. One thing, however, in return,
" I have to hope, and that is, that you will not deny
" me the firft requeft I ever make you."

"And what is it?" faid Damp Abbot; "I am at
" your fervice: on my honour, if it is in my power,
" you fhall moft willingly be obeyed."

"Truth?" faid the Lord de Saintré.

"Yes; on my falvation," faid Damp Abbot.

Then the Lord de Saintré faid to him, "All I
" would afk is the honour of entertaining you and
" Madame the day after to-morrow at dinner."

"But that!" faid Damp Abbot. "Then that I
" can anfwer for at once, for both of us. One thing,
" however, you muft engage for: there is to be no
" fort of extravagance."

Then, the beft friends in the world, and all made up
and forgotten, the two of them come together to Madame,
and the Lord de Saintré repeats his prayer. But the
inftant Madame heard it fhe as inftantly demurred, nor
would fhe liften, for a moment, to anything Saintré could
fay. Then Damp Abbot took her on one fide, and
faid to her, " Indeed, Madame, but you muft come.
" I have undertaken for both of us, and I have given
" him my word ; and you will get me both into trouble
" and difgrace, if we fail to keep our word. Befides,

"Madame, think of how matters stand between you and me: our position is ticklish enough. It is the mischief to make enemies of these cocked-up, spiteful, sneaking rascals from the Court. One should have a heed of them, as they would of hot iron. And it was for this reason, Madame, I said we would go; and you must really come; for if we do, he will be conciliated, and all forgotten. Otherwise, he will never forgive me for having thrown him."

Then Madame, who could neither divert Damp Abbot, nor yet refuse him, at last said, "Well; be it, since you are so bent on it."

Then Damp Abbot, in great glee, called the Lord de Saintré to him, and said, "My Lord; my high and mighty Lady, whom you here see, merely refused you, fearing that it might have been your purpose to offer her something altogether too unconscionable, and out of all bounds. This, she was wishing to spare you. However, I have assured her, that everything is to be as modest as she could wish."

Then the Lord de Saintré said, "Let us drop ceremony. To courtiers like ourselves, Damp Abbot, and Madame, a fine table can be but a poor treat. Now and then, to rough it, is a pleasant change. Something solid if we can; and a glass of good wine, at any rate we will manage to provide. I am sure Madame will not be difficult for once, but will put up with it as if it were better."

And when he faid this, the horfes and the cobs were at the door. Then Madame and the Lord de Saintré thanked Damp Abbot, and took their leave of him till the following day but one. And when they got outfide the gate, as hard as ever her horfe could lay foot to the ground, Madame and her people made home. And as fhe was galloping, from time to time the Lord de Saintré would bring his horfe alongfide of Madame's, and fay to her, " Ha, Madame, what is it I have done to you?
" Is there the man, in this world, who dare affert that
" I have not loyally ferved you, or loved you with my
" whole heart?"

" Truly, Sir," faid the Lady, " you fhowed as much
" when you ftrove with Damp Abbot. You will oblige
" me by troubling me no more about fuch matters, and
" leaving me to myfelf."

The Lord de Saintré, who faw, clearly enough, how matters now ftood; and who neither wifhed to be reftored to her good graces, nor would have deigned, even at her entreaty, to be again to her what he had been, in fpeaking to her, had only wanted to let her fee, that he was alive enough to the fcurvy jeft fhe had put upon him; though of her new attachment, he might fay nothing. And when they had got to Madame's hotel, and before he was able to alight, Madame faid to him, " Now you
" may go, my Lord de Saintré, for I have affairs to attend
" to in doors; and you have after to-morrow's work
" before you."

So he got his leave to go, with an "Adieu, till after "to-morrow."

Then the Lord de Saintré, whofe head was full enough with all the matter of the paſt and coming day, put ſpurs to his horſe, and made ſtraight for the town, and the quarter where all his people were to be. And in a little time he was with them, finding them all waiting where he had ordered them to attend him.

Then he called to him his maître-d'hotel, and told him, that Madame and Damp Abbot were to dine with him the next day, and that he was to uſe all the diligence he could to get together proviſions in plenty, and of the beſt ſort; and good drink as well for her as all her people. And he told him that he was to ſettle beforehand with the landlord for anything they might have ſpent, or would have to ſpend. And at the ſame time, he gave him ten écus for the uſe of the varlets and oſtlers of the hotel. And he gave orders that in the morning, his horſes and his trunks, with the maſs of his people, were to leave; ſome ten or twelve only remaining to follow with himſelf. And it was all done. And, after that, as ſoon as he was in his room, he ſent for his hoſt, and ſaid to him apart; "Good hoſt, can "you think of any Gentleman, or citizen of the place, "ſomething of the build of yonder great Squire;" pointing to one of his own people.

"Yes, my Lord," ſaid the hoſt, "more than one."

"But have they armour of the beſt, I mean the "primeſt quality?" ſaid Saintré.

Then he inquired, "Who it was had the beſt?" and when he was told, he then aſked the hoſt, "to be "good enough to requeſt the perſon named to let the "Lord de Saintré ſee him." And ſo he did.

And when the cit had come and had made his ſcrape to the Lord de Saintré, who met him with all the civility imaginable, the Lord de Saintré ſaid to him, "Jacques, who in this country has the beſt ſtore of "armour?"

"My Lord," ſaid he, "many keep it; but, without "vanity, I may ſay that I have four or five as complete "ſuits as any gentleman or townsman of the place."

"Then, by the Lord Saint Jacques," ſaid the Lord de Saintré, "it redounds to your credit. As you have "a ſuit, no doubt that fits yourſelf; do you think you "could manage to find another would anſwer to yon "knight?" indicating one of his party who was about the ſame ſize with himſelf, Saintré.

"My Lord," ſaid he, "I can ſupply you; and they "ſhall be such as you will in every way be ſatisfied "with. But what ſort of helmets will you have?"

"Jacques, my brother," ſaid the Lord de Saintré, "I want them not too heavy; and two axes and "daggers muſt be with them: and all alike; and "make yourſelf eaſy about them; you ſhall be no loſer "by your bargain."

"Loſe! what an idea!" ſaid Jacques, who could now ſcarce contain himſelf, ſo flattered was he to be in the preſence of the Lord de Saintré. "There is "nothing I have that is not at your service. But when "must you have them?"

"Why, I should like them at once," said the Lord de Saintré, "but you must bring them in a bag or a "trunk, for I would not wish anyone to see them "coming."

Then, as quickly as he could, Jacques went to his home, and brought, quietly, the two suits, all fine and furbished up, and the two axes and the daggers; and to see them, the Lord de Saintré was well satisfied. And when that night was passed, and the next day come, and the Lord de Saintré had heard mass, and sent away all his baggage and his people saving only twelve; and had seen the tables laid, and that all would be ready by his return, he got upon his horse, followed by all his company, and set out to meet and escort Madame. And when he had got about half way to her hotel, he met Madame and Damp Abbot in the fields. And when they were about to interchange their mutual salutations, Damp Abbot commenced and said, "Halt, there, my Lord de Saintré! Speak of the "wolf, and you will see his tail or his ears. My Lord "de Saintré, did you not hear our horns?"

"I hardly know, really," said he. "I rather thought "you would have been coming by the road. But have "you breakfasted, Madame, and you, my Lord Abbot?"

"We have," said Madame; "to keep out the fog, "we took a snatch, with a little ypocras, and *à la* "*poudre de duc.*"

" You certainly did right, Madame," said he, " and " you too, my Lord Abbot."

And so chatting, they all continued together; Madame, however, always addressing herself to Damp Abbot. Then the Lord de Saintré, seeing that he might as well be talking to the winds, reining in his horse, fell alongside of Madame Jehanne, thinking to enter into conversation with her. But she only told him, " that " for the present, she could dispense with his civilities."

Then he went to Madame Katherine, then to Madame Isabelle; from each of whom he met with a like reception; for they had all been forbidden to show him any attention. Then he pricked on again to Madame and to Damp Abbot; and in a few minutes after, they had all gotten to his lodgings.

Then the Lord de Saintré took Madame's arm, and conducted her into her chamber, her and her women; and then he led Damp Abbot into another. And when they were in their several chambers, readying themselves, he told his maître-d'hôtel, that as soon as he saw them all at table, he was, that instant, to have all the horses saddled, and all his people booted, and ready so to start at a moment's notice. And when the dishes were laid; and, to be brief, Madame and Damp Abbot had washed their hands, then he placed Damp Abbot, as Prelate, at the head of the table; and Madame, who could never be prevailed upon to be far from him, next. Then, the others he put at the end. But for all they could say, or do, he would never consent to be seated; but, with his napkin on his arm, kept going about, helping, firſt one, then another; now to this diſh, now to that; with plenty of good wine between.

Why need I dwell on it any more? Damp Abbot was ſo taken with the condeſcenſion and forgivingneſs of the Lord de Saintré, that it would be impoſſible for any one to be more. And preſently, when all their tubs began to be well filled, and their tripes well lined and larded, the Lord de Saintré, as if careleſſly, aſked Damp Abbot, " Had he ever had on armour ? "

" Never in my life ! " ſaid Damp Abbot.

" Hey, God," ſaid the Lord de Saintré, " but it " would become you, too ! what ſay you, Madame, " would it not ? "

" Damp Abbot would look well in anything," ſaid Madame; " and for that matter, though ſome " people might think it a good joke, I confeſs I can " ſee nothing ſo very ridiculous about it."

" Madame," ſaid the Lord de Saintré, " who is there " joking here ? I repeat again what I ſaid before : I " have rarely ſeen the man who, in my opinion, " armed, would appear to more advantage than would " Damp Abbot."

And with this, he called to Peronnet, of his bed-chamber, deſiring him " to do as he had told him." Then Peronnet brought in two boards, and laid them on treſſels, at the foot of the room; and then he put on one of them the larger and more gaudy ſuit; without, however, either axe or dagger.

And when Damp' Abbot faw this beautiful and polifhed harnefs, and heard it fo admired, he began to be delighted in his heart; for, furely, thought he, the Lord de Saintré, out of his good-nature, is going to give it to me; and it was for no other purpofe that he invited me. So he made up his mind, within himfelf, that if afked to put it on, he would do it at once, without making any fort of difficulty about it. And then to fhow him how much he was taken with it, and how deeply he felt his kindnefs, he began loudly to exprefs his admiration.

Then faid the Lord de Saintré to him, trivially, "Since it feems to take your fancy, if by any chance it "fits you, I am fure you are very welcome to it."

"Earneft?" faid Damp Abbot; "then, for the love of "Madame, I will neither eat nor drink till I have let "you fee me in it!"

Then they all began to cry out, "Away with the "tables; we have eat twice too much already!"

Then Damp Abbot, now in his glory, ftripped himfelf to his doublet.

Then the Lord de Saintré, a mallet in his one hand, with the rivets in the other, coming to him, and helping him on with the various pieces; having put the helmet on his head, made Damp Abbot all found and tight. Next he handed to him a pair of gauntlets. And when Damp Abbot found himfelf thus all armed, he began to turn himfelf, firft this way, then that; then he would ftick his hands upon his hips, all the while inquiring of Madame and her women, "What think you "now of your monk, in his new rôle of Knight? Is "he not worth looking at, eh?"

"Monk," said Madame, "such men are rarely "seen."

"Hey, God," said then Damp Abbot, "if I now had "but an axe in my hand, and any one had a mind to "settle an account, or pick a quarrel with me!" Then, as a good jest, he said to Madame, "Troth, "Madame, this same surplice is a trifle heavier than "the one in which Damp Abbot usually officiates "of a Sunday. However, since I have won it, I will "keep it." But as he was saying this, the Lord de Saintré, interrupting him, said to him, "Stay, my "friend, not so fast; you have not won it yet: in a "minute or two, however, you shall." Then he had the other harness brought in, and instantly began putting it on. And when Madame had taken more fully in what the Lord de Saintré had just said, and saw him hurrying himself into the other armour, she began to be uneasy as to what was like to come of it; so she said to him, "My Lord de Saintré, what is it you are "about?"

"Madame," said he, as soon as he was ready, "you "will see presently."

"Will see!" cried Madame; "Sir coward, and "are you then going to attack a priest?"

Without so much as answering her, the Lord de Saintré, who was now fully armed, turning to his

people, said, " Look well to the door, and see that
" neither man nor woman enters in or passes out."
Then he ordered Madame, and the other Ladies, and
the monks present to withdraw, all of them, to the foot
of the room, telling them, " that the man or the woman
" of the lot of them that budged from thence, but the
" tenth part of an inch, he would cleave them from
" the jaws to the hips."

Then might you have heard them curse the hour
they had ever set their foot in that hall. Then coming
to Madame, he said to her, " Madame, of your own
" accord, and without any manner of difficulty, you
" condescended to be judge in the affair, the other day,
" between Damp Abbot and myself; so, in return, I
" have now to beg and entreat of you, as humbly as I
" can, that you will deign again to be as much of another
" sort of a tussel, and one in which I happen to be
" somewhat more of an adept. And I have to hope,
" Madame, that you will be on my side, and second
" my proposal to Damp Abbot."

" What proposal?" said Madame. " Any insult
" offered to him, I shall take as offered to myself. He
" is under my protection."

Then the Lord de Saintré turned to Damp Abbot,
and said to him, " Damp Abbot, at Madame's request,
" and yours, I wrestled with you two times, and each
" time was thrown, as more than one aching bone this
" moment reminds me; nor, for anything I could
" entreat or urge, would one or other of you listen to

"reason. There was nothing for it, but I must go
"through with it. So now I beg and require of you,
"and for the sake of the Lady whom you have so faith-
"fully loved, that you and I may try a fall at the sort
"of combat which I have been taught to wage."

"Ha, my Lord de Saintré," said Damp Abbot, "I
"never could do any thing in armour."

"Possible," said the Lord de Saintré: "however,
"you can do at least as I did, you can try: you shall
"go through with it, or through that window, at your
"choice."

Then said Madame, now trembling before the fearful sternness of the Lord de Saintré, "Lord de
"Saintré, we will and command you, under the
"penalty of incurring our highest indignation, this
"moment to disarm; as also Damp Abbot. And if
"you do not, we will publish you everywhere for a
"coward and vindictive, and we will take very effect-
"ive measures besides to see you requited for this day's
"liberties."

And when the Lord de Saintré saw himself thus vilified and menaced, and all out of her partiality and regard for Damp Abbot, turning and looking upon her, he cried aloud before them all, "O false and disloyal
"traitress, as you are; and this to me: I who have
"so long and faithfully loved and served you; ay, as
"never woman yet was loved or served of man! and
"now for this whoreson monk I am cast off; yourself
"debased, defiled, dishonoured, and disgraced! And

Combat between Damp Abbot and de Saintré. 61

" in order that you may carry in your recollection, and " to your dying day, what it is to trifle with and to " rouse the anger of the Lord de Saintré, I will make " of you both examples, and you first, such as shall be " well remembered, and to all time, of all such apostate " dogs and bit—s." With that, raising one hand, he seized her by the hair of her head, and with the other was about to smite her on the face; but suddenly he curbed himself, recalling to his mind all the many kindnesses, on a time, he had received from her; and that, besides, it was not to be defended. Then releasing her from his grasp, he let her fall upon the form; now crying, and well nigh dead with agony, and shame, and fright. Then he called to his people to bring in the two axes and the two daggers which he had had prepared. And when they were brought, he ordered them to hand them to Damp Abbot to make his choice. Then coming towards him, he said to him, " Damp " Abbot, Damp Abbot, bethink you now of all the " injuries you that day heaped in my presence, on " Knights and Squires; Knights and Squires whose " days and nights are spent in arms, and all whose " thoughts are virtue and are honour; for now the hour " of vengeance is at hand!" With that he closed his vizor; fiercely bidding his people to do the like with Damp Abbot's. And then he went up to him; and when Damp Abbot saw that there was no possible escape for him; but that, will he, nil he, he was in for it; now furious and desperate, he raised his axe, and rushing on him, brought it down with such a force, that, had it lighted on Saintré, infallibly it had knocked him down, or killed him out of hand, for he was by much the stronger, as well as the heavier and bigger of the two. And this would have been what would have pleased Madame well. But, by the grace of God, and thanks to all the experience he had had in every kind of fray, he managed to evade it. And a moment after, thrusting his axe under a plait in Damp Abbot's armour, he carried him before him right up to the bench whereon Madame was lying. Then he tumbled him over it, Damp Abbot falling with such a crash that sure they all thought the whole place was coming in about their ears. Then when Damp Abbot saw himself down, he began to cry, " Mercy, mercy, " Madame! Ah, my Lord de Saintré, for God's sake, " mercy!"

Now the Lord de Saintré, mad with all the provocation he had received, and all the infamies and insults you have heard were heaped upon him, had determined, in his own mind, to make an end, for good and all, of Damp Abbot. And to this purpose he had raised his arm, when suddenly remembering the ever-blessed words of our LORD JESUS CHRIST, where he says in Deuteronomy, in the Old Testament, and the sixth book of the Bible: *Quicumque fuderit sanguinem humanum, fundetur sanguis illius*; and with them, so many other touching entreaties, remonstrances, supplications, instances; and which, by his own example, he had illustrated, the

Lord de Saintré relented and refolved to fpare him. However, as a juft vengeance, and as it were in obedience to the divine injunction, which, by reafon of Damp Abbot's manifeft and crying fins, had permitted him to have the better; throwing his axe from him, and taking his dagger in his hand, and opening Damp Abbot's vizor, he faid to him, " Damp Abbot, Damp Abbot, allow you " now, be God a juft judge, or be He not; when, not " all your arrogance, nor all your might, nor all your in-" folence, nor all your menaces, have been able to " fave you from this day's difgrace; ay, and before the " face of her, too, in whom was all your confidence; " and to curry whofe fmiles you have fo bafely lied, " and reviled knights and squires and their order. And " for this, your lying tongue is now about to pay its for-" feit." With that, he fplit his tongue in two; and having driven firft his dagger home through either cheek, he then left him, ere he went, enquiring of him however, " Damp Abbot, have you not now well and " honourably won your harnefs?" Then he had it taken off him; and when they were both unarmed, and he saw Madame with her hair all about her, and her clothes all difordered, lying on the floor, he faid to her, " Adieu, Madame, of women falfeft!" And as he was faying this, he looked, and fpied about her waift a belt of fatin, blue, and edged round with gold. And when he faw it, he ripped it from her with his knife, faying to her, " How, Madame! and have you then the " affurance to fhow yourfelf in fuch a colour? Blue is "the emblem of faithfulness. Ill beseems it such as "you; you shall no more of it." Then rolling it up he put it in his pocket. This done, he advanced to the ladies and gentlewomen, with the monks and attendants, who were by this all huddled up together in the farthest corner, shivering and shaking like a lot of sheep; piping, and half dead with fright; and said to them, "You have been witness to everything that has "been said and done, in all this unhappy matter; and "into which, to my infinite regret, I have been forced. "And for all the annoyance, and, I fear, fright I have "caused you, I do entreat I may be pardoned. And "now God be with you all." Then they opened the door for him, and he went down stairs, presently saying to the host, "Should Damp Abbot care to keep the larger "harness, he is to have it. But the smaller, and the "two axes and daggers, you will return to Jacques, and "tell him to let me see him speedily. Good host, have "you been satisfied?" And as he said this he got upon his horse, and setting spurs to him, called, as he vanished, to his host, "Adieu, mine own host!" And now I will say no more of him, as he went straight to the Court; but will tell you of Madame and of Damp Abbot, and of all their people, who, you need hardly be told, were not a little disturbed when they came to understand more distinctly the nature of all that happened to Madame and to Damp Abbot.

Le Roman de Jehan de Saintré.

DEATH OF THE COUNT DE BUREN.

HE Count de Buren died at Bruſſels, making, at his departure, the moſt unparalleled *exit* of which the world hath ever heard tell; and which muſt, to all time, atteſt him to have been a man of a moſt unbounded heart and ſtomach. This Knight of the Golden Fleece, finding himſelf to be ſuddenly disordered in his bed, whether ſuch diſorder were to be attributed to ſome caſual exceſs, which in his cups had been perpetrated, when carouſing, after the manner of his country, with the captains; or to the decay or corruption of his vitals, or to whatever elſe it might be, bid inquire for Andrew de Veſalius, then chief phyſician to the Emperor Charles the Fifth. Which Veſalius being quickly by his ſide, had no ſooner, upon application to his pulſe, which he found to be flickering, aſcertained the caſe to be mortal, than he very

roundly told him; suppofing himfelf not to be deceived by the rules of his art, in another five or fix hours at moft, he, the Count, would be a dead man; and that therefore he had to counfel him, as his very true friend, and that as fpeedily as might be, to fet his houfe in order, and to think upon his latter end. All which overtook him as Vefalius had foretold; and by which, his prognoftication, he became the means of enabling this Count to enact the nobleft tragedy which ever hath been performed upon fuch a ftage fince kings have worn their crowns. For the Count, not one jot amazed with the nature of the intelligence, difpatched incontinent for two of his neareft friends, the Bifhop of Arras, fince Cardinal de Grenville, his brother by adoption; and the Count d'Arembourg, his brother in arms; that he might not be denied the fatisfaction of wifhing them a laft farewell. Now was the will of the dying man expreffed, confeffion received, and the laft rites of the church to the departing adminiftered; and all, or ever the allotted fands had fled. By this, determining to rife, he had brought to him, of all which his wardrobe could afford, apparel the moft faftuous, gorgeous and fuperb. In thefe arrayed, he caufed himfelf to be armed from head to foot, even to his fpurs, in the very choiceft of his armour, and with them were affumed the mantle and the collar of his order. Then placing his fword upon his thigh, and a cap *à la Polaque*, which, to every covering, he preferred, upon his head; he had himself, thus haughtily caparisoned, to be carried into his hall of state, and where were assembled the colonels of the lansquenets, many nobles, captains, and gentlemen, as well of Spain as of Flanders, desiring once more that they might see him; for already it was cried throughout the town, that in another hour their master was a gone man. Thus planted in his chair, and upon the dias of his hall, before him lying his gauntlets, his head-piece with its plumage and its crest, he required of his brothers by adoption, that they would call before him, as well his houshold as his captains, that he might give them his last adieu. Then passed there before him, successively, in an agony, and on their knees, the gentlemen in waiting, valets, pages, grooms, laquays, porters and others; to each of whom he spoke a kind and a charitable word; recommending now this one, now that, to Monsieur d'Arras, to be compensated, each according to his several desert; gratifying this one with an horse, that, a mule; bestowing now an hawk, now a hound, or again, a change of attire; noticing all, even to a poor blear-eyed hunchback of a falconer, unsavoury and in tatters, and who durst not so much as discover himself, so wretched was his plight. For no sooner did the Count perceive him to be behind the others, even broken with anguish and in tears, than he bade him come to him that he might comfort him; curiously demanding of him touching the promise of this or of that bird with which he were then encharged. Then turning himself, and looking upon the Bishop of Arras, he said, My brother, I recommend to you this, my falconer, and have to request that he shall be so remembered in my testament, that for the remainder of his days he may eat of my bread. Alas, the poor little man has well served me, as did he my father before me, and for all which he has been, God knows, but too sorely retributed! On this no man could more contain himself; to see, on the part of so great a lord, such condescension toward so mean a person. Then having bidden a last farewell to all his captains, his household and retainers, each man being taken by the hand, he called for the mighty bowl from which he was wont to quaff, when, in the seasons of his joy, he would pledge his compeers, captains; and from it drank, standing, on either side supported by his gentlemen, to the emperor's, his master's health; expressing the very deepest sense of all the obligations which he was under to him. After this he made a fine harangue, enlarging upon all the actions of his life, and all the distinctions that he had received from the emperor; urging among other things, how he had never placed his legs beneath the mahogany of a protestant prince, or turned his face from his master, however, or by whom solicited. Then having gulped (beut le vin de l'estrier et de la mort) the stirrup cup of this, his journey to the realms of death, he handed the insignia of the Golden

Fleece to the Count D'Arembourg, to be by him reſtored to the emperor. At laſt, finding his hour to be at hand, he haſtily took his leave of the Biſhop and the Count, thanking them both moſt touchingly for all thoſe very true offices of friendſhip which they had performed for him in the article of death, and for having supported him in this, the laſt great cataſtrophe of his life. Again, a final leave was taken of all the company and captains preſent. Then turning, and perceiving Monſieur de Veſalius to be behind him, he called him to him, and embracing him, thanked him for the timely advertiſement which he had given him. Finally failing, he ſaid, Carry me to my bed; and no ſooner was he there depoſited, than he expired in the arms of his ſupporters.

Thus ſuperbly accoutred departed this great warrior, after the manner of thoſe Roman ſenators, cenſors, dictators, ediles, conſuls, captains, princes; who, enveloped in their martial and triumphal robes, and planted in their curules, abided, and on the public place, the approach of Brennus and his Gauls, and of whom they were gazed upon, as an aſſembly of the gods, till by adventure they proved to be but men; and by whom they were barbarouſly immolated. In the ſame right and royal manner would that brave queen, Mary Stuart of Scotland, die; marching to death, and to the block in the proudeſt of her yet attire; thereby. ſhewing a ſtomach and a magnanimity worthy of herfelf, and what fhe was — a queen of Scotland and of France. In like fort fhould depart all the great ones of the earth, when they too find their hour to be at hand, nor die in feathers like a duck. Here I clearly fpeak of thofe to whom it is not given to fall upon the field of battle, under the eye of their princes or their captains; a notable death, certainly; not only befitting the dignity of fo great a captain, but to be transferred unto tapeftry, that the hanging thereof for ever in the eyes of princes and of kings, might them incite alike to fuch, fo memorable an end. As much to Don Juan of Auftria was denied. But that which furprifal precluded to him when living, was performed, departed, upon his corfe. For, in fight of all the army, and before Namur, he was borne, dead, and in all his armour; fo fumptuoufly arrayed that the very buckles of his fhoes were eftimated at upwards of five thoufand ducats. All this I learned myfelf when in Flanders; where, to this day, great and fmall fpeak of the death of that famous lord, the Count de Buren; and the memory of which, from among men, fhould never be permitted to perifh.—BRANTÔME—*Hommes Illuftres.*

A GRAND, AND A SUBLIME APOSTROPHE.[1]

WHO is this gentle knight, engendered amid the ſtrife, brought forth upon the field; ſuckled in a tent; cradled in a ſhield; ſwathed in the hide, and built up of the fleſh of lions? Who, who is he in whom are met, the lynx's eye, the dragon's front, the lion's heart, the wild boar's briſtling ire, the tiger's vengeful ſpite? Who is he, intoxicate amid the fight, yet ſlumbers to the pealings, the thunderings of the ſtorm? Who is he, the whirlwind of the fray will pierce, his foe eſpy, as the falcon her prey through the miſts of the morn: as the lightning the oak, rip the man, rip the ſteed; or tumbled, them powder, as the griſt of the mill? Who is he, who ſooner than to rot his days in peace, will traverſe, not the Rhone, but Albion's wintry waves;

[1] See note B, at the end.

or, needs be, scale the rugged Jura's heights? Is he on the field of battle — as the chaff to the wind, scud the foemen before! Doth he tilt — not foot to stirrup will he deign to put; yet horseman and horse will he pin to the dust; buckler and helmet e'en cleave to the midst. There is no one thing can avail before him; nor shield, nor buckler, basenet, lance, nor coat of mail. Of the nostril the fume, the steed as he gasps; the groan, the gash, the prey; the battered shield, the shivered lance; these, these are the fights his soul doth gloat upon. Alone, on foot, it is his delight to scale the mountain; forests to prowl; to grapple with the bear, to rend the lion, and to take the stag. His helmet is never from his head; his pillow when he rests. All he has, it is but largess. — *Fabliaux ou Contes du XII et XIII Siècles.*

A VERY QUAINT, CURIOUS
AND
PLEASANT PARALLEL.

BOUT this time there was drawn, (as well do I remember,) a parallel betwixt the fortune of this great emperor (Charles V.) and that of ancient Rome, fhowing them to be of fome little parity. For even as this great city, the moſt triumphant of five parts of earth, after all the glory which had attended her from her very foundation to the times of Conſtantine; after having been the feat of emperors and of kings who had poſitively gorged her with fpoils, with trophies, and with triumphs; adorned her with monuments, with every precious thing; after having caufed to tremble earth's moſt glorious provinces; planted herſelf, as a luminary, in the heart of that Italy, itſelf the centre, backbone of the univerfe: after having caufed to run her blood, as from a ciſtern, and in her very ſtreets — yet after all

this, I say, did she, her heyday past; having cast, and behind her, all her pomps, her vanities, unsatisfying joys, betake herself to a calm, a tranquil, an holy and sincere repentance; receiving as her confessor, and into her bosom, the holy and most spiritual Father, in whose guidance, and in whose obedience, to pass her yet remaining days: thus to finish as she had begun — the fold of a shepherd.

So was it with this Charles, so many times renowned; who, after having affronted all the kings, his neighbour states; carried devastation throughout the length and breadth of Christendom; annihilated so many armies; sent to their account whole millions of his species; poured blood, as water, upon every sea and every land; taken for his prisoners a pope and a king of France; triumphed over them; finding that there was nothing further left for him to do, retired also, and withdrew himself into the bosom of the church; as well to put in practice, by such a metamorphose, her ordinances, as the old proverb, *de moço diabolo viejo hermintano:*—" Of your young devil comes your old saint."— BRANTÔME —*Hommes Illustres.*

THE VOW OF THE HERON.

N the year of the incarnation, 1338; the year in its decline; when glad birds ceafe to warble on the trees; the vine had ripened; the leaf was withering, quick ready to its fall; Edward III. held at London, in his palace of marble, a fovereign court to all his peers, lords, knights, dukes, princes, paladins; ladies, damfels, vaffals. His air was diftract and moody; his head was doubled to his breaft. With Louis he was well; he was at peace. They were kinfmen; he was his friend. He neither wifhed him, nor he thought him wrong. No; his thoughts were the thoughts of love. But when fortune turns, well I divine, turn muft we too. Venom inftilled will work its fpite. For through Robert d'Artois came, as you fhall hear, a war, which yet may rue the child unborn; which many a knight has fent to his account; woman left hufbandlefs,

child fatherlefs; good feaman fwamped; caftle razed; town, church, village, hamlet burnt. And Jefu only knoweth how all is yet to end, if forth he putteth not his hand.

Though iffue of the *fleur-de-lys*, Robert was a banifhed man. Flanders, Namur, Auvergne were clofed to him. Shelter he was forbidden. Louis willed it. Edward alone, of all his neighbours, was powerful enough to fcreen him from his vengeance. Wearied of his exile, and to diftract him of his cares, Robert, as you may fuppofe, was ever at the chafe. A falcon on his fift, he rode upon the marfhes. But before he had time to caft her off; a quarry in the fky; the bird of itfelf efcaping from him, prefently returned, a heron in her talons. Robert, indignant at the fight of fuch a prey, for the moment was difcountenanced. But quick recovering himfelf, and having for a little reflected, Ha, my bird, he faid, for this I thank thee: this will I turn to my account. And with that he detaches the heron, and calling to him his gentlemen, gave them in charge to fee that it were properly plucked, dreffed and ftuffed for the table. Then placing it between two filver difhes; accompanied by two noble damfels, two minftrels and a guitar, he boldly entered into the hall of banquet, crying as he went, Space, fpace; back, ye fcoundrel varlets, back; way for the doughty champions whom love and gallantry affemble to the feaft. Here is your proper food, ye gallants, fine!

Here, Sire, I have a heron, which this day my falcon took. No meat, my faith, for cowards, this! It is the moſt cowardous of all the birds that float; the craveneſt of the feathered tribe; for let it but ſpy its very ſhadow and it quakes. And ſo, Sir, as is but meet, to the craveneſt of the human race I now preſent it. To Edward I give it; the diſinherited of France; right iſſue of the *fleur de lys*; who for his daſtardlineſs has forfeited a crown, is allowing it to paſs from his lineage, as had this carrion heron had it been born but England's king! Furious and indignant at ſuch an affront, the monarch trembled with very rage and vexation; and riſing ſwore, Coward I have been called; coward let me be ſeen. For by the great God of paradiſe, and by his gentle mother, or ever fix years have paſsed, I ſhall have defied this King of St. Denis;[1] and I ſhall have croſſed the ſeas, I and my ſubjects. Though he be ten to one; let him not think for that to take away my birthright. What, and if I did do him homage? It was becauſe I was a brat, and knew no better. It is not worth a ſtraw. And I ſwear by St. George, St. Denis, that never ſince the times of Hector, Achilles; the great Alexander, conqueror of ſo many realms; has ſuch a raid been run in France, as, with the help of God, I propoſe to make. When Robert heard this, he was enchanted, and ſmiling malignly to himſelf, he ſaid: Thanks to thee, my

---

[1] See note C, at the end.

falcon, this day I am a restored man. And for this I praise the God of paradise. Is it not an infamy that I should be banished from this noble France, so dear; my kindred, my children, and my wife? He is my brother-in-law; yet has he not stuck to imprison my children and my wife. But, let it please to Jesu Christ, and, or ever I die, I shall so return to the presence of this King of France, whose cry is *Monjoie, St. Denis,* that to his dying hour he shall remember it. I was of his counsel, and well did I serve him; yet thus are servants furthered! With that, taking the silver dishes, the harpers with the guitar and the viols following; the two noble damsels singing as they went, *I'm away to the greenwood; 'tis love that me calls,* he next traverses the hall, and addresses himself to the Earl of Salisbury; telling him, that it was for him, as at once the most amorous, and the most valiant in all that assembly to set the example to the remainder; and that in the name of Jesu Christ, the maker and upholder of the universe, he had to entreat of him, as Edward, to register his oath. With all my heart, said Salisbury, turning to the daughter of the Earl of Derby, by whom he was sitting, and of whom he was passionately enamoured. Ha, never need I hope again to find an inspiration as the bright eyes of this fair one whose fetters I shall always vaunt to wear! Were but the Virgin among us; let her doff her divinity, and, by heaven, she were not a fairer! As an only favour, all I would now ask of her, who so often has denied me more, is, that she will but deign to lend me the tip of her delicate finger, and that she will condescend to make it the instrument wherewith to seal my right eye, so that it shall remain entirely shut. Instead of one finger she gave him two, and so effectually closed his eye, that farther use of it he had none. He then said, Fair one, is it closed? Yes, certainly, said she, and with that withdrew her hand. On this he swore by God, and by His holy mother, that never again should that eye be opened, for hail, for blast, for rain, or for storm, till o'er the plains of France he had scattered fire, sword, havoc and devastation. Nor, in fact, during the entire duration of the war, was the earl ever once seen to open his eye; and the whole army, witness of his exploits, was no less so of the exactitude with which he performed his vow. The Count d'Artois, to confirm him still more in his resolution, addresses himself to the lady, soliciting her, too, to deign to be a participator in the vows of the heron. Readily, said she, and with that she swore by the God of paradise, that never till the oath of her vassal were accomplished, would she hearken to, or permit the suit of any; be he who he might; duke, lord, earl or baron. Then, said she, let him come home to me alive, and I will make to him a free gift, without reservation, and for ever, of my person. With such a prize, incitement before him, the knight, transported with joy, felt himself to be endued with an almost superhuman courage. Now doubly burning to wreak his vengeance, Robert retakes the heron and tenders it to Sir Walter Manny. This brave knight, as became him, and to show himself worthy of the heroes who had preceded him, swore by the Virgin, mother of that God, who heaven created, the dews and the damps, not only that he would take and burn a strong town, flanked with towers, upon the marches of France, and of which Godenar de Fay was governor; that it should be ransacked, and the garrison put to the sword, but that he would come off, as should also all those who accompanied him, scathelefs from the attack. For the remainder, said he, I cast myself upon the mercy of God, and with whom alone must rest the success of our endeavour. Robert then calls upon the Earl of Derby, requiring him, for the love of God, and of the Holy Trinity, to announce his vow, as the rest. The earl, accepting the challenge, replies, Let the King of England once lead us beyond the seas, and we must needs see this terrible Louis, Count of Flanders, for so is he called of the followers of Philip de Valois, usurper of the Crown of France, and which he holds in the teeth of our monarch. We shall see him; or not a corner but I will search for him. So help me, St. Thomas; may I once get near enough to him to propose him a course! If he deny me; he cannot the satisfaction of destroying before his eyes the lands which he has not the heart to stand forth to defend.

This new triumph perfectly turns the head of Robert. Already, in imagination, he sees the Valois in the dust, his family at large, and himself re-entered upon his own. Resuming the dishes, he lays them before the Earl of Suffolk, requiring him too to append his oath to so noble a register. Suffolk then swears in his turn, that, Let but Edward carry him to France, and he would pursue to the death the King of Bohemia, the Emperor's son; he would fall upon him, hand to hand, with sword or with lance; and he would unhorse him, and take him from him, by force or by surrender. On hearing this, John de Beaumont sighed deeply. Such an outrage to be meditated to a prince of his parentage, the conqueror of an hundred fights, stung him to madness and to fury. Yes, he may hate me; but never shall I forget, he is of my blood: nor shall I forsake to love him. Nor while this arm a sword can wield, will I be found but by his side. Suffolk, renounce to your extravagant pretensions, or by the Holy Virgin, mother of God, I swear that I will bury you in the dungeons of Bohemia. Yes! and where no eye can reach you, and from which no hand can pluck you. I have said it, and no power shall hinder it. Suffolk, unwilling yet farther to provoke him, coldly replied, You are right. It had been wiser to have kept our purposes to ourselves till war had actually been declared. They had come with a better grace. We had equally been at liberty to have performed, for the honour of our ladies, the feats to which our love might prompt. Menaces are but air. The grand point is — the conclusion.

Here the Count d'Artois caused the damsels to lead forth the dance, the harpers to strike, and the minstrels to chant yet louder, still farther to provoke and to kindle the ardour of the heroes. On this, Robert, retaking the heron, advances to that intrepid adventurer, Fauquemont, requiring him also to pass his oath upon the heron, and bidding him to cover himself with glory in the quarrel which were ensuing between the two monarchs. God, said he, is it for me to talk of promises; I, who am but a poor penniless adventurer! However, what I can do, I will do. And this day, as well to mark my loyalty, as for the enhancement of my honour, I do promise and swear, that from the hour when the King of England shall have crossed the seas, by Cambray into France, I shall ever be found in the forefront of his advanced guard, affronting the enemy, carrying fire, sword and devastation upon every hand— that I will neither spare man, nor woman, nor child; nor woman with child, nor sucking babe; nor old man, nor maid; nor convent, altar, church. At these terrible imprecations, it was who would loudest extol the zeal and the devotion of so faithful a champion of the honour and the cause of his master.

Again the dishes are withdrawn, and the noble virgins proceed, singing, *True loves fond invite; which to* voice we now go. All eyes are now turned upon that famous warrior, John de Beaumont, uncle to the noble Count of Haynault. Robert, respectfully approaching, begs him to enroll himself also among the Knights of the Heron. Disgusted perhaps with the tedium of so many promises, John gravely recalled to the company the futility of all such empty and tumultuous vauntings; exhorting them rather to reserve their mettle for a season when it were more likely to be needed, and turned to account. It costs but little, said he, in a hall, mid the tapers and the dance, stimulated by the presence of the fair ones to whose favours we would aspire, to put to the rout whole armies from the field. I know well, that there are among you of Rolands and of Olivers, and who will dispose of the Aquilans and the Yaumonts: but let this be recollected, these paladins, in their turn, were compelled to succumb to others. Is it not a very farce to see an army, well armed and well mounted, making a bravado and a parade of its prowess, the enemy across the Channel! Let us keep all these fine resolutions to ourselves; or at least till they are more likely to be called into requisition. How many a pretty fellow will then find a cellar, deep as hell, scarce dark enough to hide his diminished head in! Again, I say, all this vaunting is but wind. And though I say this, fancy not that I want to elude the alternative which is placed upon me. I will explain myself. Let the King of England once penetrate

Haynault, traverfe Brabant and Cambray, fet foot upon the French foil, and I will be feen, as marfhal of his army, faithfully fupporting his fide, and caufing all the evil that I can to Philip. It is true, by this I fhall lay myfelf open to the forfeiture, not only of my territories, but of all the little which I have. No matter. I accept my fortune. By the event I will abide. But let me not be mifunderftood. If Philip, of his own proper counfel, and returning upon his better judgment, revoke my banifhment, and recall me to France, I will at once break with Edward. And if I do, who is he who will impugn? But if, on the other hand, the King of France will perfift in continuing me an exile from his country and my home, I will fecond the King of England to the utmoft of my power. I will either be his general-in-chief, or of his advanced guard.

To an explanation fo manly, fo generous, the monarch rejoined with the moft touching expreffions of his regard. Robert, the two filver difhes in his hand, once more advances, accompanied by the minftrels, the two noble damfels finging as they went; and now kneeling to the queen, affured her that there was but one thing wanting more to the diftribution of the heron, and that was, that fhe fhould open to the company the dictates of her noble breaft. Vaffal, faid fhe, by the laws and by the ties of holy church, it is not within my competence to enter into any engagement unprivy to my lord and mafter; who, at his will, it can annul, or it can bid to ftand. Stand not for that, faid the monarch; it is already ratified, at once, and beforehand. To the utmoft of my power it fhall be feconded; God but put the practicable into your mouth!¹ Then faid the queen, rifing, with a voice undaunted, unfhaken and unmoved, I am with child; I know it, for I have felt it ftir. And I fwear this day to God; to Him who died and was crucified upon a crofs, and to the Holy Virgin, His mother, that never fhall this precious fruit part from my womb, till, for the accomplifhment of this vow, you fhall have carried me beyond the feas. And let but this infant think to void his prifonhoufe, or ever the allotted hour be come which I have profcribed, and this dagger, to the haft, fhall be buried in its and in my bowels: and thus let perifh, at a ftroke, my body's foul and my body's fruit! Petrified with horror at an imprecation fo terrible, Edward forbade that the matter, one other moment, fhould be proceeded with. The heron was morfelled, and the queen and all the company partook of it.

The king, the neceffary preparations made, embarked the queen with all his chivalry, conducting her and them fafely to Antwerp. And there was fhe de-

---

¹ See note D, at the end.

livered of a fine male child, since known as the *Lion of Antwerp*. Her vow accomplished, the king, with all his hosts, departed for the plains of France. — ST. PELAYE, *Mémoires sur l'ancienne Chevalerie*.

THE PITEOUS DEATH,

Through too long a Concealment of his Attachment,

OF A GENTLEMAN OF DAUPHINY.

N the confines of Dauphiny and of Provence there was lately living a gentleman, richer much in every virtue, grace, accomplishment, than in that wealth which this world's gear, poffeffions bring. And near him there was living, as is fhe ftill living, a young perfon, whofe name I fhall forbear, out of regard to her family, which is of the nobleft, and of whom this gentleman was paffionately enamoured. And though the names I may withhold, the ftory is no lefs to be relied on. But feeing himfelf not to be come of fuch an houfe as would entitle him to raife his eyes to fuch an height, his paffion he fmothered in his breaft; for fo pure and unearthly was the love which he bore to her,

that sooner had he died than so much as harbour a thought which might have redounded to her disadvantage. Thus, inasmuch as it were hopeless ever to attain to her hand, all that he proposed to himself, as the summit of his felicity, was, to be enabled to worship her, unobserved, and at a distance, with all that perfect piety of which so heavenly a spirit were capable. And this he long did; but not with such a wariness but that at the length it came to be suspected of the lady. And she, perceiving the affection which he bore to her to be of a texture so holy and so pure; sensible to all the distinction of the attachment of so clean a spirit, met him with so much pity, so much sympathy, that the poor gentleman, who had never dared to hope for so much, could not even bring himself to wish for more. But malice, foe to all beatitude, quick nipped in the bud, an intercourse so tranquil and so happy. For first it came to be whispered about, then repeated to the mother, how much it was wondered at, that she could allow, as she did, the gentleman to haunt her house: that the gentleman could not possibly have any other than one inducement, seeing he and her daughter were so much together, in being for ever about as he was. The mother, who would not allow herself, even for a moment, to doubt of the rectitude of the gentleman, and for whose honour she would have answered, as for that of her own children, was beyond expression hurt, to find that upon such an intimacy, a construction so cruel could be placed. However, at length, fearing the scandal which was like to come of it, she entreated of the gentleman, at least for a time, to discontinue his attendance; a command to him none of the easiest of digestion; conscious to himself, as he was, that the innocence of his intentions might have guaranteed him from any such suspicions. However, as there was no help for it, and to silence the voice of scandal, he withdrew himself till such time as the affair had been forgotten; returning, to be readmitted to all his old footing; and the privation of which, you may be sure, had in no way palled his appetite. But about the very first news with which he was entertained, was, that the daughter of the house was as good as given to a gentleman, whose fortune he was unable to gather to be so much more considerable than his own, that he could bring himself to allow any such make-weight to be balanced with claims, old and standing as his own. And so, plucking up spirit, he set all his friends and kindred to work, hoping that if the choice could but be left to the maid, she would give him the preference before his rival. However, the parents, as well on his side as on her's, decided for the other, inasmuch as he was the richer; which the unfortunate gentleman took so much to heart, (knowing the poor girl to be as thwarted as himself,) that, by little and little, and without any apparent cause, he began to dwindle and to pine away; and in a very short time was so altered a man in his appearance, that the mark of death became enftamped upon his features; that death to which right rapturoufly and joyfully he was hafting. Still, fo long as he was able, he continued to trail himfelf to the fide of her whom he fo dearly loved. At length, all his forces fpent, there was nothing for it but to take to his bed, which he did; concealing, while yet he could, his fate from his friend; willing to fpare her the agony of fuch a knowledge. Now abandoning himfelf a prey to forrow and defpair, his fleep went from him, and with it all care for his meat or his drink; and fo thoroughly became he changed, that fcarce longer was it poffible to recognife him, fuch was the ghaftlinefs and the hollownefs of his features. This could not but come to the ears of the mother, who, of her own nature, kind and compaffionate, in reality at heart fo much loved the gentleman, that, had it but depended upon her, her daughter fhould have been given to him. But the parents on the father's fide were not to be gained. So, taking with her her daughter, fhe went the poor fufferer to vifit, whom too truly fhe found, as fhe had been told, rather dead than alive; for he, perceiving his end to be at hand, had, that very morning, received the facrament, nor ever thinking face of mortal to look upon again. Neverthelefs did he, within one ace of his extremity; as one arifing from the dead; feeing to be before him her, who was at once his refurrection and his life; raifing himfelf, and with a bound, exclaim,

And what, Madam, may I afk, can have poffeffed you thus to come, a man to vifit; one foot already in the grave, and of whofe death you are the caufe? Alas, faid the lady, and can it be that one fo dear to us, death fhould be receiving at our hands! Tell me, I pray you, how can this be. Madam, faid he, although I had ftruggled, as long as concealment were poffible, with the attachment which I bore to your daughter; yet have my family, in profecuting my fuit, fomewhat more noifed it, than, had it depended upon me, I could have ever wifhed, feeing the misfortune which has overtaken me. Nor is it fo much the ruin of all my earthly hopes which has brought me to this pafs, as the confcioufnefs that with no other could fhe ever have been bleffed and loved as of me. The lofs which fhe is about this day to make of the kindeft, the gentleft, and the fondeft heart which ever woman loved, afflicts me more, at this moment, than does that of a life, which, for her fake alone I had cared to preferve, and which, as it never more can be of ufe to her, it is but a fmall matter to me to part with. What was in their power to comfort him to fay, was faid. At length, faid the lady, This will never do; come, cheer up, my friend, and I give you my honour, if God will but reftore to you your wonted health, never fhall my daughter have other hufband than you; and this I now require her, and with her own lips, to confirm. This, the poor girl, in tears, as faithfully consented to. But he, who too well knew, that though his health, indeed, again he might get, yet never would he get his love; that all these fair promises were but so many prescriptions, remediate to his case, told them very plainly, that he was not to be so imposed upon; that had they but held to him such language, not three months gone, then had he been that day the blithest, the soundest and the happiest gentleman in France; but that all such comfort was now coming too late to be either credited, or to be available. However, presently, seeing them to persist in their story, after a little pause, he continued, Seeing that you are promising me what never now can be, even supposing it to be ever so much your desire; grant me, in its stead, a favour that, considering the state in which I am, I think might safely be permitted to me; a lesser than, alive, God knows, I have ever presumed to aspire to. They assured him that it should be conceded; and that he might ask, and hardily. Then, said he, Let me take into mine arms her whom you are promising me to wife; and bid her that she may embrace me, and may kiss me. The poor girl, unpractised to such a familiarity, was about to hesitate, nor knowing what to do; till her mother, seeing that there was no more life in him, expressly desired her to do as she had undertaken. On this advancing, and bowing herself upon the wretched man, she said, My good friend, for my sake, be of good heart. Then stretching forth his withered arms, scarce other now than skin and bone, he drew her to his breast with all the little strength he had; kissing with his poor, cold, pallid lips, her at whose hands his death he was accepting. And thus having held her as long as he was able, unclasping her, he said, So holy and so pure has been the love which I have ever borne to you, that never, out of the church, did I so much as desire a more perfect felicity than that which now I prove; at the expiration of which, and in the ravishment of which, right joyfully I am about to render up my soul to God; that God who himself is complete love and charity, and who well can testify to the purity of my affection and the abysses of my regard; entreating him to take, my perfect desire encompassed in mine arms, my parting spirit to his eternal keeping. And with these words, straining her to his bosom with a redoubled vehemence, the heart, unable longer to sustain the exaltation of so unwonted a beatitude, dilating to its full, its cerement burst, and the spirit, escaped, to its Maker returned. And though the poor corpse now lay without life, and for that cause could no more retain its charge; so apparent became the affection which the lady had ever borne to him, that it was not without the greatest efforts that her mother, with the servants, could detach the body of the living, if living she could be called, from the embraces of the dead; and whom they caused to be honourably interred. But the triumph of the obsequies were the tears, the sobs, the lamentations of the unfortunate girl; and which the rather declared themselves after his death, as during his life they had been stifled; and as some sort of reparation for all the catastrophe which she had brought upon him. Nor since, as I have heard, let what husband they would be proposed to her, has she ever known peace or joy of heart. — *L'Heptaméron.*

PAULINE AND HER LOVER,

Renouncing the World, betake themselves to a Monastic Life.

N the time of the Marquis of Mantua, the same who had married a sister of the Duke of Ferrara, there was living in the family of the Marchioness, a young person, called Pauline, so distractedly loved of a gentleman, servant to the Marquis, that the affair became the wonder, the talk and the theme of all; seeing that so poor and so pleasant a fellow might not unnaturally have looked to match himself, through the influence of his master, into some noble or some wealthy house. But all the riches of the world, to him seemed centred in his Pauline; and whose hand in marriage he yet hoped to obtain. The Marchioness, no less purposing, through her own personal interposition, to see Pauline more advantageously disposed of, as much as in her lay,

ought to discountenance the match: forbidding them to be together; and showing them how, should they persist in their folly, they must inevitably resign themselves to become, as well the most unhappy as the most inconsiderable couple in the land—a light in which the gentleman never could be brought to see the matter; whilst Pauline, on her part, so far as it were possible, struggled openly with her affections; still continuing, however, to nurse them in secret as before. And thus matters lingered long; supported on either side by the hope, that, sooner or later, time or chance would bring them victorious out of all their troubles; even till the war broke out; and in which war it was the fortune of the gentleman to be made a prisoner, together with a Frenchman, who, as it turned out, was no less in love in France than was his companion in Italy. And so it fell, finding themselves to be captives together, that they came to know each other's matters; and the Frenchman plainly blabbed, that his heart, as his friend's, was equally a prisoner; though the *where* he kept to himself. But inasmuch as they were servants alike to the Marquis, the French gentleman was not long in divining, that it was Pauline to whom his friend was attached; and out of the kindliness and the regard which he felt for him, no argument was left unattempted by which he might detach him from so unhappy a pursuit. But this the gentleman assured him to be a chapter beyond the reach of preachment, hope or remedy; that he might defift; and that fhould the Marquis of Mantua perfift to refufe him his love, as an indemnity for all the prifon which he had undergone, and as a return for his fervices, his fufferings, he would conftitute himfelf a friar, nor from henceforth to know, or to ferve any other mafter than God; which ftaggered his companion beyond all belief, who had never been able to detect in him any other inkling toward religion than the adoration which he bore to Pauline. Some eight or nine months gone, the gentleman, Frenchman, his companion, was fortunate enough to find himfelf at liberty, and no lefs fo, not long after, in purchafing as much for his friend; who, at the end of a very few days, was again at the court of the marquis, endeavouring, by every means that he could devife, to overcome the reluctance of the marquis and the marchionefs to his union with his Pauline. But it was all but fo much labour loft; nor would they deign to any other reply, than that the match was forbidden by the parents, as well on the one fide as on the other; or a fermon upon all the remorfe, the mifery, the privation, which a ftep fo ill-confidered would neceffarily entail. And by way of making matters fure; to preclude the poffibility of farther mifapprehenfion or mifhap, it was ftrictly forbidden to them ever again to haunt one another's company; thus hoping, that with time and feparation this moft unhappy fantafy would die out and be forgotten.

The gentleman, seeing that there was nothing for it but to obey and to retire, submitting, solicited, if it were not too vast a presumption, to be allowed at least to bid to one he loved so dear, a last adieu; seeing that he never was to see her more. Which being granted to him; coming to her, he said; It is even so, Pauline; heaven and earth are at one, not only to prevent our coming together, but even as friend and friend, to look upon or entertain each other more. For our master and our mistress have this day given commandment so strict, that well may they flatter themselves to have despatched, at a blow, two hearts of which the tenements can never now but languish: clearly showing, by such an ordinance, that love and charity alike are strangers to their breasts. I know well that it is their meaning to marry us apart, and into wealthy portions. But ah, little know they, that there is no riches to true contentment! In sum, I have suffered so much, and so heavily at their hands, that longer to remain in their service, with me is impossible. And if I well know, supposing that I never had talked or thought of marriage, they would not have been so nice but what I had been permitted to court you as beforetime; rest assured, had it been so, that sooner had I died than harboured a farther thought towards one whom I had loved with so pure an affection; to whose hand I had pretended, and would have been ready to assert against all. But seeing that to be thus tantalised had been to me too infupportable a penance; and that, in thus beholding you, this poor heart, denied of its juft contentment, would have been for ever filling itfelf, a prey to fome terrible defpair, and of which the end had been cataftrophous; I have determined, and fince long, to betake myfelf to the church. Not but what I know that falvation may be purchafed in every ftate and condition of life, but that, by an undiftracted leifure, I may be enabled more effectually to contemplate the divine Goodnefs, which, I truft, will be merciful to the fins of my youth; will give to me a new heart, as much to be enamoured of the things of heaven, as once it hath been of thofe of bafenefs and of earth. And if God will but vouchfafe to give to me the grace to be a partaker of his, my prayer to him for you fhall ceafelefs rife;[1] befeeching you, in return, by all that very true and conftant paffion which has ever been between us, that, in your orifons, I may ever be remembered; that in this, my extremity, I may be fuftained; that He will give to me an heart as great to fupport our feparation, as, in your prefence, it hath alway found of joy and of contentment. And now feeing that we are about to part, and for ever; and that never more need I hope to have of you that perfect blifs which comes of unifon; fuffer me, of a little charity, that, as a brother, I may embrace you. The poor Pauline, who till now had always treated him with rigour enough; over-

[1] See note E, at the end.

whelmed as well with the tendernefs of the requeft, as with the delicacy of the man, who, in fuch a crifis, could content himfelf with fo reafonable a prayer, for all reply, flung herfelf, fainting and in an agony, into his arms; in fuch a very deluge of tears, that, voice, breath, utterance choked; head and limbs both reeling alike; infenfible, fhe lay upon his breaft. What with love, pity, agony, alarm, diftrefs, the unhappy gentleman, incapable to the charge of fuch a burden, was feen, from a distance, to ftagger and to fall, as was the lady; he one way and fhe another. However, as fuccour was quickly at hand, with the help of reftoratives they were each brought round. Pauline, on coming to herfelf, was beyond expreffion mortified to learn the fcene, into which, through her weaknefs, fhe had been betrayed; placing, fo far as fhe could, to the fcore of pity and compaffion, the emotion which fo unhappily had efcaped her. Whilft he, in his turn, unwilling as unable again to face fo terrible an ordeal, hurried away, head and heart fo full, that, on entering his chamber, he flung himfelf upon his bed, in fuch a paroxyfm of defpair, that fure nothing lefs was concluded of all, than that that day he had made fhipwreck of the laft friend which he had in the world, or the laft farthing in his poffeffion. And no fooner was it light, and he had rifen, and committed himfelf to his Saviour, than, dividing whatever he had among his fervants, taking fome little refrefhment for his journey, and having ftri&tly forbidden to any to follow him, he went the way of the convent of St. Francis; requiring himſelf to be admitted into the order; which, as he told the monks, it was never more his intention to quit. The abbot, familiar with the man, and with his paſt, having often ſeen him, could ſcarce believe his eyes, or allow the gentleman to be ſerious; almoſt fancying the whole to be a dream, or a pleaſantry; for ſure a gentleman in France who had naturally leſs about him, the air, the cut, or the mien of a monk; or was more abundantly ſtocked, by nature and by art, with all the graces and the accompliſhments of a gallant, he knew not. But coming by degrees to take in his meaning, and ſeeing the floods of tears which kept courſing down his cheeks, he came at length to abandon his firſt impreſſions; charitably conſenting to receive him. And in a little time, perſuaded as well of the conſtancy of his reſolution as of the unfeignedneſs of his repentance, he had him to be ſolemnly allowed. All which ſhortly, as could not but be, came to the ears of the marquis and of the marchioneſs, and to whom the whole appeared ſuch a myſtery, that at the firſt, it was as much as they could do to credit it. Whilſt Pauline, as if to ſhow how completely ſhe had learned to maſter ſo unhappy an attachment, diſſimulated ſo effectually her paſſion, that the world, whom no one thing can ſatisfy, began to ſcatter, that ſhe had ſomewhat too ſoon forgotten ſo faithful and ſo fond a lover. And in this manner rolled themſelves away ſome four or five months, and without any ſort of fignification, on the one part or on the other. In this interval there was shown to her, by a lay brother, an effusion which had escaped from her lover, shortly after his entry into the convent; and which, though common enough in the Italian, I shall be obliged to turn for you into French, as best I can.

* * * * *

No sooner had Pauline read this tribute, and which she did in the silence of a cloister, than she was seized with such an agony of heart, that the very letters were saturated with her tears. And so thoroughly was she mastered, that her first thought was, to bury upon the instant, and for ever, in some hermitage, a passion so rooted and unrootable. But that prudence which had never forsaken her, conjured yet a little to defer her purpose. And however, in her inmost mind, her determination might remain unshaken, in public it was never allowed to eke; carrying with her a presence, a countenance, a mien, so accessible, so unpreoccupied, that nothing less than what she was, she seemed more to be. And this, her resolution, she covered, some six months, in her breast; to all appearance, more radiant, more reconciled to the world, than the oldest who had known her could recall: yet not so long, but that it came, one day, that Pauline, in the train of her mistress, found herself at mass in the convent of St. Francis. And who should be there and then approaching, the procession issuing from the vestry, but her unfortunate servant, who, yet in his probation year, was officiating, in attendance upon the priests; carrying the censers, covered with a cloth of silk; and he the foremost; his eyes infixed on the ground! And no sooner had Pauline detected him, mid all the glory and the halo of such a vesture; and which, if anything, seemed rather to heighten, than to detract from the heavenliness and the comeliness of his features, than in the endeavour to cloke, as much as possible, the misery she was in, she compelled herself to be seized, as with a fit of coughing. Her poor servant, to whom were sooner caught that little sound, than all the clamourings of his parish peal, could not so far refrain himself, though turn his head he would not, but that his eyes would walk their wonted ways. And no sooner had he seen her, than, dizzied and bewildered, he staggered and he fell; each and every fire rekindled, which fondly and madly he had hoped to have been quenched. However, recovering himself, to some little inequality in the pavement, he was fain to have his trouble laid. And no sooner did Pauline see, that though habit, indeed, he might have changed, heart and affections he had changed not, than she came to the conclusion, to put into execution, upon the hour, a resolution to which her mind had now been long made up—that the residue of their days should be passed in the one manner, dedicated to the one Lord; as had their prime, in the one hotel, and in the service of the one master and the one mistress. And as it was now many months since everything had been in preparation for such a step, one day she demanded permission of the marchioness, to be allowed to go to the convent of St. Clair, to hear the mass; and which was accorded to her; the lady having no manner of suspicion touching the real nature of her request. And in passing before the Gray Friars, she alighted, requiring the porter to send to her her lover, who she told him was her kinsman. And no sooner had they retired together to the solitude of a chapel, than Pauline first, and thus began. Had it been to be reconciled with mine honour, or my spirit, the step which I am this day taking had not been till now deferred. Your retirement had been my retirement. But seeing that, at length, by patience and by colour, I have broken the malice and suspicions of the world, ever prone rather to impute the worser than the better motive, I have now determined to adopt life, garb, estate, such as I perceive this day to be yours. Nor farther am I curious to inquire. If to you is well, then to me is also well. If to you is ill, that ill would I partake. The road that you do tread to paradise, that road would I; assured that He who is the fountain of the one, true, only, perfect love, us has knit, adopted to his service, by a concord pure and unearthly; and which, by his Holy Spirit, he will transform to his eternal essence: praying you, my friend, that you and I, this day, may put off, and for ever, the body of the flesh, which is of the old Adam; to be regenerate, and to be born again, in that of our Lord and Saviour, Jesus Christ. Who at this was ravished but this holy and this precious lover?— fortifying her, by every means which were in his power, in an agony of tears and of joy, in this, her pious conclusion, and telling her, that since never now could he have of her other joy than that of fellowship, he accounted it no mean blessing that they were to find themselves together in such a retreat, that, at least with their eyes, they might behold each other: that such an alleviation could not but be for the refreshment of their souls; henceforth to live, participants of the one affection, the one heart, the one spirit; emanations of the mercy of that one God, whom now he prayed them to hold in his eternal keeping; and from which none, who ever yet did trust in him, did perish or did fall. And with these words, kissing her hand, in a very transport of rapture and of tears, she signified to him to take the holy kiss of love and charity, and which he did. And in this divinest ecstacy departed Pauline.

No sooner was all this conveyed to the marchioness, and whom it staggered almost beyond the reach of credence, than she hasted, with the light, to the monastery; in the hope, that, by any chance, a step so precipitate might yet be retraced. To all which Pauline made no other reply, than that she might have been content; that it was enough to have divorced her from an husband in the flesh; the man of all men whom she the most passionately loved, without attempting to separate her from one that was a spirit, immortal and invisible; and which it should neither be in her power, nor in that of all the powers of earth combined, to effect. The marchioness, satisfied as well of the vainness of her attempt, as of the sincerity of her attendant, having kissed her, left her, with a remorseful and an aching heart. And since lived so holily and so devoutly, Pauline and her servant, that it is not to be questioned but that He, the fulfilment of whose law is charity, to them, as to the Magdeleine, at the expiration of their days, did say, that, as much they had loved, much to them was forgiven; or that now they are gathered to that blissful strand, the joy of which no eye hath seen, content of which no ear hath heard! — *L'Heptaméron.*

THE PROLOGUE
TO
THE CHRONICLES OF FROISSART.

IN order that the memorable achievements, with the noble adventures and paſſages of arms, performed as well upon the fields of England as of France, might be becomingly related, and tabled into a perpetual memory; whereby a bold poſterity might be fired to like, ſuch noble empriſe, I have determined with myſelf to treat of mighty and of imperiſhable matters. But, or ever I begin, I do firſt require of him; the great Saviour of the world, who, from out of nothing, all things did make, that He, in me, will create and will renew, an underſtanding clear and ſimple; ſo that not only every man and every woman who may ſee, or who may hear this, my book, may find in it their ſolace and enſample; but that into their grace, I alſo may be received. It is ſaid, and truly, that it is of every material that the edifice is raised, and that the mightiest river is but the gathering of the little rills. Similarly, of many clerks, is science culled and devised. That which this one is ignorant of, another can declare; nor is there any one thing which is not known; that is, of some, or in part. In order then to attain to the end, which, as I have said, I have purposed with myself, I shall take, as the basis of this, my chronicle, (invoking first, as I do, the grace of God, and of the Holy Virgin; of whom all comfort and advancement come,) that which, now long since, was compiled by my lord, Master John le Bel, canon of St. Lambert, at Liège; a man very reverend, grave and discreet; and who, with an unwearied diligence, and at an incredible pains, collected the same; his whole life being spent in the pursuit. Nor however much he may have expended, was he ever heard to grudge it; for, not only was he a man considerable, and of substance, (and, as such, could support it,) but of his own natural, generous, equal, just and liberal; dispensing with a pleasure the bounty of his hand. And moreover than this, he was, all his days, high in consideration, and very near with my lord, Sir John of Haynault, who will often be remembered, as is but just, in this book. For not only was he allied to more than one king, but himself the mainstay and the rise of many a great and memorable event. And for these reasons the aforesaid John le Bel was enabled, being about him, to see and to hear all those noble exploits which hereinafter are to be recited. And with this it is no lefs true, that by a very inſtinct I have undertaken this work; having always been curious into fuch matters; and to this intent have vifited the courts of many great and powerful barons, as well in France as in England, Scotland, and fundry other lands; and have never failed, on occafion, to inform myfelf concerning all worthy matters; wars, battles, fieges, combats, tournays; more especially since the great battle of Poitiers, where John, the noble king of France, was taken prifoner. For previoufly to that, I was very young, as well in years as in underſtanding. Howbeit, young as I was, I fet myfelf refolutely to work, to the chronicling of the aforefaid wars; purpofing from the first, to carry my work into England, as foon as completed. And which I lived to do, and to prefent it to the Lady Philippa of Haynault, queen of England, who gracioufly and condefcendingly received it at my hands, and well rewarded me for all my pains. I will not deny, but it may be found, that this, my chronicle, has neither been compiled with the diligence, nor the exactitude which a narration, fo memorable, would demand; for the honours and the ends of war, for the moſt part fo dearly bought, ought, above all other, to be unweariedly inquired into, and fcrupuloufly adjudged to thofe whofe meed they are. It is then to acquit myfelf towards all fuch, and in all truthfulnefs, that I have entered upon this undertaking, and on the foundation already fpoken to; at the prayer, and upon the ordinance of my much loved lord and mafter, Sir John de Namur, Knight, Lord of Beaufort, to whom I owe all duty, love and reverence; and in whofe grace and in whofe favour, may God continue to me the gift for ever to abide.

FROISSART.

THE DEATH, & DYING INSTRUCTIONS

OF

CHARLES V. OF FRANCE.

AT this time the king of France was overtaken with a very terrible misfortune; at which he, as well as all who knew him, were grievously distressed. For there was no help for it, but he had to die, and that too in a very little space. And all this the king well knew, as did the surgeons; and I will tell you how, and why. As the story runs, the king of France, when in his youth, and at the court of the king of Navarre, had been so subtly tampered with by that monarch, that the poison became imbibed into his system. So that not only came his flesh to dry and shrivel like a chip, but the hairs to fall from off his head, and the nails from the tips of his fingers and his toes; so that he was visibly perishing, in the eyes of all, beyond the reach of hope, art or remedy. And no sooner had his uncle, the emperor of Rome, heard of it, than he dispatched to him, in all haste, a master physician, of his own household, the most unparalleled in his science at that time alive in the world, or that, it is supposed, was ever known, or lived. And no sooner had this master physician been to the king, (at that time Duke of Normandy,) and had satisfied himself as to the nature of his affection, than he gave it, that he was poisoned, and that it went for his life. And with that he performed for him, (the since king of France,) the most astounding cure which ever was heard tell of. For he caused the venom to be so mortified, or appeased, that he was, in a little time, restored to all his wonted strength and vigour. And this by means of an issue which he practised in his arm, and through which, by little and little, the malice oozed and ran off. This effected, (and for no consideration could he be induced to remain in France,) he left with the king a receipt, to be followed as long as he should live; and distinctly told the king, as well as those who were about him, that, should the day ever come when that fistula would scab, ceasing to run, he would there and then have to die, out of hand; without let, remedy or hope; and that some fifteen or twenty days were the outside upon which he would have to calculate, for the settlement of his kingdom, and for the reconciliation and propitiation of his soul.

Death and Dying Charge of Charles V. 113

And well had the king carried all this in his memory, and forely and heavily had it lain upon him. And it was now the two and twentieth day fince the iffue had begun to flack. Nor could any other comfort be adminiftered to him than of his phyficians, who told him to be of good heart, for that with remedies of which he little thought, they would not yet fail to dompt the fiend; and fo to be of good heart and to banifh fear. Nor was this the only thing which troubled him; for to the toothache he was a fore martyr and a prey. And well took the king meafure, from all thefe admonifhments, precurfors, that longer he had not to live. And the thing, above all others, which the moft comforted him and fupported him, in all his afflictions, was, the recollection that God had bleffed him with three fair children; two fons and a daughter; Charles, Louis and Catherine. And no fooner had the iffue begun to flack, no more to run, than the king recalled to himfelf, how, by the device of the mafter leech, his hour was come. And fo, (like a wife and valiant prince, as he was,) all other matters fettled and difpatched, he caufed to be called to his fide, his three brothers; the Dukes of Berry, of Bourgoyne, and of Bourbon. His fecond brother, the Duke of Anjou, he called not, as he well knew him to be of a nature fo miferably infatiable. And no fooner were they come together than he fpake, Good my brothers, thus it is. By ordinance of nature I am now required to die; for well I know, that longer I have not to live. My son, Charles, I commit into your hands. Be kind to the lad. Acquit yourselves to him loyally in all things; as loving uncles to a nephew should. As soon as may be, let him be crowned, after my decease. Counsel him, in all his affairs, to the best of your understanding. All my hopes now rest with you. The lad is young and thoughtless; reason the more that he should be governed and advised of abler, and of older heads. See that he be indoctrined to all the state and appointment of a king; as well in what is to be attended of him, as in that which it will be for him, from his subjects, to require. Marry him into some royal and some noble house; but, any how, that it be to the profit of the realm at large. I have long known by a famous astrologer, who told it me, and assured me, that in his youth he would have perilous affairs upon hand, and that it would be consumed amid great and terrible commotions and assaults. As to what he can possibly have been referring to, I have had many a sorry cogitation. And much have I turned in my mind from what quarter the blow is like to come, if not from Flanders. For, God be praised, the affairs of my kingdom were never in better case. The Duke of Bretaigne is a man to be looked to; for one very fickle in his nature, and of an infinite subtlety, and who has ever worn an heart rather English than French. And for this reason, spare not to keep on good terms, as well with the nobles as the good towns of Brittany. In no other way is his malice to be defeated. Of the Bretons themselves, I have no cause to complain; they have invariably and faithfully served me, and helped me to defend my kingdom against my enemies. Also make Sir Oliver Clisson constable; for, all things considered, I know of none so fitting thereto as he. And for the marriage of Charles, my son; look first to Germany. If it be possible, ally him into that quarter. It will be for his and all your safety. You know how our adversary of England is seeking to fortify himself, by alliance, in the same direction. Be beforehand. The poor are sorely assessed and tormented. Remit the taxes you can, and as soon as you can. These are matters which, albeit in my lifetime I may have been compelled to wink at them, sit not, at this moment, too lightly upon my breast; though the endless undertakings, with the wars which we had on hand, in a measure constrained me to continue them. And many other like and memorable words were spoken by the said King John, which, however, I have not deemed it necessary to repeat. And although the King of France refused to see the Duke of Anjou, upon his death-bed, or to allow him any part in the government of the state, for all that, the said duke was by him at the time. For he had posts for ever on the road between Angers and Paris, and who apprised him certainly, in all things, touching the king, his brother.

And he had, farther, ſpies, who brought him word, day and night, of the progreſs of his declination; ſo that he was enabled, the very day of his deceaſe, to be in an antichamber, and by which means he came to ſee and to hear everything as it paſſed, and as I have told it you. And now we will return to the matter of the Engliſh, and whom we left on their way to Bretaigne. — FROISSART.

AN ACCOUNT

OF

TWO OR THREE REMARKABLE DUELS.

N the early part of the reign of the late King Henry II., there was a duel, at Sedan, between the baron de Guerres and the lord de Fandilles, and which originated in a difpute that occurred between them, the very identical day that the faid majefty made his entry into Paris. The caufe I fhall forbear, as it was a fomewhat dirty one, and none of the moft creditable.

* * * * *

Thefe two brave gentlemen, then, to fettle the matter between them, (for it trenched too clofely, as well upon the honour as the reputation of the baron, to admit of any fort of compromife,) demanded of the king the ufe of the lifts, and which the king, who fince the unhappy affair of my uncle, Monfieur de la Chaftaigneraye, which he never ceased to deplore, as flatly denied them. As they were not, however, to be so diverted, they had next recourse to Monsieur de Bouillon, as prince sovereign of Sedan; and where they were successful. And accordingly, on the day appointed, neither failed to appear; accompanied on either side by their parents, friends, allies, godfathers, supporters; all preliminaries and formalities enjoined by the ancient and well-known laws of the duello, adjusted and complied with. But first and foremost, nothing would suit the lord de Fandilles, (so confident and overweening was he,) but he must build himself a gibbet and roll himself a faggot, that he might be indulged in the satisfaction as well of roasting as of hanging his opponent! However, fortune stood not so much his friend as he had thought for, for he had the worst of it; but not, however, in such a manner that his adversary had any great cause to value himself upon his superior prowess. The upper parts of their persons were in armour. For all attack, the baron chose a short sword, and to the handling of which he was well up; having learnt his lesson from a priest, himself an adept in the art. At first, however, this was protested against by Monsieur le Vidasme, godfather to de Fandilles, on the grounds, that by one of the articles of the code, the use of every other weapon was forbidden, than such as was habitually worn or used by military men and persons of condition. But to this it was rejoined, that the Swiss, as brave a people as any upon the surface of the earth, avail themselves of no other. So the end of the matter was, that Monsieur le Vidasme, confident in the mettle of his godson, made no more difficulty about it; especially as the said godson seemed to hold, alike the man and his weapons, in a very perfect contempt. So now we have brought them to the camp; all the necessary preliminaries disposed of and responded to. At the very first go off, Fandilles dealt the baron so hideous a gash across the thigh, that, upon the instant, his strength began to fail, through loss of blood. And so, well perceiving the disadvantage which he was at, and was still more likely to be at, he determined, there and then, to close with his man; a trick to which he was well up; and to which he had been of purpose initiated by a stumpy little Breton priest, almoner to Monsieur de Lenoncourt, his relative. And no sooner had he brought him to the ground, himself above, than he set to to pommel him with all his might and main; for in buckling together, they had each of them necessarily been compelled to drop their weapons. But as his strength was now fast upon the ebb, it was a toss up whether he would ever live to dispatch him. Matters hanging in this doubtful state; as luck would have it, a scaffold was first seen to totter, and then to give way, whereon were standing a most unconscionable company of lords, ladies with their daughters, knights, esquires; spectators of this cruel pastime. So that what with the shrieks, the noise, the hubbub, the confusion, the attention of the company was perfectly bewildered betwixt the rival entertainments; one part remaining rivetted upon the issue of the fight; the other hurrying away to the extrication of the disconsolate and disordered fair ones, with the gentlemen, their companions and fellow-sufferers. Under cover of all this confusion, the friends of the baron, making for the centre, began to holloa to their champion, *Stop his eyes and mouth! stop his eyes and mouth!* and which, on their lives, they durst not have presumed to do, had it not been for the scandal of the scaffold; it being forbidden, by the laws of the field, and on the forfeiture of life and limb, so much as to speak, cough, sneeze, spit, hem, blow the nose, or make any sort of an inkling toward a sign or a hint. Profiting by the suggestion, the baron, though it was much as he could do, so effectually managed to bung his eyes and mouth with sand, (and with which, to insure their footing, the arena had been strewed,) that he was compelled, at least so say the friends of the baron, to give in; and who, accordingly, went about crying, *He has yielded! he has yielded!* Which the party of Fandilles as stoutly denied. But what with the confusion of the breakdown, the uproar, the noise, the scuffle, it was found to be literally impossible to come at what had really taken place between them. Monsieur de Bouillon, as umpire of the field, desired that they should be separated. And no sooner had the baron caufed his wound to be ftaunched, than he gave his prifoner to underftand, that it was his intention to treat him to the fame foup, which, before the fight, he had thought to have ladled out to him. On this there was a terrible ado between the parents and the allies, as well on the one fide as the other; Monfieur le Vidafme, godfather to de Fandilles, folemnly protefting and affirming that he had never heard one word about the rendering, or anything to the purpofe. The godfather to the baron, (if I recollect rightly, Monfieur de Pavan of Lorraine, a brave and worthy gentleman,) as ftiffly afferted the contrary, and infifted that his godfon fhould be permitted to difpofe of his prifoner as he thought right, and as, by the laws of war, he was perfectly entitled to do. But Monfieur de Bouillon, having thoroughly fifted the matter, and confulted with the divers captains and gentlemen prefent, forbade him to attempt to do anything of the fort; and told the baron, that he might be content to let matters reft where they were; feeing there was much to be faid on both fides, and that there was very confiderable doubt as to whether his adverfary really had furrendered or not.

In fact, they each of them acquitted themfelves like brave men; the vanquifhed living to ferve his king on many a hard fought field, and to fall, honourably, at the affault on Caunis, then befieged by the Marfhal de Briffac; and where, it is remembered, how he was the firſt to mount the breach, and on which he fell.

I may poſſibly have dwelt a little too long on this affair. However, as it was a remarkable one in itſelf, and as I myſelf had heard it related by the partiſans, as well on the one ſide as on the other, I did not chooſe it to be forgotten; and by which is to be ſeen the infamous and the miſerable penalties which the conquerors were permitted to impoſe upon the conquered. For, beyond any manner of queſtion, had the truth of what the baron aſſerted been but capable to have been come at, he would have burnt his man at the ſtake, and no power could have hindered him; and which God, who poſſibly may have known the wickedneſs of his quarrel, would not, for that reaſon, permit him to do.

Monſieur Olivier de la Marche, firſt gentleman of the houſehold to the Archduke Philip, Count of Flanders; as gallant a knight, unqueſtionably, as any of his time; able as well to handle his pen as his ſword, has left us, in his memoirs, an account of a combat which took place in his day, at Valanciennes, in the preſence of the ſaid duke; and which is aſſuredly uncommonly rich, as well from the character of the weapons with which it was waged, as for the pleaſantneſs of the ſolemnities with which it was celebrated. For in other reſpects, goodneſs knows, it was tragic enough;

as it ended in the hanging and the death of one of the parties. The circumſtance aroſe out of a privilege, long ſince conferred by the emperors and the counts of Haynault upon the town of Valanciennes; and which was this—That any man who had the misfortune to diſpoſe of another fairly, ſo to ſpeak; that is, in the defence of his proper perſon; without any ſort of foul play or circumvention, might, on fleeing to it, claim the ſanctuary of the good town of Valanciennes— provided always, he were willing and ready to maintain, at the point, or rather with a crack of his ſhillelagh, that he had killed his man fairly, as a gentleman, and a man of honour. Nor could the challenger, any more, preſent himſelf with any other weapon. But to his ſtory. It appeared that a certain Mahuot had killed a relative of one Jacotin Plouvier, and by the which Plouvier the ſaid Mahuot had been purſued into the limits of Valanciennes; Jacotin perſiſting, all the time, that he had taken his kinſman at a diſadvantage, and not as any fair man would have done. So the end of the matter was, that on the complaint of Jacotin, they were ſentenced by the counſel of the town, and with whom it reſted, to have it fairly out between them. The duke, who did not wiſh to appear in the affair, nor indeed well could he, as it came not within his cognizance, was neverthelefs preſent. And as ſoon as ever the multitude, which was incredible, was on the ground, proclamation was made by one carrying a bludgeon, *Beware the orders! beware the orders!* So that all were as still as mice; as it was forbidden, under penalty of loss of life and limb, to speak or stir. To the yard, which was round, there was but one entry; and facing one another were planted two chairs, covered with black, (just fancy!) on which the champions were to repose themselves whilst all the usual preliminaries were being adjusted. They were then respectively tendered the missal, and on which each of them, by oath, respectively confirmed his justification; in itself, by the way, a very old custom. They were clad alike, in a shirt or jacket of boiled leather; and as well their legs and arms as their bodies. Their heads were shorn, feet bare. And as if this was not enough, the nails had been pared, as well upon their fingers as their toes! Of the beard, there is nothing said; which to me is inexplicable; for nothing comes so handy in a scuffle, especially when long, stiff and forky, as it was then the custom to wear it, and as it is now being revived among us. For all defence, they were allowed a shield, pointed at the top; (mind you that; for it is not one of the least pleasant strokes in this affair,) as to be piqued below is only permitted to the nobles. For the attack, they had each a formidable quarter-staff, of white vine or medlar, and of a like length. This wood is excessively tough, and the best Naples bowls are made of it. The celebrated cross stick of Friar John, in Rabelais, and of which he made so good a use, was

of a fort of crab, which is alfo exceedingly tough and
ftrong. However, extremities were not proceeded to,
till they had demanded, and been allowed, three boons;
fugar, greafe and afhes! So, firft and foremoft, they
were handed, each of them, a tub of greafe. Only
imagine: what a ceremony! To the fame end the
wreftlers, among the Turks, fmear themfelves with oil,
the better to evade the clofe of their opponents. After
that they were feverally permitted, and by way of foap,
a fhovel full of cinders, to wafh away the effects of the
greafe upon their palms, and the better to enable them
to clutch their ftaves! So much for formality number
two. And for number three, there was inferted with
a fpoon, into the mouth of each, the regulation allowance of fugar; (and, mind you this, weighed firft,) and
this, the better to enable them to retain the faliva, and to
hold their breath! a pleafant myftery, truly! In Tur-
key, the pofts and couriers are likewife faid to have re-
courfe to a fimilar expedient when difpatched upon long
and exhaufting courfes. And mark you this, farther;
that of each of thefe three precious condiments, effay
was made, before their eyes, as at the tables, and before
the repafts of princes and of kings! A pleafant and
an honourable refponfibility, truly! To cut the matter
fhort, no fooner had they come to the fcratch, than
Mahuot let drive fuch a cloud of duft, of which the
place was covered, full in the eyes of Jacotin, that ere
he could recover himfelf, his head had been as good as

laid open with a fetch. But Jacotin, who, for all that, was the tougher of the two, so doggedly stuck to him, that, before he could well know what he was about, he had knocked the senses out of him, jumped on him, gouged him, finally dispatching him at a blow! After this, he dragged him, like a dog, from the lists; and hung him, there and then, with the consent of the court.

There is a story told in the "Annals of France," how, in the time of Charles VI., the lord of Courrages, by judgment of the Court of Parliament, at Paris, fought in the lists with a gentleman, named Le Gris, in the vindication of the honour of his wife, whom the said Le Gris had forced in his absence; he, for the time, being beyond the seas, and in the Holy Land. The lady, who was assisting at the scene, seated, and in her chariot, was peremptorily desired by the King, (and which was a terrible affront,) to come down from it; as it was not for one lying under so grievous a reproach to assume herself innocent, till such time as that innocence had been made to appear; and that she was to descend from out of it, and place herself upon a scaffold, there to attend the mercy of God, and the issue of arms. And which, fortunately for her, declared for the side of the lord of Courrages, who was lucky enough to have been able to dispatch his man, having first compelled him to confess his villainy upon the lady. After which he had him to a gallows, and there hung him, to the triumph and juftification of the unhappy countefs. I remember well to have feen the reprefentation of this combat, upon an old arras, in the chambers of our kings at Blois, among other curious reliques of the paft. And the firft time too that I faw it ; it was with Charles IX. ; and who, as he was naturally curious in fuch matters, had the whole explained to him. As to their perfons, they feemed to be in armour. Whilft for weapons, they had but fimply battle axes ; in fact, neither more nor lefs than the pole-axe or halbert, which the gentlemen of the body guard carry to this day ; to which, moreover, I fhould add, a dagger or fhort fword on the thigh.

We alfo read, (it was in the time of Louis the Stammerer,) that Ingelgerius, Count of Gaftinois, in bed with his wife, came fo fuddenly to die, without any fort of ailing or warning, that it was not till the morning that the latter became aware of what had happened, in the night, to him and to her. And of which fhe was no fooner convinced, than fhe difpatched, in all hafte, for the gentlemen, ladies, knights, her friends and neighbours, to fhew them all this piteous fpectacle, and which fhe did, in a vifible agony of diftrefs ; telling them how the whole had occurred. But there was one of the company, named Gothran, and of the family of the late count, who was not to be fo eafily fatisfied.

For he roundly, before them all, accused the countess as well of his death, as of adultery; telling her that she had not only played him false in his lifetime, but had now made away with him, the better to be enabled to carry on her infamous amours. As soon as all this scandal had come to the ears of the King, and with whom the count had always been a favourite, he had as well Gothran as the countess before him. And although everything was heard, on one side and on the other, nothing positive could be got at. It was but allegation. However Gothran, who had determined that the matter should not rest where it was, to urge on his quarrel, boldly cast his wager upon the ground, calling upon the lady, or her champion, on her behalf, to take it up: the lady, all the while, showing, urging and protesting the maliciousness of the charge. But Gothran, deaf to all reason, persisted in his tale, and in his determination to support it, against all comers, with the weight of his sword. Thus the matter was long debated before the barons, and everything heard which was to be heard. However, to little purpose. So the end of it was, (as was required by the immemorial precedent of France, when a challenger persists in his charge, and is prepared to support it at the hazard of his life,) that the lady was adjudged, in like manner, to provide herself with a champion to act upon her part — a verdict which was very terrible to the lady. So that turning, she looked very piteously upon all the company, her kinsmen, relatives, friends; imploring them, as well by her sighs as her tears, to see if there was none who would stand forth in defence of her life and of her honour — a trouble which she might well have spared herself. Not that any, for one moment, doubted of the virtue of the lady, or the righteousness of her cause, but through an unwillingness to encounter an adversary so terrible as was this Gothran. Accursed and craven kinsmen! say I. As fortune would have it, among the spectators of this sorry scene, was a certain young prince, Ingelgerius, Count of Anjou; a lad scarcely yet in his sixteenth year; and whom this very countess had held, an infant, upon the font, giving to him, herself, the name of her own very husband; and to whom, consequently, he was godson. This young count, seeing his godmother in such extremity, abandoned and forsaken of all her more legitimate defenders, boldly stepped from the crowd, and throwing himself upon his knees before the King, told him, that his heart burned within him; and that he neither could nor would stand by, and see his godmother thus miserably perish; and that he would accept the defiance of Gothran. How touching, on the part of the lad; and how beautiful an exemplification of the virtues of that holy sacrament! And there and then he cast down his wager, which Gothran as instantly picked up. For custom required, that he who dealt the challenge should first throw his glove upon the ground, and that the accepter should take it up. Though it has sometimes occurred, that both parties have insisted upon being the challengers; in which cases, each would take up the other's glove; as once happened in the time of Charles V., in the persons of John de Geristelles of Haynault and Peter de Bourzenel. But to this there was nothing that could be urged by the King, which was not, to divert him from so dangerous a game. His very words have come down to us. "My son," said he, "youth and inexperience too often flatter those "who are their minions, into undertakings, the nature "of which they but little know, and which invariably "will turn to their confusion. You are much too "young to measure yourself with any such man as this "Gothran. Let not your maiden spurs, my child, be "pled for on any such field. My son, think well of all "this; for, 'fore God, this day it goes with your life." But neither could prayers nor remonstrances shake the little count in his determination. So that the whole company was in an agony; crying, what a terrible thing it was to see so fine and so noble-spirited a lad, hurried, in this wretched manner, to butchery and to death! On the other hand, who was in ecstacies but the countess? being with him, comforting him and encouraging him by every means which were in her power; convincing him of the truth of all the misfortune that had overtaken her, and of the justice of their common cause. And ten of the clock, upon the very next morning, was the hour appointed for the combat. And no fooner was it light, and the young count had rifen, taken his laft farewell of the countefs, commended his foul unto God, confeffed himfelf, heard mafs, diftributed, affumed the glorious fymbol of the Crofs, than he leaped upon his horfe, and gallopped boldly to the lifts, where already the terrible Gothran was in waiting. At this ftage of the proceedings the lady was produced, and the ufual purgations were fworn to, on the one part and on the other. On the very firft encounter, the fhield of the count was carried right from him and beyond him, fuch was the violence of the fhock. But in return, fo rudely had he affailed his adverfary, that he had driven his fpear, not only through fhield, but breaft-plate, belly, bowels, reins; coming clean out from his behind. With that, he fprang from his faddle, and fevering his head from his trunk, at a blow, prefented it to the King, who received it no lefs joyfully at his hands than though he had made him the mafter of a city. On this the countefs was releafed; and running to him, fhe caught him in her arms, embracing him and kiffing him before all the company; thanking him, in an agony of tears and of joy, for all the unfpeakable obligation which he had laid her under. And the very next day, as fome approach to a return, fhe made over to him, with the confent of the King, the lordfhip of Chafteau-Landon, with fundry other fiefs and holdings in Gaftinois; and for which the count, there and then, did homage to the King.[1] And the remainder of her days were ſpent in retirement and fecluſion, mortification, prayers, alms and charity.—BRANTÔME.

[1] See note F, at the end.

A SOMEWHAT NAÏVE ACCOUNT

OF THE

DUKE DE SULLY'S COURTSHIP.

IMMERSED, as I was, in this new fort of life; obliged, in a manner, from the very nature of my avocations, to play my part amid all the gaieties and frivolities of the court, its emptinefs and its nothingnefs; in the flower of my youth; no one can be furprifed to find that I paid to the god of Love the accuftomed homage attended of us all. In fact, I had become over head and ears in love with the daughter of the prefident de Saint-Mefmin, and one of the moft lovely women of her time in France. And in this mood I abandoned myfelf, without any fort of reftraint, to all the delicioufnefs of a paffion, the firft affaults of which are fo peculiarly bewitching; indeed, fo much fo, that when I came foberly to reflect, how little defirable, in other refpects, fuch a match would be, I found that all fuch confiderations had come too late to be pitted with the regards and the expectations of the lady's family, the prepoffeffion of the moft eftimable of fathers; but, above all, the charms of fuch a miftrefs — a chain in itfelf, which, had there been no other, I had found it difficult enough to have undone. Lafond, to divert me from her, entreated me but only once to fee Mademoifelle de Courteney, who, it feems, he had pitched upon as a party in every way more fuitable; and which, accordingly, I did. And although I knew well, in my heart, that all he faid was true, the recollection of Mademoifelle de Saint-Mefmin and her charms, as quickly drove all fuch cold-blooded reflections from my mind.

Matters were in this doubtful ftage, when, one day, I happened to be fleeping at Nogent-fur-Seine; the faid Lafond, with fome few others, being with me at the time. And curioufly enough, as fate would have it, there and then were both the fair ones; Mademoifelle de Saint-Mefmin and Mademoifelle de Courteney! The fituation was delicate. For I well knew, that there was no efcape for it, but I muft break, upon the fpot, with whichever of the damfels I fhould the firft decline to wait upon; in as much as it was beyond the nature of things to fuppofe that it could be within the wit of man, or mortal, to fatisfy, in fuch a conjuncture, the expectations of two fuch women. At this moment, a little fifter of Mademoifelle de Saint-Mefmin happened to come into the room, where fhe found me in all the ftudy and hefitation of a man, drawn one way by all the weight of his affections, another by that of his better fenfe, reafon and conviction. And fo, giving full play to all the vivacity of her temperament, after fome pretty little rallying, fhe fet to to drag me off, by main force, a prifoner to her fifter's feet.[1] But before we could get there, I was overtaken by Lafond, who whifpered in my ear, "The "other door, Sir; you will there find fortune, an "extraction royal, and charms as great, when they "fhall have come to their maturity." Thefe few words, tendered fo *à propos*, at once recalled me to my fenfes, and fixed me in my refolution. I faw that the counfel of Lafond was found, and that the only difference, in point of perfonal attraction, between Mademoifelle de Saint-Mefmin and her rival, was, that the one was in the actual poffeffion of charms, which a year or two could fcarce fail to develope in the other. I refufed to vifit Mademoifelle de Saint-Mefmin, which brought down upon me a perfect ftorm of indignation and reproach. However, I ftood my ground, making ftraight for the apartment of Mademoifelle de Courteney; and to whom the facrifice was reprefented in a fomewhat more flattering light, than, to be candid, it altogether merited. With my reception, I had no

---
[1] See note G, at the end.

reaſon to be diſſatisfied. And in a little time, when I had come to ſee her oftener, I began to be more fully aware of all the virtues and the worth of my new miſtreſs; and whom, ſhortly after, I married. — *Mémoires de Sully.*

THE BIRTH OF HENRY THE FOURTH.

IT has never been precifely afcertained in what place Henry IV. was conceived. The moft generally received opinion, however, is, that it was at La Fleche, in Anjou, where Antoine de Bourbon, his father, and the Princefs de Navarre, his mother, are known to have been living from the end of February, fifteen hundred and fifty two, to mid-May, fifteen hundred and fifty three. But this much is certain, that the firft time that fhe became unmiftakeably aware of her condition, or felt her child to ftir, was in the camp, in Picardy, to which fhe had accompanied her hufband, for the time being, governor of that province; having quitted La Fleche to put himfelf at the head of an expedition againft the Emperor Charles V. And certes, it was but in character, that he, who was one day deftined to become fo mighty a prince, fhould give the earlieft evidence of his being, in a camp, amid the roar of cannons, trumpets, and the clang of arms; like a true son of Mars, as he was.

His grandfather, Henri d'Albret, as soon as he heard that his daughter was with child, sent for her, determining to take into his own hands the education of this promised fruit, and which, from a sort of presentiment, he was persuaded would one day live to avenge upon the Spaniard all the injuries that they had inflicted on his house.

This courageous princess, then, taking leave of her husband, set out from Compiegne the fifteenth of November, traversed to the Pyrenees, the length of France, and arrived at Pau, in Bearn, where her father then was, the fourth day of December; thus allowing herself but some eighteen or nineteen days for her journey. And on the thirteenth of the same month she was happily delivered of a son.

Previously to this, the King, Henry d'Albret, had made a testament, and which the princess was exceedingly curious to see; in as much as it was generally suspected to have been drawn somewhat to her prejudice, and in the favour of a certain lady, whom the goodman, upon a time, had been a little too kind to. Otherwise than indirectly, she dare not allude to it. However, to satisfy her, he promised, that as soon as she should have showed him what she was then carrying in her loins, the will would be placed in her hands; and provided alfo, that fhe would undertake to fing to him all the while that her infant were coming into the world; *fo that*, faid he, *you may not be making me a whining and a refty child.* All which fhe engaged for, and was as good as her word; finging to him, in her native *Bearnois*, amid all her fufferings and her pangs. It was remarked that the infant, contrary to the ufual courfe of nature, came into the world without any fort of crying, or apparent fuffering. And affuredly it was not to be fuppofed that a prince, deftined to be, one day, the glory and the joy of France, fhould have come into the world, amid agonies and groans and cries.

As foon as ever he was born, his grandfather took him away in the folds of his robe, having firft handed to his daughter the promifed teftament, and which was enclofed in a cafket of gold; faying to her, *Here, my daughter, this I give to you; this I referve to myfelf.* He then rubbed his little lips with a head of garlick, and poured a drop or two of wine into his mouth, in order to fortify his temperament, and render him more vigourous and hardy.

The Spaniards had formerly a trick of faying, by way of raillery, when upon the article of the birth of the mother of our Henry, *Miracle, the cow has brought forth a fheep!* meaning, by the cow, the Queen Margaret, his mother. For fo was fhe dignified, and her hufband, *The cowherd;* in allufion to the arms of

Bearn, which are two cows. And the King Henry, who never queftioned but that his grandfon would one day become famous, ufed frequently, on receiving the felicitations of his friends, and in rejoinder to the cool irony of the Spaniard, to take him in his arms, and fay, *See you not this ; my fheep has brought forth a lion !*

* * * * *

He was at firft very difficult to raife ; having had fo many as feven or eight nurfes ; with the laft of whom, however, the honours remained. As foon as ever he was weaned, the king gave him into the charge of Sufan de Bourbon, wife to John d'Albret, baron de Moiffens, who carried him to the chateau de Coaraffe, in Bearn, amid the mountains and the rocks.

His grandfather would on no account confent to his being brought up with all the delicacy and confideration, too often beftowed upon thofe of his rank ; knowing well, that a feeble and an enervate perfon is, for the moft part, mated to a timorous and a creeping foul. He forbade him either to be becomingly dreffed, or to be humoured with any fort of toys or nonfenfe ; or again, to be in any way fawned to, or remembered of his rank ; for, faid he, all thefe things but ferve to the puffing up of vanity, and rather to breed arrogance and pretenfion than noble or generous propenfities. In fact, he required him to be clad and to be treated, exactly as other children of his years. And he was made to run about and climb all day among the rocks, so as early to inure him to danger and fatigue : the better to impart a tone and vigour to his syſtem. And which was, aſſuredly, above all things to be looked to, in the nurture of a prince who was deſtined to go through and to ſuffer ſo much, for the recovery, and for the ſake of his country and his rights. — HARDOUIN DE PEREFIXE.

THE DEATH OF HENRY THE FOURTH.

UT amid all thefe preparations, there were other, and of a different kind, in progrefs, and which agitated him in a very extraordinary manner. It is of the coronation of the queen that I would fpeak. To the very thought of it, fo unfpeakable was his abhorrence, that nothing lefs than his known complacency toward that princefs could ever have brought him to confent to the fame. And no fooner had this conceffion been wrung from him, than her majefty caufed all hands to be put upon the work. I have already touched upon the drift and the nature of the arguments with which fhe was urged and poffeffed by her creatures to hurry the ceremony on; affuredly, either very prepofterous or very criminal. Immediately after, Henry was to leave Paris. And as a fortnight, at the fartheft, was the outfide which he could poffibly be detained, marching orders

had been already difpatched to all the troops, as well horfe as foot, and who, accordingly, had left by the way of Champagne.

* * * * *

As a final warning, the king had announced to all the foreign courts, how he was about to quit his capital, and this, through the medium of a letter which he addreffed to the archduke. Here it is, and exactly as it was couched and went; if indeed Villeroy, through whofe hands, as fecretary of ftate, it had neceffarily to pafs, allowed it to go unmended, which he had an uncommon reluctance to do. " My brother, unable
" to refufe to my old allies, friends and confederates,
" the aid which they have prayed at my hands, againft
" thofe who are perfifting to trouble the fucceffion in
" the duchies and counties of Cleves, Julliers, La-
" Mark, Bergh, Ravenfperg, and Raveftein; I am
" preparing, with my troops, to go to their affiftance.
" And in as much as the route, which I am purpofing
" to follow, will lie through at leaft a portion of your
" territories, I have thought it but courteous to apprife
" you of the fame; praying you, in return, to notify to
" me, Will it be your good pleafure, that I am to
" falute you as a friend, or as an enemy? In the in-
" terim, abiding your reply, I pray God to have you in
" his fafe keeping. HENRY."

I do not really know, what is either to be faid or thought of a report then current, and which was confirmed by Giraud, who had come direct from Bruffels, the feventh of March, to the king, who was then at Fontainebleau; and which was to this effect — That it was very generally believed, as well at the court, as throughout the Auftrian ftates, that all thefe warlike rumours and preparations were but fo many bugbears, on the part of Henry, to impofe upon his enemies; and that this was the real reafon why fo little preparation was being made to oppofe him. That but little preparation was being made might have been true; as, in fact, it proved; without, however, for that, the archduke being altogether, within himfelf, fo fatisfied, as to the world he affected to be. For had he really been fo, then had he been of a very different complexion from all the reft of thofe who had the real interefts of the Houfes of Auftria and of Spain at heart. No words could picture their confternation. For whilft the faction of their adverfaries, or, as it was ftyled abroad, that of France, was carrying its head erect, and confidently predicting the iffue which, on all hands, was wifhed to it; that of Auftria was cowed into filence, paralyzed, amazed; the object of an execration to which it faw itfelf the devoted victim; no poffible means prefenting themfelves whereby to evade the ftorm which was about to defcend upon it and to overwhelm it. But alas, how little is it in me thus to fpeak of, or to flight them! They had unhappily but too many refources at their difpofition to be thus lightly taunted. But it was not the shock of arms, nor yet a noble despair, which they were to oppose to a prince whom Europe had pitched upon as her avenger, and advanced to be her shield and her support. No, it but required to lop the head from off this vasty power — an infamy. And never, sure, did assassination, poison, treason achieve a triumph more worthy of themselves: a triumph so base, so execrable, so heinous, that words are wanting to me to express the one-tenth part of its villainy. I finish, trembling, what I have to tell the world concerning this most wretched tragedy; and the very thought of which, to this hour, wrings tears of blood from my heart.

What are we to, what can we think of all those gloomy presentiments with which the closing days of this unhappy prince were clouded; and with which it is but too notorious that he was possessed? They were really of so extraordinary a character, that they are something appalling so much as to think of. I have already touched upon the almost insuperable reluctance with which he at length consented that the ceremony should take place before his departure. And the nearer he found the day to be at hand, the more and the more did the agony and the trouble of his soul increase. He broke the whole to me in such an abandon of bitterness and despair, that I could not refrain from rallying him on a weakness so unbecoming and unpardonable in fuch a prince. But his own lips will better tell their tale than any words of mine. "Ah, "my friend," faid he, "you cannot conceive how this "coronation is preying upon me! I cannot tell what "it is has come over me, but my heart mifgives me. "There is fomething terrible about to happen." On this he threw himfelf into a little chair, that I had had made on purpofe for him, and which never was allowed out of my cabinet; prefently to fall into fo devouring a trance, tapping all the while, mechanically, the cafe of his fpectacles, that he feemed completely loft to everything about and around him; and from which at length he ftarted, as from a dream, beating frantically his fides and his hands; exclaiming the while, "O my God, my God! never am I more to "leave it: I am to die in this town. They will kill "me. It is their laft chance. Ah, curfed, curfed "crowning; you will be the death of me!" "Good "God, Sir," faid I to him one day, "to what extra-"ordinary hallucinations are you giving yourfelf up! "If this is to be the way, better far to quafh the whole "affair at once; war, coronation, voyage, and all to "boot. Will you that it be fo? Say the word, and "they fhall be countermanded; it is the affair of an "inftant." "Yes," faid he, after that I had, on more than one occafion, fimilarly interrogated him: "Yes; "ftop the coronation, and let me hear no more about "it. It is the only way to get out of my head, ima-

"ginations which nothing elfe will. I fhall get off "from the city, and there will be nothing then to "fear." By what poffible traits are the infcrutable and unerring inftincts of the heart to be detected, if not by thefe? "I will not conceal from you," faid he to me, on another occafion, "how I have been told, "that I am to perifh in my coach, and at the firft "folemnity which I may happen to attend." "Sir," I rejoined, "I never heard you refer to this before; "and now that I think of it, I have often been amazed "to fee you fo nervous in a conveyance; you, who "ever carry yourfelf fo undauntedly amid the cannon, "the lances, the guns and the pikes. But feeing that "thefe prefentiments have now fo unrootably taken "poffeffion of your mind, were I in your place, I "would be off this inftant; and I would either allow "the ceremony to go on without me, or I would poft-"pone it till a more propitious occafion; and, for a "time at leaft, I would forbear to fet foot either in "Paris or in a coach. Will you that I fend upon the "fpot, to Nôtre-Dame and to St. Denis, and ftop the "whole affair?" "I would certainly like it very "much," faid he, "but what will my wife fay; fhe "has this crowning moft marvelloufly at heart." "Let "her fay whatever fhe likes beft," faid I, feeing his eyes to gliften at the fuggeftion; "but it is never to "be fuppofed, once fhe comes to underftand your "majefty's repugnance, and all the mifchief which "you are perſuaded to be like to come of it, that ſhe "will perſiſt in her oppoſition."

Nothing now were required but to obtain her majeſty's conſent, to proceed to the interruption of the whole affair. And it is not without very much reluctance that I find myſelf compelled to ſtate, that, do or urge what I would, I could not prevail upon her majeſty to gratify her huſband in this regard. I paſs without a comment the prayers, the arguments, the entreaties with which, for three ſucceſſive days, I continued to weary her. It was for the prince to yield. Though, to be candid, as he was the firſt, at times, to rally himſelf upon his apprehenſions, he at length ſo far maſtered them, as to be able to keep them to himſelf, and to forbid their being mooted to the queen. But no ſooner were the workmen again upon the work, than with them returned all his old miſgivings; for ever muttering to himſelf, and in my ears, "Ah, my "friend, I ſhall never leave this town. They will "murder me. O wretched, wretched crowning; you "will be the death of me!"— words which I ſhall not readily forget.

In all this affair, throughout, there were divers more ſecret paſſages, which I have judged it to be more judicious to ſuppreſs. This diſcretion, I would even have puſhed yet farther; were it not mere affectation to pretend to myſtery, or delicacy about matters known as well to my ſervants as to many. The following is of this character. Schomberg, who was then living with me, and almost upon the footing of the household, was one day sitting at table, when I suddenly perceived a page to come, and stealthily slip a billet into his sleeve. At first I amused myself in bantering him about it, supposing it to be a *billet-doux*, or to relate to some intrigue, nonsense, or affair of gallantry. He replied, without so much as looking at it, that he thought he might safely undertake to say, it was not of the character which I seemed to imagine; but that, let its nature be what it might, he would pledge himself to acquaint me with it. The scrap contained but two words. As soon as he had finished, he retired to a window to make himself master of its contents; which, when he had done, he placed it in my hands, adding, that it was from Mademoiselle de Gournai; a name in itself sufficient, had I then been acquainted with that lady, to have disabused me of all my previous imaginations. It was simply a line requiring him to wait on her immediately, and on a matter of the last importance. He promised me to return as soon as he could discover what it was all about; and, in fact, he was back within the half hour.

It appeared that Mademoiselle de Gournai had learned, through a female who had been in the service of Madame de Verneuil, that a conspiracy had actually been entered into against the person of the king; and having, farther, inquired of the woman, Who were the parties concerned; she had named Madame de Verneuil herself, Monsieur N———, and certain others. Her first thought was, through one of the women in waiting, named Catherine, to acquaint the queen, who, in her turn, would apprise his majesty. But Mademoiselle de Gournai, on farther reflection, alarmed lest such a course might be inadequate to the exigency, bethought herself of Monsieur de Schomberg, as a party who might safely be entrusted to break the matter directly to the king. Schomberg, as soon as he had put me in possession of the facts, told me to observe in what a delicate position he was placed; at the same time asking my advice as to how he was to proceed. The affair was by much too serious to be pooh, poohed, or concealed; on the other hand, to carry it to his majesty, was infallibly to bring down upon himself the implacable hate of all those who might be compromised, and whom the prince would questionless challenge. No one but my wife was present at this consultation. And the conclusion which we came to was this; That Schomberg should open the matter to the king, with all the tenderness and circumspection possible; and that if his majesty should call on him to name the accomplices, he was to refer him to the two females, already mentioned, as his authority, and as the parties most likely to be able to satisfy him. It is notorious to all, that this Catherine was sent for and examined; that she stuck unflinchingly to her deposition, and, to her dying day, persisted in the same. This, I think, is something which will not readily be forgotten by those who may be disposed to draw their own inferences from the unwarrantable manner in which so many pieces were suppressed, connected with the examination of this wretched parricide.

The ceremony of the coronation began, however, to be proceeded with, and on all the scale of usual magnificence. It was to be spread over several days; the last and principal of which was to be Sunday, the sixteenth of May. The king, out of complaisance to her majesty, consented to assist at a ceremony, the very thought of which was a dagger in his breast. However, he had resigned himself to it, determining, it once over, that nothing should delay him another hour in Paris. And the very morning of the next day, Monday, the seventeenth, was the one fixed on for his departure. So far as I myself, personally, was concerned, I had been off ere then, had not the reopening of an old wound in my neck compelled me to place myself in the hands of my physicians, and by whom I was prescribed the use of the hot bath for three successive days. I had not a particle of curiosity to assist at all those pageantries, which those who, still behind, were hurrying, on every hand, to see. The miserable forebodings of our Henry had rendered the very mention of them as odious to me as to himself. To add to this, the count de Soiffons, willing to have himfelf thought to be diffatisfied with the precedence affigned to him in the ceremonial, retired in a pet from the court.

The ceremony having been fufpended on Friday, the fourteenth of May; that moft miferable of days; the unfortunate king had been purpofing to pafs a portion of it in conference with myfelf; as it was the laft time that he would have an opportunity of feeing me previous to his departure. I know perfectly well what it was that he was wifhing to fay to me. A moft malicious report was then abroad, to the effect, that at the very moment when he appeared to be the moft determined to fall upon the houfe of Auftria, with a power the moft overwhelming, he had already, in fecret, an underftanding with it; not only, that he fhould not proceed to extremities, but to betray his own proper allies; Auftria, on her part, confenting, that he was to retain for himfelf, Cléves, with the remainder of the fucceffion, in the caufe of which he had oftenfibly taken up arms. To this there was added another ftipulation, that Spain was to give up into his hands, the prince and princefs of Condé. Henry, no doubt, was wifhing to reaffure me againft a report fo prejudicial to his reputation.

*   *   *   *   *

It was then, as I prefume, to give me fome more preffing injunctions about the commiffariat, that Henry

sent to me, by La-Varenne, early on Friday morning, to say that he wanted to take a little turn alone with me in the gardens of the Tuileries, and so I was to come. He found me in my bath, but seeing me about to dress myself, in order to obey the summons of his majesty, he bade me to stay where I was, adding, that he was sure his majesty would sooner prefer to cross, himself, to the arsenal, than to allow me to go abroad in the state in which I then was, and that he would be seriously displeased to find me exposing myself without any sort of real occasion. At any rate, said he, wait a moment : give me the time to go to him and to return, and let us hear what he himself will say. And, in fact, he was back at the end of half an hour ; and these are the very words which he brought to me. " Sir," said he, " his majesty requires you to
" continue in your bath, and, farther, forbids you to
" leave the doors to-day, in as much as Monsieur du
" Laurent has told him, that you are in no way fit to
" be about. He also desires me to tell you, that he
" has a little errand to do today in town, and of which
" he will acquaint you ; but that tomorrow morning,
" towards five o'clock, without any fail, he will be at
" the arsenal, to have it all over with you ; for he
" was determined to be off, come what would, on
" Monday morning. He says, that he has found
" everything which you told him about his voyage,
" and the rest of his affairs, to come true ; and that

"nothing now can stand between him and his pro-
"jections *but the default of one or other of us.*" (They are his very words which I am using.) "He farther "orders you," said La-Varenne, "to expect him in your "dressing gown and night cap, as he will not have you "to be huddled out of your bath;" and I was also to say, "that if he found you dressed, he would be se-"riously angry with you." To all which La-Varenne added, on his part, that he had followed my advice in dispatching the letter to the archduke, though indeed it was little better than an idle ceremony; as he was determined, one way or another, to let the world see that he was in earnest. One and all my servants afterwards told me, that they had been struck with the extraordinary lassitude into which I fell immediately after the departure of La-Varenne, and the cause of which they were unable to surmise; nor, indeed, was there any.

I had just entered my wardrobe; it was at about four o'clock in the afternoon, when I heard a piercing shriek, and then another, as well from Castinet as from my wife; each of whom was crying wildly, Where was I? The whole house seemed, in an instant, to be filled with howling and lamentation. With every instant, blow upon blow, it came, "Ah, my God, my "God; all is lost; France has perished!" I rushed out upon the spot, all undressed as I was. At every turn I was met, "O Sir, the king has been mortally "wounded in the side;" or, "Oh, Sir, the king has "been stabbed." I was not long left in doubt, for, almost upon the instant, Saint-Michel, who had as good as seen the blow struck, came rushing in, the knife, which he had been able to secure, yet reeking in his hand. "Ah," I cried, with raised hands and eyes to heaven, and in a desolation the most unutterable, the most inconceivable, "this, this is the hour "the wretched prince had always told of: God have "mercy on him, on us and on the state. If he is "dead, then is it all over with us; for never would "Providence have permitted such a violence, had it not "been to prepare the way for the pouring forth of the "vessels of his wrath. Ah France, it is into strange "keeping that thou art about to fall!"

No one need think here to find the details of this most execrable parricide; the recollection of which transpierces my very soul with agony, renews itself at every instant, and to the last hour of my existence shall never be effaced from mine eyes. Nor can I, for the soul of me, conceive, of what mould they can be, who can talk, or coolly hear talked, to this day, of the greatest calamity which possibly could have overtaken their country. And such is the extremity of horror with which this loathing possesses me, that, even to this hour, I shut my eyes, as far as may be, upon this deplorable catastrophe; and that my tongue refuses so much as to name the accursed monster, causer of all our woes, as inwardly I invoke the vengeance of the God of heaven on him, and on all thofe who fteeled him to it. The public indignation has already fufficiently indicated, and in a manner the moft unequivocal, the originators of this thrice deteftable confpiracy. I cannot, however, refrain from ftigmatifing, with all thofe who heard of it, a fcandal, well nigh known to all, and which is this — That, when firft feized, the affaffin was fo little looked to, in the houfe to which he was carried, that, for more than four hours, all forts of perfons had accefs to, and were permitted to fpeak with him. Among whom were fome, (whofe names it is no wife neceffary fhould figure in this place,) who ftuck not fo unfcrupuloufly to avail themfelves of that liberty, that they even went the length of conjuring him, all the while calling him, "*their good friend*," "to have a care," (thefe are their very words,) "*how* "*he would compromife good catholics, innocent and re-* "*fpectable parties;* for that fuch would be a crime irre- "miffable in the eyes of heaven, and worthy of eternal "damnation." And it was not till more than one, fcandalifed at fuch a licenfe, had begun loudly and everywhere to remonftrate, that meafures were at length taken to prevent an indifcriminate accefs to the prifoner.

From wherever it came, fuch was the tragical end of a prince, on whom it would feem that nature had determined to heap her every boon, with the exception of such a death as had become him. I have already said, that he had the frame and all his members cast in that mould which constitutes, not only what we call a well built man, but farther, one firm, athletic, sanguine, nervous. He was of a vigorous complexion, and all the features of his face were animated and pleasing; so that the result of the whole was a physique the most sprightly, gentle, engaging, bewitching. To all which were mated a carriage, an approach so familiar, so reassuring, that, let what majesty might be thrown into his port, that airiness would ever mingle with it, for which he was so notorious. I could add but little to what is already known as to his temperament and constitution, were I to say, that he was naturally kind, sympathising, compassionate, affectionate; manly, straightforward, generous; piercing, intelligent; in a word, endowed with all those perfections which the reader will so often have had occasion to admire in the perusal of these memoirs.

His people he loved with the devotion of a father, and the state, as a head of a family. And this it was which invariably recovered him, how apparently soever immersed in his pleasures, to the loadstar of his course, namely, to the task to see his people happy, and his kingdom flourishing. Hence that fecundity of conception, that unwearied attention to the classification of the various offices and departments of the state. No inconsiderable portion of his labours has been already specified.

In a word, I may conclude by obferving, that it were hardly fo much as poffible to conceive office, precedent, ftate, profeffion, function, calling, to which he had not turned his attention, or with regard to which he had not fo contrived, that it fhould not be in the power of any, after his deceafe, to deftroy the good foundation laid; as had but too often heretofore been the cafe in this monarchy. "It is my ambition," faid he, "that my clofing years may be fo paffed, that "they may be alike pleafing to God and ufeful to "man." Grand, noble and generous fentiments; rare and exquifite emotions and fenfibilities, harboured themfelves, as it were naturally, in his breaft; fo that he had brought himfelf to look on adverfity but as a paffing cloud; profperity as his natural element. He had caufed various marfhes to be drained, as a fort of preliminary to a yet greater undertaking that he was contemplating, which was, to put in communication, by means of canals, the two feas and the great rivers. Time was the only thing which was wanting to the completion of thefe, his magnificent conceptions.

He often faid, that ten things he required of heaven; and whence came the faying, *The ten wifhes of Henry*. To all of them, it was not his felicity to attain. They are thefe. 1°, Spiritual gifts and grace. 2°, To be permitted the enjoyment, to the laft, of all the faculties of his foul, and of the members of his body. 3°, To fee the church, to which he had formerly belonged, settled and undisturbed. 4°, To be rid of his wife, (it is of his first that he speaks,) and to be fortunate enough to find another, more accommodate to his temper, and who would bring him children while he could yet reasonably hope, in the course of nature, to be spared himself to rear and to instruct them. 5°, To restore France to all her ancient splendour. 6°, To take either Navarre, or Flanders and Artois from Spain. 7°. To gain a victory, in person, over the King of Spain, and another over the Grand-Signor; a distinction in which he envied Don Juan of Austria. 8°, To be enabled to crush, without having recourse to extreme measures, the Huguenot faction, and of which the dukes de Bouillon and de La Trimouille were the chiefs. For a ninth, he joined this, that he might see these two men, with the duke d'Epernon, constrained to implore his clemency. It was long before he could be prevailed upon to name the tenth, which regarded the carrying through of his great designs; and which might be divided into two heads. The first was matter of religion. It was his wish to reduce to the three principal denominations, the infinite number of sects with which Europe is overrun; seeing it to be impracticable to unite all the world in one. The other was purely politic, and regarded the number, the distribution, the balance of the different powers, and which he proposed to consolidate into one great republic, upon the basis that I shall presently refer to.

I should be giving the lie to all those professions of candour which I have ever made, if, after having lauded this prince for an infinity of qualities, truly admirable in themselves, I should conceal, that they were balanced by frailties and defects, and those even considerable ones. I have neither disguised his passion for the sex, nor yet his love of gaming, nor his easiness, facility, too often degenerating into weakness, nor his propensity to all sorts of pleasures. Nor have I, any more, concealed the indiscretions into which they betrayed him, nor the sums that they caused him sillily to fool away, nor all the precious hours which they lost him. But at the same time, I have taken care to qualify all this, by remarking, that his detractors have, beyond all conscience, exaggerated on all these heads. He was, if you will, a slave to women; but when did one of them meddle either in the choice of a minister, or with the fate of a servant; or make her weight to be felt at the council table, or at the board? The same with the rest. And to sum up, in one word, the whole; we have but to recur to all which he had achieved and carried through, to perceive, that there is no manner of comparison to be drawn between the more marked and the less defensible sides of his character. And seeing that the calls of honour and of glory had always been sufficient and able to tear him from his pleasures, it is but reasonable to presume that these were the mastering passions of his soul.

I have ſtill by me a letter which he once wrote to me by Loménie, becauſe, ſaid he, owing to a ſlight hurt, I am unable myſelf to hold my pen. It is headed from Chantilly, and bears the date of an eighth of April. There is no year. The reader may not, perhaps, be altogether indiſpoſed to hear Henry himſelf upon ſuch an head. What firſt induced him to think of writing to me ſuch a charaƈter of letter, was, as he himſelf aſſerts, in the opening lines, a deference to public opinion ; it being his amuſement to have retailed to him, daily, all the cenſure, news and goſſip of the town, by Roquelaure, Frontenac, La-Riviére, du Laurens, d'Arambure, Morlas-Salette, La-Varenne, Bonniéres, Du-Jon, Béringhen, l'Oſerai, Armagnac, Jacquinot, Perroton and others ; who, for the moſt part, acquitted themſelves ſufficiently roundly with him ; in obedience to his commands, to conceal nothing from him.

He commences by ſaying, (they are his own words,) that his enemies and detraƈtors accuſe him of ſlighting, and even deſpiſing the greateſt and moſt conſiderable of the realm ; and of ſquandering, in idle and frivolous expenditure, ſums which, according to them, had been more meetly appropriated to the gratification of their requirements. " Some," ſays he, " blame me as being " too fond of building and coſtly undertakings ; others, " as too much attached to the chaſe, my dogs, my " birds ; others, to dice, cards and different ſorts of " games ; others, again, to women, good cheer, balls,

" the comedy, dancing, running the ring, and such like
" diversions; where, say they, I am still to be seen,
" despite my grey beard, as youthful as ever, as tickled
" to have run a good hit, to have carried off the palm
" two or three times ; or, say they, laughing, to have
" won a forfeit of a fair one, as ever I had been in my
" younger days, or as the most conceited young rascal in
" the court that day could be. I will not deny," con-
tinues he, " but that in all this there may be some truth.
" But it also seems to me, that, nothing being carried
" to excess, all this should rather be made a subject of
" felicitation than of reproach to me ; and that, in any
" case, some little allowance should be made for recre-
" ations which no one can pretend to be the source of
" either damage or incommodity to my people, and as
" being, in some sort, compensatory for all the fatigues,
" the dangers, the privations in which, from my youth
" to my fiftieth year, my days have been consumed."
. . . " I have heard you yourself say," adds this
prince, " when some one had happened to have been
" blaming you in some particular or other, That scrip-
" ture does not require of any man to be absolutely free
" from crimes or weaknesses; in as much as these are
" infirmities inherent to the very necessity of our
" being; but only, never to suffer them to get the
" upper hand, or to become the arbiters of our actions.
" It is for this medium that I have always striven, as
" farther was not to be looked for. No one knows

" better, from many a scene which has passed between
" me and my mistresses, (and women, every body knows,
" or at least thinks, to be my master passion,) whether
" I have not often been on your side and against them;
" even to the length of telling them, to their faces, that
" I had rather lose ten such mistresses, as one of them,
" than one such servant as you. And it is what, I
" give you my honour, you will yet see me do, when
" the proper moment shall have come to put in ex-
" ecution the glorious projects, which you know, since
" long, to have been occupying my mind. I will let
" you then see, that at the call of honour and of glory,
" I can quit, without a struggle, mistresses, dogs, birds,
" gaming, buildings, fêtes. It is my highest ambition,
" my duty to my God discharged, to my wife, my
" family, my faithful servants; my people, whom I shall
" always love as my own children; to be accounted
" a prince to be relied on; of his word and of honour."

But it is time to return to the painful narrative of the occurrences which followed upon the death of this good prince. However distressing it may be to me, these memoirs cannot, with any propriety, be brought to a close sooner than with the times when I ceased to be a participator in the affairs of the state.

Miserable as was the affliction into which I was thrown by a report so horrible, it suddenly occurred to me, that, even supposing him to be mortally wounded, he might yet have some little time to linger. And in this imagination, fondly clinging to this poor fpark of hope and comfort, I called in hafte to my fervants, "Here, my things, my boots; faddle the horfes in-" ftantly, I cannot wait for the coach. Let all my "gentlemen be in attendance: I will go and fee for "myfelf." For the moment, but two or three of my people were forthcoming; for the remainder, concluding me to be fafe, and in bed for the reft of the day, were difperfed right and left, all over the town. But before I could be ready, the rumour of the death of the King had recalled them, and with them an hoft of others, more or lefs dependent on me. So that before we had fronted the refidence of Beaumarchais, more than an hundred gentlemen, mounted, were following me; and in a very few minutes more than half as many again had joined in; as, at every ftep, I was met by one or other loyal fervant of the king's, hafting to me to know in what manner they were to carry themfelves in fo unexpected a conjuncture. The confternation and the general forrow bore a fufficient teftimony to how paffionately this prince was beloved in his capital. It was really fomething amazing to fee in what various and what affecting ways, the citizens and the populace of this vaft city evinced their forrow and their attachment. The tears, the groans, the cries, the ftupefaction! One would clafp his hands convulfively; another raife his eyes diftractedly to heaven, a third would fmite upon his breaft. Some, looking piteoufly on me, kept fobbing out, "Ah, Sir; we are all loft: "our good mafter is dead."

In the rue de la Pourpointerie, a man whom I did not fo much as fee, let alone recognife, coming alongfide me, flipped into my hand a little note, which I immediately handed to thofe who were about me. It confifted but of two or three words. "Sir, where is "it that you are going to? It is all over. I have "feen him dead. Enter once the Louvre, and you "will never leave it any more than he." This wretched note, putting paft all doubt the terrible truth, and which was quickly confirmed through a thoufand channels, I could no more refrain myfelf, but burft into an agony of tears. Du-Jon, whom I met near the Saint-Innocents, faid to me, "Sir, our cafe is paft "remedy. God has even fo difpofed of him. I "know it, for I have feen him. Look to yourfelf; "for this is not the kind of thing to reft here." At the head of the rue St. Honoré, another warning of the fame nature was thrown into my lap. However, in fpite of everything, I ftill kept making for the Louvre, probably fome three hundred horfemen in my fuite, when I was encountered by Vitry, at the place where the four roads meet. He came to me, and embraced me. I never faw, nor can I figure to myfelf, a man in a more deplorable condition. "Ah "Sir," he faid, "they have killed our dear mafter; "there is nothing now for it but to die. For my own "part, I know that I have not long to live, and am resolved to quit the country, never to return. We have seen the last of all that rectitude, good order and discipline, by you and him established." It was then to continue; "But where, Sir, are you going to with all this crowd? You will neither be permitted to enter, or to approach the Louvre with more than two or three persons. With such a retinue, for obvious reasons, I cannot advise you to be seen. The end is not yet, or I am much mistaken; for I have already seen faces that seem to be so little penetrated with the loss which they have experienced, that they are unable so much as even decently to wear the semblance of that sorrow which all good men, this day, are feeling. The very sight of them had like to have split my heart in twain. And if you, Sir, had seen them, as I have done, you would think as I do of all this matter. It is my advice to you," he concluded, "to return to where you came from. You will have enough to look to elsewhere, without going to the Louvre."

Such an accordance of counsel, notes, apprehensions, warnings, finished at length by startling me. I halted clean short; and after some little confultation with Vitry and some ten or twelve others of the more confiderable of my party, I came to the conclusion, that it were the safer course to retrace my steps, and to content myself with sending to the queen the tender of my services and of my duty. I caused her to be assured, at the same time, that till it should seem good to her to transmit to me her commands, I would look, with a redoubled vigilance, to the Bastile, the arsenal, the troops, artillery, and matters in general; whether governmental, or within my own more immediate jurisdiction.

I had hardly reached the rue Saint-Antoine, and by which time it was impossible that the message which I had dispatched to her majesty could have been delivered, when I was overtaken by a gentleman, on the part of the princess, begging me to come, in all haste, to the Louvre, and to be accompanied of as few as might be, as she had matters to discuss with me of the last importance; and adding, that immediately after, I was to be at liberty to return. A proposition of such a character; to go alone, as it were, to the Louvre; to deliver myself up, bound, into the hands of my enemies, with whom it was filled, was not exactly the one the best calculated to dispel my already aroused misgivings. Add to this, that, at the very same moment, I was apprised, how a captain and a detachment of the guard and archers had been already seen at the outer barriers of the Bastile, and that others had been sent to the Temple, where the powder was, and to the treasury, to make sure of the mint. All which appeared to me to be of so ugly an aspect, more especially as it had been done without any sort of communication with myself, that I was not long in determining upon the reply which I was to make to the queen. So I sent her word, by her gentleman, that I was willing to believe, that, so soon as she should have heard the party whom I had had the honour of deputing to her, she would allow for the reasonableness of my apprehensions, and come to be of my way of thinking; and that, acting on such a presumption, I would attend, at the arsenal or the Bastile, the commands which she would deign to send me; from which places it was not my intention to stir.

But her majesty was not to be so satisfied. One after another she sent to me, and on her part, messieurs de Montbazon, de Praslin, de Schomberg, La-Varenne; and, after them, my brother. I did not know what to make of these reiterated commands, coming thus one upon the top of another, every fifteen minutes. My imaginations increased; and I resolutely determined to stay where I was, at least for that day. And assuredly, if every other had been wanting, the condition to which I was then reduced, might have been a sufficient apology for my so doing. The effort that I had made on quitting my bath, and on an almost empty stomach; the agony of my mind, even more distressing than that of my body, altogether had thrown me into so violent a perspiration, so miserable a prostration, that, on entering, I was forced to change my shirt and to take to my bed, where I remained till the following day. Messieurs the constable and d'Epernon sent, by their gentlemen, to inquire for me, and with the tender of their services. The manner in which they pressed me to go and see the queen, and which in some manner satisfied me that the step might be taken with safety, determined me at length to waive the restrictions which had been placed upon the visit, namely, that my train was to be dispensed with; and I accordingly, promised to go on the following day.

Some three hundred gentlemen, on horseback, had been in waiting, since daylight, as on the preceding day, to escort me to the court. They were all either of my friends or of my kindred; or of those who, neither the one nor the other, were either hoping, from this visit, to see me reinstated; or more likely, ashamed too suddenly to abandon me. I thanked them all; giving them, at the same time, to understand why it was that it would be more agreeable to me to be allowed to proceed with my ordinary attendance, and to dispense with the company of any whose presence, at such a moment, could impart a significance to my visit. It was then simply with my own retinue, in all about twenty persons, that I entered the Louvre. It was only upon the countenances of those who had been more immediately attached to the person of the late king that I could perceive a trace of real sorrow. These all, subalterns as well as officers, seemed to be deeply sensible of the public loss. As I passed successively through the various doors, they kept coming to me, the tears in their eyes, either to fall upon my neck, or to groan out in my face : "Ah, Sir, we are undone; "in loſing our good maſter, we have loſt all;" conjuring me, in the moſt affecting manner, never to abandon the children, after having, ſaid they, ſo faithfully ſerved the father.

But to ſcenes like theſe, the interior of the palace preſented, I am compelled, with pain, to ſay it, a very marked contraſt. For if I there met with ſome faces, comported indeed to all the livery of ſorrow, it ſimply diſtreſſed me the more, as it was too evident that it was only by a ſtruggle that they were ſo; or others, again, affrontingly enjoying themſelves, it was but to heap indignation to the unſpeakable anguiſh which oppreſſed me. And no ſooner had I come to the preſence of the queen, than all the little firmneſs that I had been muſtering up, completely forſook me, and I burſt into an agony of lamentation and of tears. Nor, on her part, was ſhe any more miſtreſs of herſelf; ſo that between us there was a pretty ſcene. She ſent for the king, and the endearments and careſſes with which he received me, were for me ſo new and ſo overpowering a ſhock, that it was as much as ever I could do to ſupport it. I have not the remoteſt recollection of what this young prince ſaid to me, or, again, of what I ſaid to him. I can only recall, that it was with the greateſt difficulty that they could tear him from me, ſo paſſionately did I cling to him : all the time, the queen, his mother, repeating to him, "My "son, this is Monsieur de Sully. You must love him. "He was one of the best and most faithful servants of "the king, your father; and I have to trust that he "will continue to be the same to you." Some farther discourse passed between us, without, however, that either could find a moment to allay our tears. She has since allowed, that, with another, I was the person whose presence the most deeply affected her.

A reception so marked, so full of confidence and distinction, put all the princes, lords, ministers, who were about her majesty, under a necessity of outvying one another in their protestations of service, attachment, devotion. Most assuredly they did not impose upon me, for I knew as well what was passing in their inmost souls as they did themselves. I could not but know, that, in the projects which they had formed; their determination to turn the present conjuncture to account; to raise themselves to honours, to wealth, to distinction, at the expense of the realm at large, and to the derogation of the crown, I had nothing for it to expect, but to be sacrificed, a prey to their machinations. For they saw clearly enough; that there was no other barrier now remaining to interpose 'twixt them and their practices, save the resolution of my character and the severity of my restrictions. They had had but too much experience already, on such heads, not to be aware that there was no other chance left to them of eventually attaining to their ends, than by refolutely fetting to, to work out of my hands all care of the adminiftration. So that later, when they had brought all their ordnance to bear, to render me odious in the eyes of the queen; (even fuppofing that they had not already made a beginning, when the Jefuits and their followers had fet on the nuncio to pronounce the decree for my removal;) when my colleagues at the council board and in the finance, through Concini and his wife, had infinuated to the two princes of the blood, how impoffible it was that they could ever be poffeffed of any real power in the ftate fo long as I remained at the head of affairs; and that, were I once removed, the direction muft neceffarily fall into their hands: when they had made it clear to all the reft, that to depend upon Concini was to depend upon the real Sully; when, in fine, I found all parties, with an equal ardour, labouring for my deftruction; then, I fay, did nothing come about which I had not, from the beginning, forefeen and foretold.

The firft proceeding of the parliament, as foon as it was certified of the death of the king, having been to confer the regency upon the queen-mother, it was deemed defirable that the king himfelf fhould affift in perfon at his own high court, there to confirm the nomination. The next day after the death of the king having been appointed for that ceremony, I was fent for by her majefty, about break of day, to accompany her upon that occasion. I exhausted every sort of excuse; I even feigned myself to be so unwell as to be unable to leave my bed; such was the indescribable repugnance which I felt to what they were requiring from me. However, I was compelled to yield; so pressing and reiterated were the commands of her majesty. Encountering on every hand, some new provocation to sorrow and to bitterness of heart; transpierced with all this din of trumpets and of arms; conscious that a face, now furrowed with tears, was but sadly out of place amid all these tokens of joy and of festivity, I plunged into the crowd, and was among the first to enter the hall of the Augustins, where the parliament was then sitting.

* * * * *

I was not long in divining, that, however much, upon the surface, it was affected to adopt the precedents which, for the most part, are preserved under a legitimate regency; although it was wished to be made to appear, that the alterations in operation were no other than such as are necessarily called for under any change of government; in fact, though they laboured to convey the impression, that the government had no other desire than to impart a greater lustre to the accession of a king, a minor; those who were about the queen had nothing less at heart, than to work, under such a mystification, their own individual ends. But coming to be envisaged more closely, all these seeming regularities clean vanished away; and in their place were seen novelties and mismanagement which could not but alarm, among the lookers on, the few really well meaning and well principled. I thought myself to be privileged, and, in some sort, called upon, to make it to be felt and understood, that I both saw and disapproved of these attempts. But the season for remonstrance, which the distress of the first, and the awkwardness of the second day, had permitted to pass, with the third had entirely disappeared. Every effort at decency, or the semblance of regret; in a word, the insufferable mask which they had been compelled to assume, and was now no longer to be borne, was completely dropped. Sheer stupefaction, for want of a legitimate contentment, produced this effect on some; mere levity on others; in others, again, the natural and necessary resumption of every day life, public or domestic; but, above all, the necessity of conforming to the deportment of those, from the cue of whom the carriage of a court is to be caught.

This then, at the end of the third day, was the aspect of this new world. To all outward semblance, and as far as the eye could reach, nothing appeared to be changed at the Louvre. The mournfulness of the decorations seemed to have cast their awefulness over everything around. To judge from the hangings, the walls, the drapery, the furniture, with all the thousand indications of a general and a nation's loss, one had supposed the state apartments to have been the abode of sorrow and the court of death. But things began to wear a very different aspect, when the countenances of those to whose lot it had fallen to be chief mourners, in this sad ceremony, came to be more closely regarded. For if among them you might still detect the falling tear, the sigh, the sob, there was still too much to form a painful contrast. But it was only on descending to the chambers beneath, or to the *entre-sol*, as it is called, that some real idea could be formed as to the tone and direction of men's tempers and expectations. All that magnificence which had been banished from every other portion of the palace, there found to itself a refuge, an asylum. Gold, purple, embroidery, the most lavish, costly furniture, were all in their profusion; making of it, as it were, an enchanted scene. It was not without an aching heart, that I, with some few more true Frenchmen, could look on such like orgies, in an hour of so unparalleled a visitation. And I am ashamed to say, that all the care which could be taken was unavailing, to conceal from the world this most heartless and most shameful exposure. The roars of laughter, the songs, the merriment which were heard to escape from those localities but too sadly divulged it. So that they were filled with people who either were, or fancied themselves to be happy. It was there that the real court had ensconced itself, and that were held such public counsels, as, for decency's sake, it was still judged politic to obferve; or privy ones, in which any good, which might poffibly have been refolved on in the firft, was as fpeedily negatived, frowned on and made light of. — *Mémoires de Sully.*

BONS MOTS

AND

ANECDOTES OF HENRY IV.

HEARING this, he ordered the viscount de Chartres, Palcheux, Brasseuse, Avantigny, with three or four others, to enter the wood, and, if possible, to secure some prisoners. They were quickly back, bringing with them the Count de Belin, whom they had taken. The King, recognising him, advanced to meet, and laughingly embraced him. The Count, who, with all his eyes, was looking for the army, could not, for the soul of him, refrain from expressing the astonishment which it caused him to find his majesty thus poorly escorted. " But, my friend," said Henry, in a like tone of pleasantry, "you must remember that you do not see them all. " You have forgotten to take into the account, God and " a good cause; which both are on my side." Habituated, as I was, to be about the prince, even I was amazed to fee him, in fuch a moment, with an air, a countenance, thus tranquil, calm and ferene; blending, as it were, the moft imperturbable coolnefs with the moft uncalculating audacity; impreffing his foldiery, and all who faw him, with the fenfe of an almoft fuperhuman prefence; infpiring and firing them with the laft of ardour.

Henry IV. to Pièrre Grillon. Hang thyfelf, brave Grillon, we fought at Arques, and you were not !

Adieù, brave Grillon, through thick and through thin will I love you. *Henri.*

The mayor of this town, (Chartres,) which he had juft taken, made him a long harangue; telling him, among other things, how he was at length compelled to allow, that the town had become the property of his majefty, by the human law and by the divine law. " Yes," faid Henry, interrupting him, "and add, by " the *cannon law.*"

La-Varenne, having placed his fon under the tuition of a gentleman, told the King, " how he had juft put a " gentleman with his fon." " Strange ! " faid his majefty, " to give your fon to a gentleman, that I " could underftand ; but to give a gentleman to your " fon is what I cannot underftand." This La-Varenne was a man of the moft egregious vanity. His firft introduction to the court had been in the capacity of cook to Madame. He excelled, above all things, in the faculty of larding, or *piqueying*, as it is called. If it be true, what is related of him, that, one day, fhortly after his advancement, this princefs, meeting him, accofted him thus, "La-Varenne, you have made a "better thing of it by carrying pullets to my brother's "table, than you ever did by ftuffing them for mine," one might be tempted to conclude, that the methods by which he had ingratiated himfelf with Henry were none of the moft creditable.

I cannot fay, fays Sully, whether the following is anything better than a mere invention. If it is not, Sancy has much to anfwer for in fpreading it. However, fuch as it is, I give it. Alibour, firft phyfician to the crown, having been fent by his majefty to Madame de Liancourt, who, it feemed, had paffed a reftlefs night; (it was about the time when his majefty's affiduities, toward that lady, were firft commencing,) returning, told him; "that, in fact, he had found her "to be a good deal agitated, but that his majefty need "be under no fort of apprehenfion, for all would come "right at laft." "But will you not purge and bleed "her?" afked the King. "God forbid," rejoined the plain old fellow, with no lefs abruptnefs, "it might coft "them both their lives." "Ho! good man," faid the King, with all his eyes, angered and amazed to the laft degree, "where is it that you are allowing your tongue "to wander to? You muſt be either dreaming, or have "taken clean leave of your wits!" However, Alibour ſtuck to what he had ſaid, urging, for the ſatisfaction of his majeſty, the grounds upon which his concluſions were baſed: which, again, his majeſty as ſtoutly ſpurned; confidently hinting to the old gentleman, how very ſlight and recent was the intimacy between them. "I neither know, nor want to know," ſaid the old boy, with the moſt imperturbable coolneſs, "what "has been, or has not been between you," and finiſhed by telling him, "that if he could not ſooner be per- "ſuaded of the truth of the matter; ſix or ſeven "months hence he would know more about it." Henry broke from him in a moſt towering rage, making ſtraight for the chamber of the fair diſordered, who quickly found the means to ſet to rights all that the old fellow ſo unhappily had ſet to wrong; ſo that no one could ever detect ſo much as the trace of a miſunderſtanding to have been between the King and his miſtreſs. It is nevertheleſs true that the prediction of Alibour was, to the letter, fulfilled. But it is to be ſuppoſed that Henry, on farther recollection, was diſ- poſed to place the miſconception to his own account; for inſtead of diſowning the infant of which Madame de Liancourt was delivered, at Couſſy, during the ſiege of Laon, it was frankly placed to his own behalf, and baptized by the name of Céſar.

Sancy did not fail to embellish and make the most of his discovery; nor did he any more omit to let the world know, how La-Regnardiere, who had taken the liberty of collating with his majesty, certain passages touching the antecedents of the lady, and which were not, by him, particularly relished; found himself compelled, a day or two after, to make himself scarce from court; or how it had been given out, as a blind, that he had broken a lance with the Admiral. Sancy had even something to say on the death of the good man, Alibour; professing that it would have appeared to him to have been more consonant to the ordinary course of nature, had it not fallen out simultaneously with the fulfilment of his prediction.

"It is not counsel that I want," said Henry, "but support:" to those who were urging him to mount, and to flee upon a splendid Turkish courser which they had in readiness, "it is less perilous to "follow than to fly."

Certain deputies of the town of Arras, taking occasion, in the course of their harangue, to enlarge upon the virtues of the third Henry, told him, "what a "good prince he had been." "Yes," said he, "he "was a good prince, but he feared you. But I, I "neither fear you nor love you."

"There are three things," said Henry, "that the world will never credit, but which, neverthelefs, are true—that the Queen of England, (Elizabeth,) died a maid; that the archduke is a great captain; and that the King of France is a right good Catholic."

The King, during his progrefs, was wearied with endlefs receptions. L'Etoile has preferved fome few pleafant enough repartees, on the part of his majefty, to thefe moft wretched haranguers. One of them having fairly worn him out with the recapitulation of all his various titles and attributes, moft high, moft mighty, moft merciful, moft gracious, &c. "And add," faid Henry, interrupting him, "moft weary." Another, clearing his throat with, "Sir; Agefilaus, King of Lacedemon," "Hold there, friend," faid the King, cutting him fhort; "belly of St. Gris! I have heard before of this fame Agefilaus; but he had dined, and I have not." On another occafion, having repeatedly befought a mayor to be pleafed to curtail his difcourfe, and finding him ftill to go on as before, he turned on his heel, telling him, "that he might retail the remainder to Monfieur Guillaume." Monfieur Guillaume was the court fool.

One day, at Fontainebleau, his gardener lamenting to him, how impoffible it was to get anything to thrive in so poor a foil; "Stock it with Gascons," said Henry, eyeing the Duke of Epernon as he spoke; "they thrive everywhere." Another time, vaunting to the Spanish Ambassador, "that he would breakfast at " Milan, hear mass at Rome, and dine at Naples;" this ambassador replied, "Sir, with so much expedition, " your majesty may possibly be in time to attend his " vespers in Sicily." He never resented, or took ill, repartees launched in a spirit like this.

On a man who was a notorious glutton being admitted to his presence; he told him, swearing by his usual oath, *Ventre de St. Gris*, belly of St. Gris, "that " if he thought there were six other such fellows as him- " self in France, he would swing them all up; for they " would be enough to induce a famine in the land."

"All the forests in France," he used to say, "would " not suffice to furnish gibbets, were he to hang all " those who had written or preached against him."
When he was shewn the calumnies which were in circulation touching the late queen, his mother, he only said, "O, the rascal! Let be; he returned into " France on the faith of my passport, and I will not " have him questioned." He had, however, none of the like indulgence toward offences which did not, personally, regard himself. Once, upon his fête day, and on his way to church, where he was to receive the

facrament, Monfieur de Roquelaire, conceiving the occafion to be propitious, advancing, craved his majefty's interpofition in favour of Saint-Chamaud, (François d'Hautefort,) who was his relative, and who, without any fort of provocation, had groffly infulted Lt.-General de Tulles, (Pierre de Tulles, Lord du Teil,) and on whom the King had defired an exemplary juftice to be done. The King liftened to him. But when he had got the length of telling his majefty, "that he was willing to hope, that he would forgive "the offending for the fake of Him, whofe body and "whofe blood he was about to receive, and who had "never profeffed to pardon any but thofe who, them- "felves, did pardon others," Henry, looking fternly upon him, interrupted him, and bade him to begone, and to leave him in peace; telling him, "that he "was amazed how he could have pitched on fuch a "moment, when he was about to undertake, in the "face of heaven, to difpenfe of juftice in his realm, "and to crave of the Almighty, pardon for all the oc- "cafions where he had failed therein, to make to him "any fuch prayer."

At Ivry, as foon as the two armies were fairly facing one another, and the trumpets about to found, Henry advanced from the ranks, and with raifed eyes and hands to heaven, called upon God, that day, to teftify to the finglenefs of his purpofes, and to be with him in the fight ; befeeching him to bring home to the rebels, to make them to fee and to underftand, how it was in his perfon that the legitimate claims to the crown were centred. " But, Lord," he continued, " if it is thy " will that it be otherwife ordained ; if of thofe kings " I am to be, whom Thou, in thy wrath, doft difpenfe, " and giveft in thy fore difpleafure ; withhold not thine " hand : life and crown rend from me. A propitia-" tion, accept me, in thine eyes ! With my days, let " end the woes of France : let my blood be the laft " which is to be fhed in this unhappy quarrel ! "

Immediately on this, he called for his helmet, with its three white plumes, and having placed it on his head, as he was about to clofe the vizard, he thus ad-dreffed his foldiers ; " Comrades all ; if you this day " run my fortune, I, no lefs, run yours. It is my de-" termination, this day, to conquer or to die with you. " Above all things, ftick to your ranks. If in the " heat of the melée, you are compelled to break them ; " make for a rallying point. This is the fecret of war. " Make for yon," faid he, (pointing to three apple trees, upon the right,) " and if any of you mifs, or " enfigns, trumpets, cornets, chiefs, then have a look " for my white feathers ; and where the road to victory " and to glory is, there you will be like to find them."

The King, on his return from hunting, found all his army in a regular panic ; the very generals in a ftate of despair. Neither heart nor head failed him. His concern he kept to himself. Giving his orders without any sort of emotion, he wore his countenance as radiant, and talked as jauntingly as at the close, or on the morrow of a victory. He marched his troops, upon the instant, to the field of battle, which he had pitched on three days before, being some eight hundred paces from his lines. From whence envisaging the deliberate attitude of the Spanish troops, and the miserable confusion of his own; the weakness of his position, which it was now too late to fortify, he was most profoundly agitated; conceiving there to be no possible escape. Presently he was seen to lean himself back in his saddle, and next was heard, with bared head and raised eyes to heaven, to cry, " Ah, Lord, if this be the day which " Thou hast appointed to meet to me the meed of thy " wrath and of my deservings: thy will be done! To " thy stroke, I bow. Spare not the guilty. Yet, Lord, " in thy mercy, think of this poor people. For the " fault of the shepherd, smite not Thou the sheep!"

No one can so much as conceive the effect produced by these few words. They ran like wildfire through the camp; and it seemed as if heaven itself had interposed in their favour, banishing every fear of their foes.

* * * This threw him into incredible straits, difficulties and embarrassments; for, not only was he unfurnished with the means to carry on the war, but he clearly foresaw, from the murmurings which were already afloat, that if he attempted to lay any farther burdens upon the people, it would bring down a perfect storm of indignation about his ears. In this extremity, he had recourse to the highest remedy which is ever proceeded to, and that only when the kingdom is emperilled—a convocation of the States-General. And in as much as the exigency was by far too pressing to admit of all the formalities which had been requisite to enable so heterogeneous a body to be assembled, he simply confined himself to summoning the princes, notables, the chiefest of the nobility; the prelates, the lords treasurers and justices.

The assembly was held, by his orders, at Rouen, in the great hall of the abbey of St. Ouen; in the midst of which there was placed a chair, in the form of a throne, and elevated upon a dais. At his side were the prelates and the great lords; behind him, the four secretaries of state; beneath him sat the first presidents of the sovereign courts, with the deputies of the high officers of state.[1] He opened the session with a fine harangue, well worthy of a true prince, who will ever know that real greatness and power do not so much consist in the exercise or possession of an unlimited prerogative, as in the welfare and salvation of a people.

"If it were my ambition," said he, "to be ac-

[1] See note H, at the end.

"counted a great difcourfer, I had rather come to you, this day, ftocked with fmooth and flowing phrafes than loving inclinations. But it is to a fomething haughtier than merely to be efteemed an eloquent orator that my ambition afpires. I afpire to the more glorious title of Liberator of France — Reftorer of my country. Already, thanks to the favour of heaven, to the counfel of my faithful advifers, and to the right arms of my brave and my chivalrous nobility, (and among whom, you, my princes, too, I count; for, than *gentleman*, higher denomination there is not, below,) I have already recovered her from degradation and from ruin. It is now my wifh to carry on the good work; to reftore her to all her priftine fplendour, to all her ancient ftrength. Continue with me, my faithful fubjects, fellow labourers to this generous conclufion, as you have been in the beginning. I have not bid you to my prefence, as princes, my predeceffors, have done to their's; blindly to conform yourfelves to my imperious will. No, I have called you to this place, your counfels to hear, in them to put my truft; to follow them; in a word, to lend myfelf generoufly and confidingly to your plans. This is not a fantafy which oft will crofs the brains of kings; but leaft of all of greybeards like myfelf; captains and conquerors as I. But fuch is the love which I bear to my people; fo ardent my defire to the fervice of the

" ſtate, that this declenſion is as delightful, as, I truſt,
" it is honourable to me."

It was whilſt this affair, ſays Sully, was proceeding, that Henry, now returned from Fontainebleau, and giving the moſt of his time to pleaſure and the table, firſt heard tell of Mademoiſelle d'Entragues; his curioſity being piqued by the account of his courtiers, ever ready to pander to his weakneſs for the ſex. One ſo lovely, ſo attractive, ſo *ſpirituel* as ſhe was repreſented to be, he determined to judge of for himſelf; and no ſooner had he ſeen her than he was irrecoverably gone. Could he but have foreſeen, at that moment, all the miſery which that unhappy paſſion was deſtined to cauſe him in the end! But it was the doom of Henry, that this wretched penchant, which was for ever ſullying his fame and his reputation, was to be the empoiſoner and embitterer of his days.

The lady was neither a novice nor a ſimpleton. And though ſenſible enough to all the honour of ſeeing herſelf purſued of ſo great a prince, ſhe was no leſs ſo to the poſſibility, (viewed the preſent conjuncture of affairs,) of being able to throw in her hand, as a complement to the price of her complaiſance. She was, therefore, in no particular hurry to comply with his petition. Pride and modeſty, by turns, were interpoſed, and laſt of all avarice. She demanded no leſs a ſum than a hundred thouſand crowns, as the price of her laſt condeſcenſion. When ſhe had thus, with her higgling; ſo much more calculated, as it would ſeem to me, to damp than to inflame the ardours of a generous attachment, ſtill farther wrought him to her purpoſe, it required nothing ſhort of violence, on his part, to extract the money from me. After ſuch a proof of his weakneſs, everything was felt to be attainable, and other batteries were brought to play. She alleged the watch which her family had over her, and the vengeance that would inevitably overtake her on her fall. All this ſqueamiſhneſs the prince talked down, as beſt he could; ſtill little to the ſatisfaction of the lady; who at length told him flatly, (having well choſen the moment for ſuch an exerciſe of her authority,) that ſhe would comply with nothing, till ſuch time as he had given her his promiſe, under his own hand, to marry her within the year. It was not on her own account, ſhe added, accompanying this moſt unheard of ſtipulation with all that diſtreſſing modeſty, remorſe, ſo well calculated yet farther to inflame the paſſion of the prince, that ſhe aſked for ſuch a pledge; his word had been enough for her; or, rather, ſhe had not required ſo much as that; aware, as ſhe was, that the diſtance between them was much too great, ever to permit of her pretending to ſuch an honour. All ſhe wanted it for, was, to be able to urge it to her parents, as ſome ſort of palliation of the weakneſs into which ſhe had unhappily been betrayed. Seeing the King to heſitate, she had the tact to slip in, that, for her own part, she looked on the whole thing as a mere farce; as she well knew, that it was not within the competence of any court, or tribunal to compel compliance on the part of his majesty.

Assuredly a rare ensample of the power and tyranny of love! For Henry was not so blinded but he could very well see that the girl was determined to overreach him. Nor need I recur to other, and good cause which he had, to suppose her to be anything rather than a vestal; nor yet to the conspiracies in which her father, her mother, her brother, and even herself had been detected, and for which that whole house had been forbidden the capital: an order which I myself, by his majesty's direction, had lately transmitted to them. Yet, despite all this, this weak prince consented at last to the terms imposed, and gave her his word that she should have it.

One morning, at Fontainebleau, as he was booted for the chase, he called me aside to a gallery, and placed in my hands this most discreditable compact. It is but a piece of simple justice which I owe to Henry, seeing that I have never attempted to conceal his faults, to admit, that even to the most unjustifiable extravagancies into which he was betrayed, he was ever the first to allow; and to submit them to the examination of those whose censure they were the surest to provoke — an instance of rectitude and of magnanimity such as one but rarely encounters in princes and in kings! During all the time that I was reading this document, and every line of which, to me, was a fresh dagger, Henry was in tortures; one moment averting his face, to conceal his confusion; the next endeavouring, by a word, an ejaculation, to win me to his side; alternately justifying and condemning himself. For my own part, I was literally absorbed and lost in the contemplation of all the possibilities which might eventually come of this most fatal pledge. The clause, to marry a mistress, provided that, within the year, she should bring him a male child, (for these were the very terms in which it was conceived,) appeared to me, on the face of it, to be preposterous, and palpably null. Though there might be consolation in this; I could think of nothing to re-assure me on the score of all the misery, bitterness, contempt, which, sooner or later, could not fail, on the divulgation of such a secret, to overtake his majesty. Nor did the obstacles that such a discovery would throw in the way of the divorce, which was then in negociation, any more escape me: and these imaginations deprived me of all utterance.

Henry, seeing me to replace the paper in his hands, however coldly, with an agitation which was not to be misunderstood, said to me, "La, la! out with it; and "do not be making such a face about it." It was some little time before I could command words, that would be fitting to employ on such an occasion.

There is but little call to touch upon the caufes of my embarraffment. It were but too eafy to account for it, at leaft to thofe whofe misfortune it has been to be the confidants of princes, when called upon, by honour and by confcience, to combat their refolutions; ever rooted, fixed and imperious. His majefty again affured me, that I might do and fpeak hardily, and as my confcience prompted me, without being in any way afraid of incurring his difpleafure. "It is an in-"demnity," faid he, "which I fairly owe to you, in "return for the three hundred thoufand livres that I "managed to get out of you." This affurance, I made him repeat to me two or three times over, and even to confirm with a fort of oath. After that I did not hefitate another fecond, to let him fee me in my true character, and to let him know the man whom he had to deal with. I took it from his hands, and tore it to ribbons before his eyes. "God's blood!" faid he, altogether taken back with the hardinefs and the fuddennefs of the move, "what is this that you have "prefumed to do? I verily believe you are mad." "It is too true, Sir;" faid I, "I am mad; and would "to God I were the only man in France this day were "fo!" I had made up my mind, within myfelf, to rifk everything fooner than to betray, by a mean compliance, my duty and my confcience. So defpite the choler and vexation which were vifible upon the countenance of his majefty, as he ftooped to recover the fcraps, I did not forbear to imprefs upon him, with all the earneftnefs of which I was capable, confiderations which readily enough will prefent themfelves to the mind of every intelligent reader. Irritated as he was, he heard me to the end; but maftered, no lefs, by his paffions, his refolution was not to be fhaken. All the victory which he could gain over himfelf, was, to refrain from profcribing a too faithful fervant. He quitted the gallery without condefcending to addrefs to me a fingle word; and ordering Loménie to bring his writing materials, he went into his cabinet, and from which he iffued, at the expiration of a quarter of an hour, having employed that interval in the production of a duplicate. I was at the foot of the ftairs as he defcended. He paffed me without deigning to appear to be in any way confcious of my prefence, and mounting his horfe, took the direction of Malefherbes, hunting as he went, and where he remained two days.

It did not feem to me, that this incident fhould, in any way, interrupt the negociations in the affair of the diffolution, or prevent our continuing to be on the look out for a wife for his majefty; but, on the contrary, furnifh an additional reafon for hurrying on the one and the other. So the reprefentatives of his majefty, at Rome, were inftructed to demand, on the part of the King, the hand of the princefs, Marie de Médicis, daughter to the grand-duke of Florence. His majefty left the matter entirely to ourfelves; naming, though by sheer dint of importunity, the constable, the chancellor, Villeroi and myself, as the parties who were to treat with the agents whom the grand-duke was to send to Paris. We did not let the iron cool. For no sooner had Joannini, who was the duke's man, arrived, than, in less than no time, we had agreed, on each side, on the articles; had had them drawn, engrossed, and signed.

It fell to my lot to have to apprise his majesty of the result of our labours; who, it seemed, had little calculated on such an expedition. So when, in reply to his inquiry, as I entered, " Well, what is it that you are " all come about?" I rejoined, " Why, Sir, to marry " you!" he remained for a full quarter of an hour, for all the world like a man who had received a thunderbolt in his head. He then set to to pace the room with frantic strides, tearing his hair, biting his finger ends; and altogether in so horrible a commotion, that it was some time ere he could find words wherewith to reply. During all this, I clearly saw, that what I had said to him had not been without its effect. At length, coming to be cooler, and with all the air of a man who had screwed himself up to go through with an unpleasant piece of business, he broke out, working his hands, all the while, one in another, " Ha, well; " in God's name, if it must be, and there is no way of " getting out of it. Since you tell me, that it is for " the benefit of my people that I must marry, I suppose "it muſt be done." He frankly confeſſed to me afterwards, that it was the dread of making, in a ſecond, as unlucky a choice as he had done in his firſt wife, which had been the real cauſe of all his unaccountableneſs. O, the inexplicable inconſiſtency of the human mind! to ſee a prince who had extricated himſelf, almoſt without an effort, from a thouſand ſcrapes, dilemmas, dangers, as well on the field as in the cloſet, trembling at the bare apprehenſion of familiar and domeſtic jars; and ſeemingly more agitated, at their very proſpect, than he had been in the preceding year, when, through the information of a capucin of Milan, he had ſeen an Italian ſeized, in the middle of the court, who had come expreſſly to Paris to diſpatch him! The marriage thus agreed upon was to be conſummated in the enſuing year.

* * * * *

The month of June had now come; without, however, for that, Monſieur de Savoye ſhowing the ſlighteſt inclination to ſtand to his engagements. So that his majeſty began to ſee clearly enough, that it was only by dint of force that he need ever hope to get anything out of him. But in addition to the bias of the courtiers, who ſeemed, one and all, to have ſold themſelves to the Duke of Savoye, yet another, and more weighty logic was weighing with the prince. And that was, his attachment to his new miſtreſs, whom he had now raiſed to the dignity of Marchioneſs of Verneuil. He could not prevail on himself to think of leaving her. And I am perfectly ashamed to say, that when, by downright bullying, I had at last prevailed upon him to set out for Lyons, he still kept hesitating, to the last moment, whether he should not take her with him; a step to which he was sufficiently encouraged by but too many who were about him. She was then with child, and in such a state of affairs, the promise which she had extracted from him, and then had in her hands, became for him a matter of the last anxiety. However, heaven, as usual, stood his good friend. For the lady miscarried of a still born child, through the fright which she had undergone in seeing the lightning, during a terrible thunderstorm, pass under the very bed on which she was lying. It was at Moulins, which he had just reached, that Henry first heard of this mishap; and many a wistful eye thence he turned toward the quarter where his mistress lay. However, certain reflections presented themselves to his mind, and which were not without their sobering influences. He kept on his course to Lyons, where his troops had been ordered to meet him.

* * * * *

When the King arrived, (all this is gathered from the most credible historians of the time,) the Queen was at supper. And as he was curious to steal a look at her, ere formally announcing himself, he came in, exactly as he was, as far as the outer hall, which was then crowded with people. But he had no sooner set his foot among them, than he was recognized by all about, who, of course, at once made way for him; so that he was forced, upon the instant, to retire. The Queen, from so unusual a movement, immediately suspected his majesty to be present; of which circumstance, however, she took no sort of notice, nor seemed to be in any way affected thereby, farther than by pushing the dishes from her, one after another, as they were placed upon the table; eating little or nothing; in fact, as if she had rather sat down for ceremony's sake, than to satisfy her appetite. As soon as the cloth was removed, she retired to her room. The King, who had only been waiting for this, immediately went to her, preceded by Monsieur le Grand, who knocked so audibly at the door, that her majesty at once divined it could be no other than the King. And so, advancing, she met them at the moment when Monsieur le Grand was about to announce his majesty; instantly to throw herself upon her knees before him. The King immediately raised her and embraced her; on which some little time was dedicated to mutual congratulation, caressing, kissing, felicitations. As soon as these compliments and ceremonies were ended, his majesty took her by the hand, and led her to the fireplace, where, for some quarter of an hour, they spoke more seriously together. His majesty then retired to supper; of which, however, he but slightly partook. After that he sent

Madame de Nemours to the Queen; bidding her to tell her majefty, "that he had foreborne to bring any fort "of bed with him, as he was willing to hope that her "majefty would be pleafed to permit him a portion of "hers; and which he farther hoped would, from that "day, be common to them both." This meffage having been carried by that lady to the Queen, fhe brought him back word, in return, "That fhe had "come to France for no other purpofe than to oblige "his majefty, and to conform herfelf, as his moft "humble fervant, to his very lighteft wifh." Henry, hearing this, immediately undreffed and proceeded to the apartment of the Queen, who was already in bed.

This father Gonthier [1], a Jefuit, launched out, in the prefence of the King, who was prefent at mafs on the Friday, Saturday and Sunday of Chriftmas week, into the moft terrible and reiterated abufe of the Huguenots; calling them *rafcals, vermin, fcoundrels*, &c. And falling foul, at length, of the newly appended article of their faith; that the pope was Antichrift, he continued, "If, Sir, it be true that the pope is "Antichrift, what becomes of your marriage? What "the worth of the difpenfation? What becomes of "the Dauphin?" On this the Marfhall d'Ornano took occafion one day to fay to his majefty, "Sir,

---

[1] See note I, at the end.

" had a Jesuit so far forgotten himself, in my presence,
" at Bourdeaux, as this man has done in your ma-
" jesty's, I would have had him chucked clean into
" the river, as soon as ever he came down from his
" chair."

On another occasion, as Henry was assisting at the same church, at a sermon preached by the same Gonthier; this father, justly scandalized at the irreverence displayed, at such a time and in such a place, as well by the Marchioness of Verneuil as certain other ladies present, who were laughing and giggling, and in divers ways endeavouring to arrest the King's attention; suddenly stopped and apostrophised his majesty thus; " When, Sir, will you forbear to come thus to the
" house of God, with a whole seraglio in your train;
" or to provoke so crying a scandal in so holy a place?"
The King, instead of committing him to the Bastile, as all the women were wanting him to do, came again to hear him the next day. All the notice which he took of what had passed, was, to whisper him quietly in the ear, as he was on his way to the pulpit, " that he was
" obliged to him for his reproof of yesterday, and that
" he had nothing to fear; only he had to request, that,
" another time, he should not be made the subject of
" public censure."

Biron, says Perefixe, had by him certain papers, written in his own hand, and wherein the articles of

the conspiracy were detailed at length. Laffin repre-
sented to him, how dangerous it was for him to keep
any such documents, or even to show them, as his
handwriting was so well known; and that the best
way would be, to let a duplicate be taken, and then to
destroy the originals — advice which Biron considered
to be so well worth attending to, that he immediately
placed them in his hands; instructing him to make
the copies as he proposed; and which he did, transf
cribing them at a table, whilst Biron was lying on his
bed. He then handed him the copy; at the same
time tearing up what was, or rather, what Biron conceived to be, the original, and throwing it in the fire;
whereas he had adroitly substituted other papers in
their place. Most assuredly a matter of so high an importance, the marshall should have looked to for himself; for this piece of negligence, with God's permission,
was destined, later, as we shall presently see, to cost
him his head. * * * *

Biron was perfectly aware that Laffin had repaired
to, and been seen in court. But it put him under no
sort of anxiety; feeling as confident of his man as he
was of himself. Besides, his bosom friend, the baron
de Lux, had assured him, that Laffin had been as true
as steel, and that not a breath had escaped. No doubt
de Lux fancied that it was all as he said, having
overheard the King, on turning from Laffin, and as
though an incredible weight had been taken off his

mind, to say, "I am right thankful to have seen that man; he has completely set my mind at rest, and shown me that I was wrong in my suspicions."

All this time Biron's friends kept writing to him, that he would be a fool to run his head into the lion's mouth, or to show himself at court: that it was a much safer plan to place his affairs in the hands of an intermediary, than his person in those of the King. However, in spite of all this, and of all his remorse of conscience, after some little deliberation, he set out, post, for Fontainebleau; arriving just as his majesty was about to set out, himself, to bring him to reason, having long since given over all expectation of otherwise succeeding.

Many, and more or less circumstantial accounts have been left, by the historians of the time, of the trial, imprisonment and death of this marshal. I shall content myself with resuming the whole.

It is hardly possible too much to wonder at the blindness and infatuation of this wretched man; or sufficiently to extol the goodness and long suffering of the King, who exhausted every conceivable means to soften, to tame, and to subdue him. Frankly to avow our faults is the first evidence of a sincere repentance. The King, taking him aside, most passionately besought him to open to him the whole; to tell him frankly what was his understanding, and who were his agents, with the duke of Savoye; promising him most faithfully, if he would but make a clean breaſt of it, that all ſhould be forgotten, as though it had never been. He farther told him, that though he himſelf was in poſſeſſion of the lighteſt particulars, he would alſo wiſh to hear them confirmed from his own lips; and even went the length of ſwearing to him, that, let his crime be the greateſt which ſubject could fail in toward his prince, if he would but allow to it, all ſhould be forgiven. Biron, inſtead of humbly thanking his majeſty, or, at leaſt, warily and temperately parrying the thruſt, and as had become him, in the preſence of his juſtly-incenſed ſovereign, inſolently told him, "that he was "innocent, and that it was to vindicate himſelf that he "had come to court; to find out who were his calum-"niators; and to ſee, if juſtice were not inflicted on "them, whether he could not manage to take it for "himſelf." Although, by this haughty retort, his crime had become doubly aggravated in the eyes of his majeſty, he did not, for that, forbear to tell him gently, that he hoped he would a little reconſider his propoſition, and that the next time he ſhould ſee him he would find him better adviſed.

The very ſame evening, after ſupper, the Count de Soiſſons came to him, on the part of his majeſty, earneſtly entreating him to throw himſelf on the King's mercy; concluding his remonſtrance with the words of Solomon, "*That the wrath of a king is as the mes-*"*ſengers of death.*" But it was only to meet, if poſſible, with a loftier reception than that which had been deigned to his majefty.

The following day, during a turn beneath his elms, his majefty, a fecond time, entreated him to confefs his crimes; but he could get nothing out of him fave proteftations of innocence, menaces and recriminations. Seeing his perfiftence, his majefty found himfelf to be troubled to the very abyffes of his foul; drawn now this way, now that, nor knowing in what manner to proceed. On the one hand, the ftrong perfonal regard that he ever entertained for the man, the recollection of all the fervices which he had done him, alike withheld his arm. On the other, the heinoufnefs of his crime, his horrible pride, his obftinacy, called loudly for a public example, and urged him to let juftice take its courfe. Joined to this, he no lefs clearly faw the danger to which he himfelf, perfonally, as well as the ftate, was expofed; and which there was no other means to avert, than by crufhing, in the bud, a plot, the ramifications of which he were unable to trace.

In this agony of indecifion, he retired into his clofet, and falling upon his knees, befought of God to put into his heart, the courfe which it would be befitting for him to purfue. For thus he was in the habit of doing on all momentous and perplexing occafions. Providence he took to be his moft faithful counfellor and his fureft ftay. On rifing from his knees, as he afterwards faid, he found his agitation to have fubfided;

and he determined, there and then, to place the marſhal under arreſt, ſhould his council, on view of the evidence which was then in hand, pronounce him to be guilty. To this end, he ſelected four from among the council, Bellievre, Roſny, Villeroy and Sillery; placing the papers in their hands. They declared, to unanimity, that the proofs were overwhelming.

Even after this, he determined, a third time, to attempt this haughty ſpirit. Prayers, remonſtrances, aſſeverations, promiſes of forgiveneſs, for the laſt time, were again employed, to induce him to avow his crime. But it was to little purpoſe; he ſtill replied as before; and, in fact, adding, "that if he could but make out "who his aſperſers were, he would knock their brains "about their ears."

At length the King, fairly wearied and difguſted with all this bragadocio, madneſs and infatuation, turned on his heel, difmiſſing him as he went; (and they were the laſt words that he ever addreſſed to him;) "Then "I muſt get it out of others: *Adieu, baron de Biron!*" A ſalutation which broke upon him, as the clap of thunder which precedes the bolt. The King, in thus, in an inſtant, and by a word, diveſting him of all the eminent dignities to which he had been raiſed, giving him clearly enough to underſtand, that it was his intention yet farther to degrade him.

As he was about to retire from the apartments of her majeſty, and where he had been playing at cards;

Vitry, the captain of the guard, demanded of him his sword, telling him that he was to confider himfelf his majefty's prifoner. Another captain of the guard, Praflin, made fure of the count d'Auvergne; and in the morning they were taken together, under an adequate efcort, by water, to the Baftile.

* * * * *

When they came to the confrontment and examination of the witneffes, and Laffin was placed in the box; inftead of impugning his evidence, as that of a man whom an hundred infamies might be objected to, Biron admitted him at once to be a man of honour and a gentleman. But no fooner had he heard his evidence read, than he immediately turned round, calling him *traitor, fcoundrel, forcerer*. A recognition which now came too late; his qualifications were no more attended to.

Renazé, whom he fancied to be his prifoner, faft and fafe, in Piedmont, but from whence he had efcaped, fome few days before, ftepped next into the box. And when he firft faw him to enter the court, he verily believed that it had been a phantom. After that, he never fo much as opened his lips, allowing him to proceed, without any fort of interruption, in his depofition, which was in every way conformable to that of Laffin. They each depofed, that an opportunity was to have been fecured to the governor of the fort St. Catherine to cut off the King, whilft engaged in reconnoitring the place; that Biron was to have been with him, though walking a little ahead, and armed in a particular device, so that he might be the more readily distinguished. They farther alleged, that another scheme was, to secure his majesty whilst hunting, or otherwise unattended, and to carry him away into Spain. * * * *

On the morrow, the last day of July, it was put to the vote, and out of one hundred and fifty voices, there was not one dissentient. All were for his death. He was declared *to have been tried for, and to have been found guilty of high treason; of conspiracies levelled against the person of the King; of having been in communication with his majesty's enemies, he, the while, a marshal of France. And as an atonement for the said crimes, he was adjudged to forfeit all his lands; to be destituted of all his titles, honours, dignities; to lose his head, upon the Place de Greve; his goods and chattels, moveable and immoveable, to be transferred and confiscated to the crown. His patrimony of Biron was farther declared to be incapable of being again erected into a barony; and this estate, with all his others, to be annexed to the domains of the crown.*

The King, under colour of conferring a grace upon the family, but in reality out of the apprehension of a tumult; for the marshal had many friends at court, and was the darling of the swordsmen; remitted the place of execution, consenting that it should be at the Bastile.

The chancellor, with the first prefident, conducted him to the chapel, where, at fix o'clock in the morning, his condemnation was read to him; and which he liftened to fubmiffively enough, and on his knees, till they came to the charge of *attempts upon the perfon of the King.* For at them he rofe, exclaiming, "*That is* "*falfe; take that out.*" After this, the chancellor, with the ufual formalities, demanded of him the collar of his order, his ducal coronet, with the truncheon of his office. The two latter, he had not about him; the firft he drew from his pocket and handed to him.

It would be idle to recall the thoufand exculpations, exclamations, recriminations, extravagancies, (for they were nothing lefs,) to which he abandoned himfelf.

At fix o'clock in the evening, he was conducted to the fcaffold, where his head was ftricken from his body. It was remarked that the head pofitively bounded three feveral times from the ground, fuch were the effervefcence and exaltation of the fpirits of the man, and fuch the prodigious quantity of blood which had mounted to his brain. And, in fact, a greater ftream was noticed to come from the head than from the body. He was laid in the fepulchres of St. Paul's, without any fort of ceremony; but in the prefence of a marvellous affemblage of people, among whom there was fcarcely to be found a dry eye: every one lamenting to fee fo noble a fpirit thus brought, through an overweening and a preposterous ambition, to a miserable and a shameful end.

The coronation of the Queen, says the marshal de Bassompierre, was being proceeded with upon a scale of unusual magnificence. His majesty was in the highest spirits. . . . . The King said one day to him, (Monsieur de Guise,) and to myself, "Ah, you people "little know me now, but when I am gone, and taken "from you, as I shall be, one of these days, you will "then better understand my real worth, and all the "difference that there is from me to other men." "Good God, Sir," was my reply, "will you never "cease to be distressing us in this manner; telling us "that you have but a little time to live! Sir, these are "not pleasant things to hear. You will yet be spared, "an' it please God, many a long and a happy year. "Sir, there is no felicity on this earth which is com- "parable unto your felicity. You are in the very "prime of your life. You are in the possession, and "in the enjoyment, of every faculty of your mind and "member of your body. Honour is yours; if ever it "was permitted to mortal. You are now seated, and in "the most undisturbed tranquillity, upon the throne of "your progenitors—the greatest in Christendom; loved, "adored of your people; every blessing is heaped upon "you—lands, houses, wealth, inheritance; a lovely "lady to your wife; fair mistresses; a beauteous off-

" spring growing up around you; what farther, Sir, is
" it in the power of man or mortal, to conceive of, to
" wish for, or to want?" "Ah, my friend," said he,
with a sigh, " all these things must be forgotten; they
" must be all left." — Various Sources.

THE STORY OF PATIENT GRIZZEL.

IN Lombardy, upon the confines of Piedmont, there is fituated a noble land, and which is called, The country of Saluces; and the lords of which, time out of mind, have ever borne the rank of marquifes. And of all thefe marquifes, the moſt powerful, as well as the nobleſt, was one known by the name of Walter. He was fair, pleafing, well built, handfome; adorned with every bounty, gift of nature; but he had one fault, and that was, to be a little too much enamoured of the freedom and the licenfe of a fingle life, and a little too much indifpofed to allow for the natural uneafinefs of his barons and his vaffals, upon fuch a head. For ferioufly difquieted they were. So that at length, with one accord, they came together, and, deliberation made, an embaffage was deputed to carry to him the following remonſtrance. "Marquis, our only mafter, true and "fovereign lord; it is the love alone that we bear to

"you which has now begotten in us the boldness to
"address you. Your lightest action, Sir, is meet and
"pleasant in our eyes; and happy do we account our-
"selves in such a lord. But, dear Sir, years, years are
"rolling over us apace, and time adventured returneth
"not again. And be it, Sir, that now you are in the
"flower of your prime; yet age, with stealthy step, is
"creeping on; and death, which never yet did spare,
"approaches fast. And so, our lord, remembering of
"these, we, your vassals, whose chiefest joy will ever be
"to love and to obey you, humbly entreat they may be
"permitted to take upon themselves the pleasing task,
"to find to you a noble dame; high, fair and virtuous;
"such as it would become so great a prince to take to
"wife. Deign, Sir, so far to meet the wishes of your
"faithful people; so that, should, by any unforeseen
"event, which heaven avert, our lord be taken from
"us, to such a sorrow might not be added the misery
"of seeing the marquisite exposed, a prey to litigation
"or to arms."

To this discourse, Walter, profoundly touched, replied as follows—"It is true, my friends, that it is a de-
"light to me to pasture in that freedom which my state
"allows, and which in wedlock is not to be looked for;
"that is, if the testimony of those who have already
"entered it is in any way to be relied upon. And there
"is another, and a very serious drawback attached to
"matrimony; and that is, that we cannot always be

"perfectly certain that those children which we have been so ardently desiring, when we do have them, have been of our own begetting. However, my friends, your wishes shall be attended to. I promise you, the wife shall be had; and I trust, with the divine mercy, to be enabled so to choose, that she will prove one with whom I shall be permitted to live in harmony and in happiness. But first and foremost, there is one stipulation which I must make with you, and that is, that you will pledge yourselves; be she whom she may that I do choose; be she rich man's daughter, or be she poor man's daughter; to respect and to acknowledge her as your sovereign lady; and that there shall not be a man among you who will presume either to blame or to cavil at the object of my choice." To the conditions imposed by the marquis, the company as faithfully subscribed, humbly thanking him for having thus graciously acceded to their prayer. And there and then was the day fixed for the approaching nuptials, to the unspeakable delight of the country of Saluces.

Now, not far from where the palace of Saluces stood, there was a village, inhabited by poor, simple, labouring people; and this village the marquis often had had occasion, in going to, or in coming from the chase, to pass. And among these poor people there was one, an old man, named Janicola, wearied and worn with age and with infirmities; and who could now no more so much as walk. But as often will the sun of heaven descend upon and light the wretched hovel, as the palaces of princes and of kings. Of which this good old man was proof. For with an only daughter, Grisélidis, God had blessed him; of a person the most matchless; but the graces, perfections of whose mind, no tongue or pen could paint. And in her was all his comfort and his joy. His sheep, by day, upon the hills she fed; with eve them to the fold returned; his wretched supper on the hearth to warm, or help him to his sorry bed. In a word, every duty, return, which daughter to a father could extend, did this admirable woman to her's.

Now, for a very long time, the marquis, by common fame, had heard speak of the extraordinary virtues, and the devotedness of this most glorious and incomparable girl. And often and often had it happened, in going to and returning from the chase, that he had involuntarily loitered to behold her; and communing with his heart, to himself had said, "If ever I take to myself a "wife; that woman shall be the one."

And now the day was come which the marquis had appointed for the wedding. The halls were thronged with lords and ladies, knights, burgesses, and citizens of all degrees. With one exception, the company were assembled. It was to little purpose that they stared for the bride. Nay, so much as who or where she was, not a man of them could divine. At length the marquis, as though he would have gone to her encounter, placing his hat upon his head, stepped forth of the hall; the lords and company following, to see how all this mystery would end. And in all this state he proceeded to the village and the door of the good man, Janicola; and announcing himself, said, "Janicola, I know that "you have ever loved me; I am now going to put "your professions to the proof. I want you to give "me your daughter to wife." The poor man, aghast at such a proposition, humbly and reverently replied, "Sir, you are my lord and my master; it is but meet "that your pleasure should be my pleasure."

All this time, the poor girl, crimson with confusion, stood, trembling behind her old father; for, sure, never before had she entertained such an assembly within her doors. Presently the marquis, turning to her, said, "Grisélidis, it is my wish to take you to be my wife. "Your father, you see, has passed his consent. Yours, "I flatter myself, will not be withheld. But before "we proceed any farther; one question, and in his "presence, I must put to you. The woman who is "to be my wife, I expect to be submissive to me in all "things; to be one who will never will but what I "may will; and who, let my whims or my commands "be what they may, will be consentant, on the instant, "to conform to them. In agreeing to become my "wife, will you farther undertake to abide by these "conditions?" "My lord," said Grisélidis, "since

"such be your desire, never shall word, or thought, or
"deed escape from me, otherwise than conformable to
"your expressed will. Bid me to lay down my life,
"and it shall cheerfully and unhesitatingly be done so,
"at your feet." "It is enough," said the marquis,
and with that he took her by the hand, and led her
forth, presenting her to all his barons and his people, to
whom he said, "My friends, behold my wife. See
"your future lady; and whom, as you love me your-
"selves, I now require you to love and to honour."
And having so delivered himself, he caused her to be
conveyed to the palace, where, by her ladies, she was
stripped of all her rustic habiliments; enrobed in satins,
in jewels and in silks; in fact, as became the bride of
such a prince. That she trembled and she blushed, I
need not say. And had you, yourself, reader, but seen
her, one moment a poor peasant wench, and in a hovel,
and the next a crowned queen, and in her palace;
doubtless, your amazement had been no less palpable.

The marriage and the feast were alike celebrated on
the one day. The tables groaned; the halls resounded
with mirth, the viol and the song. Everything was
forgotten in the general joy. The people, no less than
their lord, were enchanted with the object of his
choice. Till then Grisélidis had been famous for her
virtue and her devotion; but from that day, gentle,
affable, winning, conciliating, she began to be as beloved as heretofore she had been respected. And

whether from among those who had known her before her elevation, or those who came to know her after, there lacked not one to rejoice in her good fortune.

Soon after this she found herself to be with child, and gave birth to a daughter, which promised, one day, to be no less fair than herself. And though as well its father, as the commons, would have preferred a son; there was not, for that, the less rejoicing throughout the country. The child was brought up by its mother, at the palace. But no sooner was it weaned, than the marquis, who had long been devising with himself in what way to put to the proof the virtues of his wife; though every day more enamoured of her; having come to her, addressed her thus; "Grisélidis,
"you have not, doubtless, forgotten who you were,
"and what you were, ere you came to be advanced by
"me to the position which you this day hold. For my
"own part, I had well nigh forgotten it; as all the
"kindnesses which you have received at my hands
"abundantly must satisfy you. But now for some
"time, in fact, ever since the birth of your daughter,
"my barons murmur, and loudly complain, that one
"day they must see themselves vassals of the grand-
"daughter of Janicola. So that I, something more
"than whose mere interest it is to conciliate these men,
"now find myself compelled to make this cruel sacri-
"fice; the very thought of which is like to rend my
"heart in twain. However, I could not bring myself

"to put it into execution till such time as I had broken it to you. I now come to ask your consent, and have to implore you to call into requisition all that patience which you avouched for in the day that you became my wife." "Dear Sir," was her meek reply, nor ever once allowing so much as a symptom of emotion to escape her, "You are my lord and are my husband; I and my child are yours. Dispose, as you will, of it and of me; for never shall I forget or betray that submission which I undertook for at our marriage, and which I owe you." So much gentleness and condescension amazed the marquis, who retired, seemingly a prey to sorrow and to thought, but, in reality, penetrated to the very soul, with fondness and admiration of his wife. And no sooner was he alone, than he called to him an old and faithful domestic; one who had been some thirty years under his roof, and breaking to him his purpose, dispatched him to his mistress. So coming to her, he said, "Madame, I do beseech you to see before you the unwilling instrument of a very sad commission. I am charged to demand of you your child. My lord requires this sacrifice at your hands." From the nature of the commission, recalling so fearfully the commotion and the dark hints of the marquis, she at once concluded the terrible fate which was reserved to it. Nevertheless, her tears she stifled, her apprehensions she smothered; nor even once so much as indulging herself with a sigh or a sob, she stepped to the cradle where the child was sleeping, took it in her arms, kissed it, signed it with the cross, making it over to the man, who as faithfully recounted to the marquis all the admirable courage and devotion, to which he had been witness, on the part of his lady. Walter was perfectly lost in admiration of the fortitude and virtues of his wife; and when, on the top of this came the tears and the innocence of the poor little babe, it was as much as ever he could do to steel himself to so rude a trial. But such better determinations too quickly passed, and he gave it into the hands of his servant, desiring him to carry it quietly to the countess d'Empêche, his sister; and to charge her to see it brought up with such a wariness, that no living soul, no, not so much as her own husband, should have any inkling of the mystery. The servant, to the letter, discharged his commission; and the countess undertook to gloss the affair, even as her brother had required.

From the time of this excision the marquis continued to live, as aforetime, with his wife. And often as he would peer into her eyes, as though to read her inmost soul; were sorrow or remembrance there? so often would she meet him with all the fondness and the love of yore. Nor did she ever allow so much as the shadow of a bitterness to appear; or the name of her lost one, either in his presence, or behind his back, to cross her lips.

Four years paſſed away, and again ſhe found herſelf to be with child. This time it proved to be a ſon; to the joy and the enchantment of its parents and Saluces. And from her breaſt ſhe nouriſhed it, as ſhe had done her daughter. But no ſooner had this long deſired and dearly loved infant attained to its ſecond year, than the marquis, determined, yet a ſecond time, to put to the teſt the patience of Griſélidis, coming to her, as before, again inſiſted to her the murmurings of his barons and his ſubjects.

O what, at ſuch a moment, muſt have been the agony, the yearnings, of this incomparable woman; already bereaved of a daughter, and now her ſon, her only hope, her only joy, about to be taken from her and deſtroyed! Where is, I will not ſay, the tender mother, but the mere ordinary, ſympathiſing, human breaſt, which, on hearing ſuch a ſentence, could ſtifle the pangs of nature in its depth? Queens, princeſſes, ladies, women of all degrees, harken the reſponſe of this one to her lord; attend, and profit by it! "Dear Sir, I have ſworn to you before, I ſwear "to you again, never to know or harbour other will "or thought than yours. What you will, I will. "The day in which my wretched rags I dropped, that "day my proper will I doffed; no other than my "lord's to know. And were it but within my power "to divine, or ever they were expreſſed, the wiſhes of "my lord, his lighteſt thought had been anticipated.

"With me but to die, and I shall die; for death itself "were not so terrible to me as the misfortune of in- "curring your displeasure."

Walter was more and more astonished. Another, or a stranger, might have been disposed to place all this stoicism to mere insensibility and apathy of heart. But he who, a thousand times, her infants at her breast, had witnessed the yearnings, the abysses of her maternity, could place it to no other account, than a sense of the affection and the duty which she bore to him. Nevertheless, as before, the sergeant came to claim the child, and carrying it to Bologna, it was brought up together with its sister.

After two such terrible ordeals, the marquis might well have remained satisfied on the score of the patience of his wife, and have foreborne to subject her to yet a farther. But there are some dispositions, by nature, so incorrigibly imaginative that nothing can, or will cure them; whose jealousy, once aroused, never can be allayed; and whose chiefest pleasure is the torture of another's breast. Not only did she appear to have stifled all the memories of the causes of her former sorrows, as though they had never been, but she daily seemed to be becoming, if possible, even more devoted, attached, tender and subdued. Yet for all this did he still determine to try, to torment and to prove her.

By the time his daughter had reached her twelfth year, and his son his eighth, he at length bethought

himself to recall them to their homes. And accordingly to his sister he sent, praying her to come and see him, and that his children might be with her. And at the same time he caused a report to get wind; how he was about to put away his wife, and to take another. It was not long ere this heartless scandal was whispered to Grisélidis. It was told to her, that a young person, of a noble house, accomplished, lovely, fair as a fairy, was about to arrive and to be new lady of Saluces. If she was thunderstruck at such a blow, I leave you to consider. However, summoning up all her resolution, she awaited in silence the hour when he, whose will was her will, should think proper formally to acquaint her with it. Nor had she long to wait. For the marquis, sending for her, and in the presence of all his court, addressed her thus. "Grisélidis, during all the
"time that we have lived together, now twelve years
"gone, I owe it to you to say, that never but content-
"ment have I taken in your sight; for it was to your
"virtues and not to your descent that I looked when
"I took you. But one thing is wanting. Saluces
"must have an heir. My barons require it; Rome
"permits it. I must have a wife worthy and becoming
"such a prince. Such an one is already upon the
"road, so prepare yourself to cede to her your place.
"The portion which you brought, you may retake.
"You are at liberty now to retire, and you must bear
"all this as best you can." "Sir," said Grisélidis, "I

" am not so ignorant as not to know, that the daughter
" of Janicola never could have been destined to be the
" wife of such a prince. And I take my God to wit-
" ness, that, day by day, as, in this palace, and of
" which you raised me to be the queen, I have re-
" turned him thanks for all the mercies which he had
" heaped upon me, I have never ceased to confess,
" how unworthy I was, so much as of the least of
" them. Since such is your pleasure, the scenes, the
" haunts of all my former joy, I quit, my lord, without
" a pang; returning, in my cabin, these eyes to close,
" as first they saw the light; and where, happily, again
" I may repay to an helpless father those duties that
" I have been compelled to devise to another. As to
" my dowry, Sir, of which you speak; you know, that
" to my chastity, I did but bring my hodden, sub-
" mission and devotion. My jewels, my robes, my all
" are yours. Allow me a moment to change them,
' for those that once I wore. They are yet by me.
" Here, Sir, is the ring with which you wedded Gri-
" sélidis. Naked came I from my father's door, and
" naked will I thither return; nor shall I carry any
" other consolation with me than the trust to be re-
" membered as the spotless widow, as I have lived the
" wife, of so great a lord."

So passionately moved was the marquis that he was forced to retire; unable in any way to master his emotion. And presently Grisélidis, despoiling herself of all her bravery, her jewels, her finery, and cafting on her back her peafant's frock, returned on foot to whence fhe came, accompanied by an hoft of lords, of ladies and of knights, melted to tears at the beholding fo fad a change. She alone, of all, appeared to be unmoved; walking in filence, with bended eyes upon the ground. Thus efcorted, fhe arrived at her father's, who did not feem to be in any way furprifed at fuch a vifit. From the firft, he had invariably continued to look on the match as unfuitable, and always feared that, fooner or later, the marquis, fick of his daughter, would not fcruple to return her upon his hands. The old man tenderly embraced her, and without evidencing any fort of emotion, whether of joy or the reverfe, kindly thanked the company for the honour which they had done his daughter in thus accompanying her; exhorting them to love their lord, and to continue faithfully to ferve him.

Now juft fancy what Janicola muft have been inwardly undergoing; thus to fee his daughter, who had paffed fo many years in abundance and in fplendour, condemned, for the remainder of her days, to penury and want! But to look on her, one never could have fuppofed her to have known other, or better. All her joy, her care, was to comfort and beguile her aged father.

But by this, the count and countefs d'Empêche were arriving, with the two children; accompanied of many knights and nobles, ladies, followers. Already they were within two days' journey of Saluces. The marquis,

to carry through his terrible experiment, sent again for
Grisélidis, who instantly appeared, on foot, and as she
was, in all her peasant trim. "Daughter of Janicola,"
said he, "to-morrow, as you know, I am to receive my
"expectant bride; and seeing that there is no one of
"all my court who is so well acquainted as yourself
"with all its ins and outs, and all the ways that please
"me; and as it is my wish to see her, as well as my
"brother and my sister, with all their company, enter-
"tained in a befitting manner, I have determined to
"place in your hands the entire charge of their recep-
"tion; but more especially of that of the young person
"of whom I spoke." "Sir," said Grisélidis, "so many
"obligations am I under to you, that, so long as God
"shall spare me days, it shall be my choicest pleasure to
"do to you that which shall be pleasing in your eyes;"
there and then retiring to give her orders to the servants
and purveyors. Her eyes were everywhere. With
her very hands she made the bed in which but yester-
night she lay, and that now was destined for another.
And on the appearance of the young people, far from
allowing to escape, as one might have anticipated, a
sigh, a wince, or a tear; or being in any way ashamed
of the homeliness of her appearance, she went respectfully to meet the bride, saluted her, and led her to her
appointed chamber. By a sort of instinct, and the
bottom of which she could not fathom, she found herself to be irresistibly drawn towards these children; nor

could she keep from marvelling at their beauty, or once take her eyes from off them.

¹ The day of the feaſt being come, and all the company at table, the marquis, having ſent for Griſélidis, and indicated to her his deſtined bride, now radiant with beauty, youth and every charm; attired in all her finery, bid her tell him, what ſhe thought of his intended? "Sir," ſaid ſhe, "your choice could "neither have fallen upon a lovelier or a worthier "object. And ſhould, Sir, God but hear the prayers "which daily to his throne for you I raiſe; long and "happily ſhall ſhe live in your poſſeſſion. But, Sir, if "it may be, ſpare to her the trials which have been "proved of another. She is but young; too tenderly "has her youth been led. Alas, Sir, ſhe knows not "what it is to ſuffer. May hap ſhe might want the "ſtrength: if ſhe came to die. . . . . ."

At theſe words the marquis could no more refrain himſelf, nor one other moment diffimulate. Loſt in admiration of the immoveable firmneſs and the indomptable virtue, which nothing could cauſe to falter, or recoil, he cried aloud, "Griſélidis, dear Griſélidis, this "is paſt endurance: this is too much. To put to the "teſt the force of your affection, I have paſſed you "through a ruder proof than ever man who lived be- "neath this ſun ſo much as dared to think of; yet

---

¹ See note J, at the end.

"never have I found in you but obedience, lovingnefs,
"fidelity." With that he drew her to his arms,
watering her, as he leant over her, with his tears.
Prefently, recovering himfelf, before all the company
he cried, " Incomparable woman, yes, yes, you alone
" are fitting to be my wife, and you alone fhall be.
" You have thought me to be the murderer of my
" children: fo did my court. They were but removed.
" My fifter, to whofe hands I committed them, this
" day reftores them. See them with your eyes. And
" you, my children, come and throw yourfelves at the
" feet of your admirable mother." It was too much.
So perfect a felicity was not to be borne. Swooning,
fhe funk upon the ground. And no fooner was fhe
reftored to herfelf than fhe ftrained them to her bofom
with fuch an abandonment that it was as much as ever
could be done to tear them from her. The whole
affembly was in tears, nor was there any one thing
heard but exclamations, fhouts and rapture. And thus
this fête, which the marquis had fo inaufpicioufly in-
augurated, was turned, for his wife, into a fource of
felicity, of joy and of triumph.

Walter caufed the old Janicola to be carried to
the palace of Saluces; and whom, up to this time, if
he had neglected, it was fimply to try his wife. And
he was had in honour for the remainder of his days.
And the marquis and his wife lived together yet twenty
years, and in an intercourfe the moft undifturbed.

They faw their children married, and they faw yet their children again. And after them their fon inherited the land, with the unqualified confentment of Saluces.

Fabliaux ou Contes du xii et xiii Siècles.

THE LIFE OF MARY, QUEEN OF SCOTS.

HOSE who may, at any time, propofe to themfelves to write of this illuftrious Scottifh queen, will ever find two very ample themes to be at their difpofition; her life and her death. The one as unhappily befriended as the other, of a countenancing fortune; as will, by the following fketch be feen, and which I merely offer, as a fort of abftract; leaving to thofe who may be better informed, and abler penmen than myfelf, the charge of an higher and an ampler expofition.

This queen, then, had for her father, King James, as well a gallant and an able gentleman, as, at heart, a right ftaunch Frenchman. This James, having become a widower, by the death of Magdaleine, a daughter of France, befought the French king to find him fome worthy and virtuous princefs of his line, or kin; being defirous, above all things, to perpetuate the alliance with France.

The French king, who could not think of any party more likely to be acceptable to this good prince, proposed to him the daughter of Monsieur de Guise, Claude de Lorraine, the then widow of Monsieur de Longueville; a lady whom the king discerned to be so beautiful, so excellent, so wise and so virtuous, that he was delighted with the offer, esteeming himself most fortunate in the tender of such a choice. And as he judged her at first, so he found her, as did the estates of Scotland, which she continued to govern with an happy success, upon his decease, which fell out some few years after their marriage, but not till such time as he had begotten upon her a noble scion, who became this beautiful, and, for the time in which she lived, most beautiful princess of the universe, our queen, of whom I write. Scarcely was she more than born, for she was yet at the teat, when there came so hideous a raid, on the part of the English, that her mother was obliged to fly with her from one corner of her kingdom to the other, to avoid its imminence. And had it not been for the timely succour which she received from Henry II., she had almost infallibly been taken. At length, for her more perfect security, it was deemed advisable, committing her to the mercy of the winds and of the waves, to transport her into France, where alone she could be safe. And certes, the maliciousness of that ill fortune, which, till that day, had persisted to persecute her, nor daring to step with her on board, was contented to remain upon a more congenial foil, ceding to the good to take her by the hand. And there, in meafure as her young years budded, proportionally was her every charm unfolded to the world, and did her rare perfections difplay themfelves. So that, coming to her fifteenth year, her glories began to break upon the world with all the refulgence of the mid-heaven fun, fo perfect an emanation was fhe of the divine. And as for her foul, it was the fitting prieftefs of fuch a temple. So thoroughly had fhe maftered the Latin, that fhe delivered, publicly, being but thirteen or fourteen years of age, in that tongue, before the king and all his court, in the great hall of the Louvre, a difcourfe which fhe had written herfelf, maintaining and afferting, in the teeth of prevalence, that it was becoming for the female mind to be adorned with, and inftructed in polite literature and in the liberal fciences. Juft fancy, how rare and exquifite a thing, to fee this lovely and accomplifhed queen thus haranguing in Latin, which fhe could exceedingly well deliver as well as write. * * * * Two hours a day were regularly fet apart for ftudy and reading, that is, as long as fhe remained in France; fo it came that there was hardly any conceivable fubject on which fhe could not enlarge herfelf with felicity. Above all things, fhe revelled in poetry, and delighted in the frequentation of the mafters of that art, but more efpecially of Monfieur de Ronfard, Monfieur de Belley and Monfieur de

Saint-Fleur, who had dedicated to her many an elegy and a noble effufion, and which, oft and oft, on a time, have I feen her read, as well in Scotland as in France, the tear in her eye, and the bur in her throat. Sometimes, too, fhe toyed, herfelf, with poetry. And I have feen fome admirable lines of hers, and quite another thing from thofe amorous ditties that have been laid to her door, and were faid to have paffed between her and Bothwell. They are far too grofs, coarfe and unfinifhed, ever to have proceeded from any fuch pen. Monfieur de Ronfard was entirely of my way of thinking about them, as, one day, together, we happened to be reading them. She wrote in an incomparably higher and a rarer vein, and with an admirable facility; running into her cabinet, and coming out again the next moment, to read what fhe had written, to us, or to whoever elfe might happen to be prefent. Farther, fhe could exprefs herfelf admirably in profe, efpecially in her familiar letters, many of which I have feen, and which were very high and eloquent. With her converfation it was different. For nothing could exceed the fafcination, the prettinefs, the gentlenefs of her demeanour and intonation; blending, in the moft charming manner, all her incomparable majefty with a certain indefcribable, bewitching and enchanting familiarity, but, above all things, grace. Even the language of her native Scotland, in itfelf outlandifh, heathenifh and barbarous, either to fpeak or to hear, as dropping from her lips, became positive music to the ear; which, most certainly, it was very far from being, in those of others.

And such was the triumph of all this beauty and this grace, that it was able to transmute very heathenism into an acceptable propriety and a felicitous conformity. And believe me, when I say, that, when attired, (as I have seen her,) *à la sauvage;* after the barbarous manner of the savages of her own country, she appeared, all mortal as she was, and under all this hideous disguise, a very goddess. And none who have seen her thus dressed, or her picture, so taken, but must be compelled to admit as much. And I have heard it stoutly argued before our king and queen, that never was she seen to more advantage, or did she appear more lovely, more attractive, than in this costume. If so, judge how incomparable must she have appeared, arrayed in all the majesty of France or Spain; or say, with an Italian bonnet on her head; or again, in all the transparency of her white court mourning, which so surpassingly became her. And sure it was a strife, from the marble of her cheek to the milkwhite of her veil, which would outvie the riven of the snow. But it was to the fuller to succumb. No artifice could touch the matchless brightness of her flesh; as an ode, which was once written upon her, in her mourning, commemorates.

*   *   *   *   *

So that from whatever point of view this lovely princefs was envifaged, it was to be feen to advantage; were it barbarous, courtly or auftere. And as if this was not enough; ftill farther to turn the heads of the beholders, fhe was poffeffed of this other attraction; a filver and a fweet toned voice. For fhe fung uncommonly well, accompanying herfelf to her lute, and which fhe touched divinely, with thofe exquifitely moulded fingers; fingers which Aurora herfelf might have envied. And though this may be enough, I fhall yet an inftant revert to a conceit which was drawn betwixt this queen and the fun of her native Scotland, and not a little to the difparagement of the latter. For it was alleged, that, whilft he, for a certain portion of the year, was but feen above the horizon for fome few hours, fhe, on the contrary, never ceafed to fhine, by day or by night. So that, of her own proper rays, fhe heated and fhe fired that difmal realm, of all others the darkeft and the dreareft, by reafon of its hyperborean altitudes.

Aha, Scottifh land; dark now thy days, I ween; thy days more fhort, thy nights more long, bereaved of the light that lit ye! Ye were too unkind to her, ye were ungrateful to her; ye were unworthy of her, in that ye knew not to pay her your duty and devotion; and as even now I will bring home to you!

In fine, this lady and this princefs was fo acceptable to France, that, in return, fhe prayed the French king to admit her into his family, and that she might be given to the Dolphin, his dearly loved son, and who, on his side, was passionately attached to her. The nuptials, then, were solemnized at Notre Dame and in the palace, at Paris; where this lovely queen was seen to move, an hundred times more airy than any goddess of the sky; whether, as with the dawn, she marched, in all her glittering majesty, to her espousals; or, as, in the evening, she tripped it, at the dance; or with the taper, as maidenly, half frightenedly, half scornfully, she retired to the bridal couch, to slacken and to render up her virgin zone. So that it was the theme of all the court, of every tongue; to be re-echoed and responded to, throughout the length and breadth of that vast city; blessed an hundred-fold were the prince to whose lot had fallen so peerless a woman; and that, let the worth of Scotland be what it might, it was never to be weighed with its queen: and that even, supposing her to have neither been possessed of crown, or of sceptre, her person alone, in itself, were to be priced with a realm; but seeing that she was a queen, she brought with herself a double dower.

And this is no more than was in the mouth of everyone. And presently she was styled, The Queen-Dolphin, and her husband, the King-Dolphin; they two living together in the most perfect love and harmony.

But presently upon this, this great king coming to die, they respectively became king and queen of two moſt potent kingdoms; France and Scotland. And happy, moſt happy, might they have continued together, had not the King Francis, her huſband, died, thus leaving her a widow, in the young April of her bloom; having barely taſted of all theſe felicities, enchantments, delights, a good four years.

A ſhort-lived felicity truly! And after ſuch an aſſertion of the imperiouſneſs of her power, one would have thought that fortune had been content to waive her reſting ire. But ah, the falſe one, thus miſerably to purſue this wretched princeſs, who, herſelf, on the occaſion of her ſorrow and her loſs, indited theſe following lines:—

*   *   *   *   *

It was thus that this unhappy queen diſburdened herſelf of her ſorrows and her cares, and which declared themſelves, if poſſible, yet more piteouſly in the withering of the pallor of her face. Nor from the day in which ſhe became a widow, did a trace of the carnation e'er fluſh afreſh upon her cheek; at leaſt for ſo long as I had the honour to be about her, whether in France or in Scotland; where, to her inſupportable ſorrow, and at the end of her mourning, ſhe found herſelf obliged to go, for the pacification of her kingdom, then torn to pieces with religious diſſenſions. I have heard her, myſelf, many a time to ſay, That ſhe dreaded the thought of that change, as ſhe did the thoughts of death itſelf; and that ſhe would infinitely rather remain in France, a simple dowager, contenting herself with Poitou and Touraine, which had been settled on her at her marriage, to returning to her own barbarous country. But her uncles, or at least some of them, were so instant with her, that she was compelled to submit. The grounds which moved them, I am not going to give. Suffice it to say, that, till it was too late, they saw not their mistake.

And touching this departure, it is not to be questioned, but that if the late King Charles, her brother-in-law, had been then of age, for he was but quite a lad at the time, and had he also been possessed of the same predilection for her, which he later betrayed, never had she been allowed to leave, and infallibly he had married her. For so inordinately was he taken with her, that, once having allowed his eyes to wander to her portrait, it was as much as ever he could do to bring himself to withdraw them; so entranced, so fascinated was he with its brightness. And he was wont to say, that she was, beyond all comparison, the most peerless princess, the most lovely conception which ever alighted on our orb, and that too happy did he esteem his brother to have enjoyed so beauteous a woman; protesting, that by no construction, could he be said to have been unfortunate, or, young as he died, to have been cut off from his portion of felicity, seeing that for ever so brief a moment he had been permitted to taste of so supreme a pleasure, which, in itself, were worth the price of fceptres. So that, had fhe remained behind, beyond a doubt he would have married her, all fifter-in-law though fhe were. The then Pope would have made no difficulties about according him the neceffary difpenfations; efpecially as he had already granted as much to one of his majefty's own fubjects, Monfieur de Lové. And alfo fince, and in Spain, we have feen the Marquis of Aguilar procuring fuch a licenfe, and many others, in different countries, where fuch impediments are not allowed to weigh, as in France, with the inconveniences and prejudices which too often accrue to the children from the neglect of fuch confolidation.

Everything which was agitated, as well on her part, as on that of others, touching this affair, I purpofely omit, not to wander too far from the matter of our queen; who, having been at length perfuaded, as I have already faid, to return into her own country; the voyage now remitted to the fpring; fo manœuvred, on one pretext or another, that fhe did not finally leave till the month of Auguft. And it may be worth while remembering, that that fpring in which fhe had originally purpofed to fet out, came fo late, and when it did come, fo fad, fo cold, fo difconfolate, that it was not till the month of May that fhe had the heart to deck herfelf in all her robes of green, to paint the meadows, or to clad the groves. So that all the gallants of the court went moralizing and publifhing about, How the spring refused to doff her wintry and her mourning robes, or to array herself, in such a moment, in all her frolic, budding, young and piony attire; the very seasons deploring the departure of this princess, the crown and glory of the year. Monsieur de Maison-Fleur, a right accomplished knight, famous as well for letters as for arms, dedicated to this occasion, a very happy elegy.

The beginning of autumn being at length at hand, it was no longer possible for our queen, now at the end of her resources, any more to dally. So she set out, by way of Calais, accompanied by her uncles, Monsieur de Nemours, the greater part of the court, together with their wives; and with them, Madame de Guise; alike disconsolate, and with burning tears, lamenting the departure of such a queen.

Two galleys which were lying in the port, one of them commanded by Monsieur de Mevillon, and the other by the captain d'Albize, together with two store ships, composed her whole fleet. And having remained but six days at Calais, as soon as she had taken a last and piteous farewell of all the company, from the greatest even to the least, she stepped on board the galley of Monsieur de Mevillon, as it was the most commodious; and with her, of her uncles, Messieurs d'Aumale, grand-prior, d'Elbeuf, Damville, the now constable; and sundry other nobles, among whom I was one.

And, behold, no sooner was the anchor weighed and had the oars begun to play, than under our very bows a ship went down, and with her most the hands on board; having accidentally missed the channel or the tide! So that she burst out into tears, passionately exclaiming, *Hah, my God, what an augury is this!* And as soon as ever the galley had gotten out of the port, a gentle breeze sprung up, the sails were hoisted, and the oars were shipped. All this while, the poor queen, lost to everything which was going on around her, kept hanging, her head upon her hand, upon the poop; the great tears rolling down her cheeks, her sad eyes fixed on the shore and spot, where last her France she left. Or if she woke, it was in her choked utterance to sob, *Adieu France, France adieu!* And in this piteous exercise she continued some four or five hours; even till the shades of night were closing fast around her, and it had been asked her, Would she not descend and partake of a little refreshment? It was then that with redoubled vehemence she began to cry, her tears even falling faster than before, *Ah, France, dear France, now is the appointed hour that for ever I must lose you; seeing that the dark and envious night, jealous of my too much joy, is about to cast her mantle o'er thee! Farewell, then, dearest, dearest France, now fading on the scene; for never, never more shall I behold you!* With that, withdrawing her eyes, she observed to those who were around her, How opposite was her case to that of

Dido's; for that Dido had never ceased to peer upon the waters, when Æneas had but lately quitted her, whilst that she, she never ceased to gaze upon the strand. She refused to sup, or to retire to the berth which had been prepared for her below; so that they had to knock up a sort of pallet for her upon the deck; and where she lay all night, in a very stupor of sorrow and distress. But before she had lain down, she charged the helmsman on no account to fail to signify to her, if, with the break of day, the shores of France were still in sight; and not to be afraid of wakening her. In which, her desire, fortune favoured her; for, with the night, the wind had dropped, the mariners betaking themselves again to the oars. So that but little way had been made, and yet were to be perceived the cliffs of France. And no sooner had the helmsman told her, that France was still to be descried, than she stood up in her bed, and fixing her eyes upon it, never once refrained to gaze on it, till it had passed for ever from her sight. For as the galley continued to retreat, so did her contentment; till at last it was for ever gone. Then it was, that in a very paroxysm of emotion, she cried, *It is finished: adieu France; France adieu; a long, a last adieu, for never more shall I behold you!*

The navy of England, which she knew to be riding in the channel, above all things she prayed that they might encounter, so that they would be forced to carry her back to France. But Providence did not think proper to grant her this interpofition, for, without any fort of let or hinderance, we arrived fafely at Leith. Of the incidents of this voyage, I fhall only notice one; how, as it was drawing on to dark, on the firft evening that we were at fea, and they were about to light the lanthorn, the lord de Chartelard, the fame who was fince decapitated in Scotland, for his felffufficiency, and not for his mifdemeanours, (and he was an exceedingly worthy gentleman, and as well a fwordfman as a man of letters,) hit upon this happy word; *That we had little call for flambeaux or for lamps to light us o'er the deep, for that the bright eyes of our queen were in themfelves fufficiently luftrous and confuming, to illumine, nay, to fire the very depths.*

It is to be noted, that the previous day, a Sunday morning, to that on which we landed in Scotland, fo unaccountable a fog arofe that we could not fo much as fee the length of the fhip; which put the captains and the pilots to their wits' end. So that we were obliged to caft anchor in the main deep, and to heave the found, in order to afcertain upon what land we had fallen. This fog continued the live-long day and night. And the next morning, about eight of the clock, we firft defcried ourfelves to be in a fhoal water, and fo lying, that, had we drifted, but ever fo little, to the right or to the left, we had infallibly foundered, and all on board perifhed. When they told this to the queen, in return, fhe affured them, "that fo far as fhe herfelf,

" perfonally, was concerned, fhe could have gone down
" without a pang, nor would it have coft her a ftruggle;
" as, than death, there was nothing now which fhe
" more ardently defired; but that in her capacity of
" queen, it was her duty and her wifh to live. She
" owed it to her country." With the light, the fhores
of Scotland appearing, there were not wanting thofe
who augured of this fame fog, how it fignified, that
they were about to fet their foot upon a land of darknefs, and mourn and terrible.

[1] We made for and took footing at Leith, where were
already in waiting, the principal inhabitants of the
country and of Edinburgh, which was fome little way
off. And incontinent were mounted the queen and
all the lords and ladies of her train, upon the fcurvy
fhelties of the country, with harnefs, as fcurvy, to
match.

No fooner did the poor queen perceive herfelf in
fuch a cavalcade, than fhe began to weep. " Where
" now," fhe cried, " the pageant and the pomp; the
" prancing palfreys and the rich caparifons of France!
" but let me be patient." And as if this was not enough,
in the evening, after fhe had retired for the night, there
came together, under the windows of her lodging,
which was in the palace of Holy Rood; (unqueftionably, a noble edifice, but altogether out of place in fuch
a country,) fome five or fix hundred fcoundrelly fellows

[1] See note K, at the end.

of the town, forsooth to give her a concert on their accursed drones and violins, which they are for ever strumming throughout the length and breadth of the land. And, above all things, it was psalms that the rascals were singing, and with such a whining and a twang, that nothing more confounded could be conceived. Ha, what a reception, and what a repose for such a night!

The very next morning, they had like to have finished her almoner; and if he had not taken refuge, on the instant, in the chamber of the queen, they had served him, as they after did her secretary, David Rizzio, who, although he happened also to be a man of wit and parts, the queen had merely taken into her service on the score of his facility to business. Yet they stuck not to dispatch him before her eyes, in her apartment, and at her feet; so close that her very robe was drenched in his blood. What an indignity! And many another, like it, did they offer her. So that we have little cause to be amazed, that men who could presume to make so free with the person of their sovereign, should have the effrontery to make themselves equally so with her reputation. After such an experiment as this, she became dolent and foreboding. *This is certainly a notable earnest*, she said, *of the promised attachment and submission of my subjects. What the end of all this will be, I cannot tell. But certainly, so far, it has an ugly complexion.* And in this, her prophecy, the poor princess proved herself to be as true a Caſſandra, as, already, in beauty she was allowed to be.

Once there, she remained, in her widowhood, three whole years. And had it only depended upon herself, so would she have continued to the end, nor wishing to disturb the manes of her husband. But she was overruled by the States-General of her kingdom, who never ceased to be instant with her, requiring her to marry, so that some noble prince might be engendered of her, such as he who, this day, is sitting upon her throne.

There are not wanting some who say, that, at the beginning of our wars, the king of Navarre was anxious to marry her; in order to which, he was prepared to put away his wife; taking religion for his pretext; but that the queen would not so much as listen to it; protesting, that she had a soul to be saved, or to be lost, and that so she would not emperil it, were it to sit on the throne of the universe; evidencing an invincible aversion to connect herself with an actually married man.

However, at the length, she remarried with a young nobleman of England, who, though of a great house, was yet still far from being her equal. This union was anything but a felicitous one, either for the one side or for the other. It is no part of my purpose to relate, how the king, her husband, was murdered; sent flying, through an infernal machine which had been introduced into his apartment. All about it is in print, and has now become matter of hiſtory. But hiſtory though it be, yet is that part of it falſe, which has not ſcrupled to aſſert, that it was compaſſed with the privity of the queen. It is nothing but lies and ſcandal, for never was this queen cruel; on the contrary, ſhe was all heart and gentleneſs. Never, when in France, was any ſuch charge laid to her account; nor did it ever give her any pleaſure to hear of poor criminals being quartered or butchered, nor had ſhe the bowels to ſee them, as had many another fair and great one, whom I could name. And during all the time that ſhe was on board, never once would ſhe allow one of the galley ſlaves to be corrected; and ſo ſhe told the Grand-prior, her uncle; and expreſſly forbade the mates to do anything of the ſort; telling them, that the very ſight of men condemned to ſo grievous a ſervitude, was enough to drive her ſick at heart, without being called upon to witneſs ſuch an enhancement of their miſery.

To conclude, never did or could inhumanity harbour in ſo tender and ſo fond a breaſt. And they are nothing elſe than impoſtors who have had the aſſurance to aſſert, or to inſinuate the contrary. Among others, Miſter Buchanan. And in the article of which, he made to his queen, a very unequal return for all the obligations that ſhe had conferred, when in France, as well upon the man, perſonally, as upon his order. He might have turned his matchleſs diſcernment to a very much better account, than to the artifice of detecting fonnets to be hers, which any one, ever fo little familiar with her ftyle or her endowments, would know never to have proceeded from any fuch pen. And as much might he have divined of the gallantries, which he has afcribed to her and to Bothwell, had he but had the candour, or the indifferency, to look clofer into them. For this Bothwell was as ugly and ungainly a fellow, as one would care to lay eyes on. But if there are thofe who have written fcandaloufly of her; again, there are not wanting others who have undertaken her vindication. I myfelf have feen at leaft one admirable book, wherein her innocence and her life were afferted and eftablifhed; and that, too, in fo convincing a manner, that the moft incredulous were compelled to come over to her fide; however it may have been cried down by her detractors. But her deftruction being now determined upon, they never ceafed to perfecute and to hunt her, till they had her into a ftronghold in her own country; I think it was St. Andrew's; and in which fhe lay, miferably, a captive, for about a year, till at length fhe was delivered by a ftout and valiant gentleman, a fubject of her own, and of a good family, named Betoun, whom I both knew and had often feen; and who told me the whole manner of it, one day, when we were together on the river, near the Louvre. He had come over expreffly to carry the intelligence to our king. He was nephew to that archbishop of Glasgow who was ambassador to France; one of those excellent men and worthy prelates, the like of whom are but rarely to be encountered. To her latest hour, he proved himself to her, a staunch and a faithful servant, and after her decease, a no less loyal one to her memory.

Once again, the queen at liberty, there was no more temporizing; and in an incredibly short time she had gotten together an army, composed of those whom she fancied were the likeliest to be relied upon. And next we have her at its head, straddled on a sturdy cob; no other defence upon her than a simple petticoat of taffeta, white, and a veil of cobweb lawn upon her head. And many a one have I seen lost in wonder and astonishment, and among others, the queen-mother; to see a princess, so tender and so dainty, nursed in the lap of ease and of indulgence, thus sternly resigning herself to all the hardships and the miseries of war. But, in return, what is there which mortals will not undergo, to taste the sweets of absolute power; or princes, to be avenged of a rebel race, and to compel them to reenter into their duty?

So now we have brought our princess, bright and magnanimous as another Zenobia, to the forefront of her army, conducting it to glory and to the battle! But woe, the change; and in how little! Just on the instant, when the pikes were levelled, and as she was exhorting them with words that might have touched the very stones; behold, as suddenly, the pikes are raised, and, rushing into each others' arms, an eternal amity is sworn, on the one side and on the other. And there and then, it was settled of the whole pack, confederated and sworn friends, to seize upon her body, and to carry her away, a prisoner, into England. Monsieur de Crosy, steward of her house, (he was a gentleman of Auvergne,) recounted the whole matter to the queen-mother; having crossed expressly to that end. I, after, saw him at St. Maur, where, with some others, we had it all over.

So the end of it was, that she was hurried away into England, where, for eighteen years, she was retained in a captivity so close, that never again did she leave it, even till the day of her death, which was persisted in, on the strength of a too cruel sentence; based upon sundry charges that had been scraped together, and may be seen in that instrument. But not the least inconsiderable of them, as I have good reason to know, and from the first authority, was, that the queen of England never could endure her, and had been, from the first, and all her days, jealous of those superior attractions, which she so well knew to eclipse her own. What a demon is this jealousy; especially, when is mated to it, the fury of religious hate! So the long and the short of it was, that this princess, after all this cruel incarceration, was condemned to lose her head. And this sentence was passed upon her two years before it was carried into execution. Some say, that all suspicion of it was studiously kept from her, till the moment had arrived when they were prepared to go through with it. Others, again, that she was informed of it, two months previously; among whom the queen-mother was one, who first learned it at Cognac; and was marvellously cut up with such a knowledge, at the time. And in connection with this, another curious thing was asserted, that, as soon as they had officially broken it to her, they changed the tapestry and hangings of her room and bed to black. When this was told to the queen-mother, nothing could exceed her pity and admiration; protesting, that she had never encountered, nor heard tell of so invincible a constancy, as that which was shown by the queen of Scotland, in all her adversities. I, for one, and I was then present, was not of those who imagined, that the queen of England would ever have allowed extremities to be proceeded to, or could have steeled herself to it; not judging her, in her natural, to be cruel. However, in this case, she proved herself to be so. And Monsieur de Bellievre, no less, whom the king had commissioned to intercede with her majesty, was of our way of thinking; but it all came to nothing.

So, in fine, to come to this piteous death, and which it is impossible so much as to touch upon, but with commiseration; on the seventeenth day of February, fifteen hundred and eighty seven, the commissioners deputed by the queen of England, (the names, I need not give; for to what good?) arrived, betwixt two and three of the clock, in the afternoon, and there and then, in the presence of Paulett, her guardian or keeper, opened to her the nature of their commission; at the same time telling her, that on the following morning it was to be carried out, and admonishing her, on her part, to be prepared for the same, by the hour of seven or eight.

She, without evidencing any sort of emotion, thanked them for their welcome tidings; assuring them, that nothing could be more acceptable to her, than to find herself, at length, to have arrived at the goal of all her miseries; telling them, that since long, she had held herself in readiness, and was willing to die; even from the day when she had first been carried into England. The only favour which she had to ask of them was, that they would accord to her some few moments, to dispose of her testament, with one or two other matters which required to be attended to; a competence which she believed to be within the latitude of their commission. To which the Earl of Shrewsbury only replied, and rudely enough, for that matter, *Not so, Madam, you must die. And see that you are forthcoming between the hours of seven and eight o'clock; for not another instant will be granted to you.* One of them, as it appeared to her, with more of the milk of human kindness in him than was in his fellows, did what he could to comfort her and to fortify her, at the aspect of so terrible an hour. But she told him, in reply, that she had no need of any consolation, at least from such a quarter; and that if they would but allow her poor conscience to depart in peace, her almoner be admitted to her, so that she might confess herself, it would be conferring an obligation upon her which would surpass every other; adding, that as to her body, she could never suppose that they would deny to it the rites of sepulture. But he told her, that such a thing was not to be thought of; so that she was forced to leave her confession under her hand, and which runs as follows.

"Father, I have this day been buffetted for con-
"science' sake, and been compelled to entertain the
"consolation of the heretic. You will hear by Bour-
"yong and others, that firmly I stood by that faith, in
"which I am about to die. What was in my power,
"I did, to be permitted to make to you my confession;
"and to receive, at your hands, the body of our
"Lord. But they have been barbarously denied to
"me, as has also, to my bones, the right to rest amid
"the sepulchres of my fathers. Nor have I, any
"more, been allowed to leave a testament behind me;
"unless, indeed, such an one as I should be prepared
"to indite in their presence, or with their hand. So
"seeing, then, father, that it cannot be otherwise; I
"now confess to, in the block, the grievousness of all
"those shortcomings, which, in detail, had it been per-

"mitted to me, you should have heard; beseeching
"you, for the sake of Him who died for us, that you
"will watch and pray for me this night, for the propi-
"tiation of my sins, and that you will send me your
"absolution and your pardon for all the offences, by
"me, committed in the flesh. I will make a last
"endeavour to see you, though it must be in their
"presence. They have promised me as much; and,
"if practicable, you shall give me absolution. Hasten
"to me the most proper prayers for this night, and for
"the coming morn; for the time is short; nor more,
"can I spare to write. You shall not be forgotten,
"any more than the rest. Your benefices shall be
"continued and assured to you; and you have been
"spoken of to the king. I have no more time. Let
"me know, by a line, what you may conceive to be
"most conducive to my welfare. After that, I shall
"have but to dedicate my thoughts to heaven. MARY."

Whatever she did, she lost no time. And the little which remained to her, (enough, God knows, of its sort, to blanch the stoutest heart; but contrary, to her, who never knew the fear of death, and even longed to be escaped of all her miseries,) she employed in writing to our king, the queen-mother, whom she had always respected; to Monsieur and Madame de Guise, and other private friends; letters, one and all, most piteous certainly, and tending alike to let them know, that up to her latest breath, she had not forgotten them;

and expressive of all the satisfaction with which she was about to be released from the calamities, that, for twenty long years, had overtaken her. She sent them all mementos; sorry enough in themselves, but, such as they were, all that yet remained to this poor captive princess to bestow.

After this, she sent for her household, from the greatest to the least, and requiring her coffers to be opened, she took out any little money which remained, dividing it among them, as far as it went, and in proportion to their several claims. Among her women, she distributed her jewels, her nicknacks and her robes, telling them, that she was only distressed, it were no better in her power to recompense their services; that, however, they need be under no anxiety, as her son would see that they should not be losers on her account. And she farther charged her master of the household, to tell her said son, and to whom she now sent her benediction, that he was on no account to think of attempting to avenge her death, but to leave all to God, and to his divine appointment. With that, and without even a tear or a sigh, she bid them all adieu. On the contrary, she comforted and consoled them, telling them, that they had no occasion to distress themselves, seeing that she was about to make so blessed an issue out of all the miseries of this wretched life. After this, she caused all but her maidens to withdraw.

As soon as it came night, and she had retired to her oratory, she prayed, and upon her bare knees, for two hours together; for so she was seen, by her women, who watched her. After that she arose, and coming into her chamber, said, *Sweet hearts, I think that I had better eat a mouthful, and then lie down, a little, so that to-morrow I may not be betrayed into any unbecoming weakness, or anything unworthy of myself.* What a spirit and greatheartedness! And this she did; eating a morsel of the fillet, dipped in wine. After that she threw herself on her bed, hardly sleeping, however; the remainder of the night being spent in prayer and heavenly offices.

Two hours before the light, she rose; dressing herself as expeditiously as possible; though, however, with a more than ordinary regard to appearances. Fixing on a robe of black velvet, which was the only remnant that remained to her of her former estate, she said to her women; *My friends, I had sooner bequeathed to one of you this gown, than that which yesterday I wore; and I had done so, only, you know, it is necessary that I should appear in some little state and grandeur on the approaching occasion. See, here is a handkerchief, which I also kept; it is the one with which my eyes are presently to be bandaged. To you, sweet heart,* turning to one of them, *I give it; for it is you whom I count upon to do for me this last charitable office.*

Again she withdrew to her oratory, having first bidden them all farewell, and kiffed them round; and, farther, charged them with many particulars to be carried to the king, the queen and all her kin; none of them fuch as would, in any way, tend to inflame them to vengeance on her account; but the reverfe. She then proceeded to take from her own hands the bleffed facrament; adminiftering to herfelf a confecrated wafer which the good pope, Pius the Fifth, had fent to her, to be availed of in her agony; and which fhe had kept by her, right curioufly and hallowedly treafured.

Her orifons finifhed, which were long, and it being now high day, fhe came forth to her chamber, and fat herfelf down by the fire; all the while talking to her women, and comforting them, when one would have fuppofed, that it had been for them to have comforted her; and telling them, "How poor and inconftant a "thing was this world's felicity, by her example, might "be feen and read of all, from the greateft even to the "leaft. Here was fhe, a queen of Scotland and of "France; the one by birth, and the other by fortune; "after having plunged over head and ears into a very "fea of triumph and felicity, and ridden the lighteft "there, reduced at laft to end her days upon a fcaffold, "all innocent as fhe was; and which, her innocence, "was her only confolation. The hardeft thing that "they could fay againft her was, that fhe was a good "catholic; and for which, her faith, fhe was now "called upon to die; and which, to her lateft breath,

" she would never cease to profess; for in it, she had
" been baptized." She told them, " that she had only
" one thing more to ask of them, and that was, that
" they would undertake to carry to France, where they
" were about to return, the constancy with which she
" died; that all her ambition was now limited to that;
" and that, although she well knew it would be to them
" a bitter draught, to be the spectators of such a tra-
" gedy, she must still entreat them to be present, so
" that they might be faithful witnesses to the death
" of Mary Stuart."

She had scarcely finished these words when a horrible rapping was heard at the door. Her women, in their agony, were about to bar it. But she bade them to desist; saying, *Good friends, to what purpose? open it.* And in there stalked a fellow with a white rod in his hand, who, without so much as saluting a soul, began incontinent to strut about the room; parenthetically informing himself, that, *Ha*, *here he was; here he was.* The queen, convinced by this, that her hour was come, immediately took into her hand, a little crucifix of ivory.

Presently after, entered the commissioners. And as soon as they were seated, the queen said to them, *And so, gentlemen, you have come to fetch me. I am both ready and willing to die. I am under an infinite obligation to your queen, my good sister, for this, her last and greatest courtesy; and to you, my lords, no less, who have made this tedious journey, to convey it. Let us proceed.* They, beholding so much firmness, mingled with such a gentleness, and all, too, in so incomparable a person, were beyond expression amazed; for never, even in her best days, had she appeared to more advantage; a gentle flush o'erspreading every feature.

Boccacio has told as much of Sophonisba, in the presence of Masanissa, when in her adversity, and after the capture of her husband and her capital. You would have thought, said he, that her very misfortunes but served to the heightening of her beauty; rendering her every grace, more glowing, more chastened and subdued.

These commissioners found themselves sorely tempted to show her some little indulgence. However, as the procession was being formed, they were for refusing to allow her women to accompany her; alarmed, lest by their tears or their lamentations, the executioner might be unnerved; or, otherwise, a scene induced. But she, turning to them, said, *What, gentlemen, may not my women be with me at the block? of a little charity, I pray you, suffer it.* At length, on her undertaking for their silence, the point was waived, and it was engaged that they should be called in at the proper time.

The place of execution was a hall, in the midst of which they had erected a sort of scaffold, of twelve feet square, and two high; the whole covered with a dingy piece of black cloth. And into this hall she marched, with a no less stately port, a no less majesty and grace, than though it had been the salon of the Louvre; where, so often, she had figured in the days of her magnificence. Nor did her countenance ever once falter.

As soon as she arrived at the foot of the scaffold, she beckoned to her master of the houshold, saying to him, *Friend, lend me your arm to mount; it is the last favour which I shall ever ask of you;* at the same time recalling to him all that she had already charged him with to carry to her son. Now planted upon the scaffold, she next inquired for her almoner, entreating of the officers present, that he might be sent for. But this they refused her flat; the earl of Kent telling her, that he could not but admire, to see her thus infatuated with superstitions which long since had been exploded; and that it was in the heart, and not the hand, that the cross of Christ was to be carried. To which she replied, that, for her part, she thought that it would be a very difficult thing to carry such a symbol in the hand, and the heart not to find itself thereby sympathetically touched; and that the course which it were 'most befitting for all true christians to pursue, when in the article of death, was, to bear upon them the true mark of their redemption. But perceiving that the point was not to be carried, she sent at once for her maids, as they had promised her that she might. One of them, on entering the hall, and seeing her mistress in such a plight, mid the headsman, the axe and the black, broke out into a paroxysm of wailing and of tears. And it was not till the queen, by raising her finger to her lips, had recalled to her her promise, that she was at length enabled to compose herself.

Her majesty then began distinctly to protest, that never had she practised against the government, or the person of the queen, her good sister; though admitting, that she had sought to recover that liberty of which she had been deprived; as, by nature, she supposed, all captives were inclined, or permitted to do. She said, she well knew that religion was the true cause of this sentence; and affirmed, that it was a cause in which she rejoiced that it was given to her to die. She prayed her good sister of England to pardon her poor servants, now in prison, and whose only crime had been the efforts which they had made to release her, and a too much attachment to their mistress; requiring, that her blood might be allowed to expiate for all.

They then brought to her a minister of their own church, that he might pray with her. But she only rejoined to him in English, *Ha, my friend, be patient;* telling him plainly, that she could not communicate with him, or with any of his sect; that she was prepared to die without any other consolation than that which came from within; for that such as he could tender, would neither bring to her comfort nor support.

Despite her entreaties, seeing that he would persist in

his jargon of a prayer, she had nothing for it but to continue her own in Latin; elevating her voice, so as to drown that of the minister. These finished, she then entreated them to believe, that it was accounted of her, a greater privilege to be permitted to seal with her blood, the testimony of her faith, than longer, as she had done, to continue to drag on her days beneath the sun; and that she could not any more tarry to be dissolved; protesting, that she had so unbounded a confidence in Him, whose image was expressed in her hand, that she was satisfied, that this transitory moment, which, in his cause, she was about to traverse, would open to her the way, and prove the cartel to the abodes of angels and of blessed souls, departed; who would receive, and would present her about to be spilled blood, as a propitiation, at the throne of grace; interceding with God, that it might be accepted, as an atonement for all her vileness in the flesh.

Such were, in substance, the prayers that she offered up, on the scaffold, and on her knees, and which were tendered in a spirit of the deepest piety. To which, also, were added others, at the same time, for the pope, and the kings of France and of Spain. Nor even was the queen of England forgotten; beseeching God to illuminate her with the light of his spirit; remembering too her son, as also the nations of England and of Scotland, that they might be recovered to the true faith.

This finished, she called for her women, that they might help her to remove her veil, her head dress, with her other ornaments. And as the executioner was offering to assist her, she shrunk, instinctively, from him, exclaiming, *Ha, my friend, forbear.* However, do what she would, she could not manage to shake him from her. For after they had lowered her robe to the waist, the infernal villain laid hold of her by the arm, and tore her linen and her under garments from her back, so that her matchless breasts and form, more whiter than any alabaster, were left naked and exposed to the company.

Seeing herself in such a plight, she made all the haste which she could, observing, that she was not in the habit of unrobing in a hall, or in the presence of such a company; (so many as four or five hundred, as I have heard, were present), nor yet to be waited on of such a gentleman of the bedchamber.

The headsman next craved her pardon, on his knees. She told him, that she forgave him and all those who were partakers in her death, as heartily as she trusted that all her sins, too, would be forgiven of God. She then called for the woman, to whom she had committed the handkerchief, desiring it to be given to her. In her hand she held a crucifix of gold, on which were relieved the image of our Lord, graven in a morsel of the true cross, and which she was purposing to present to one of her ladies. But this, the executioner would not consent to; even though she passed him her word, that the lady would make up to him the worth, three times over.

At length, everything being ready, and having kissed her maids, she desired them to leave her; first, however, signing them with the cross. But seeing one of them to persist in her tears, she imposed upon her silence, telling her, that she had passed her word for them all, that they would be composed, and that the proceedings should not be disturbed with their disorder. Again she told them quietly to retire, and, till it were over, to occupy themselves in prayer to God for her; and, after that, to be true and faithful witnesses of her end, and of how she had died in the catholic, true, only and ancient faith.

As soon as the last of them had bandaged her eyes, incontinent, she threw herself upon her knees, and with a most invincible courage; nor even allowing so much as a symptom of alarm or agitation to escape. Such was her constancy, that there was not one present, even of her enemies, who was not melted to tears; so stricken were they with her undauntedness, and with the remorse and misgivings of their own consciences.

And in as much as these ministers and executioners of Satan; of whom the one, fain, would kill the soul, as the other the body, were distressing her; the former, distracting her with his prayers, and swelling his voice, so as to throw her out, she commenced, as she could, in Latin, this psalm of David, *In te, Domine, speravi, non confundar, in æternum;* which, being interpreted, is, *Lord, in thee have I trusted; let me never be confounded;* continuing through with it, to the end. This finished, she laid her head upon the block; and as the words were passing from her lips, *In manus tuas, Domine, commendo spiritum meum; Lord, into thy hands, I commit my spirit,* the headsman gave her a terrible gash, driving her head gear right into the nape of her neck. Nor was it till the third descent, that he had been able to sever the head from the body; as if determined, by this butchery, to render yet more illustrious, this ever memorable martyrdom. Though, in truth, it is not so much suffering, as the cause, which constitutes martyrdom.

This over, he takes the head, and holding it aloft, to all the company, pronounces, *God save queen Elizabeth; thus let perish the enemies of the Gospel!* And having so delivered himself, as if to mock her, he undid her hair, discovering all her tresses, already gray. Not that she had ever been ashamed, when yet alive, to let them be seen; or to dress, or to curl them, as in her best days, when she had them so silken, graceful, fair. For it was not age which had blanched them, seeing she was but five and thirty when they turned; (and at her death she was no more than forty;) but the cares, the reverses, sorrows, privations, that she had undergone, as well in her prison as in her government.

This wretched tragedy over, her poor women, naturally solicitous for the honour of their mistress, came to Paulett, her keeper, begging of him, that the executioner fhould not be permitted to meddle with the body, and that they might be allowed to lay her out, after all the company had retired; fo as to preclude the poffibility of any indignity being offered to her perfon; and undertaking faithfully to place in his hands whatever they might find upon her, and to conceal nothing. But the inhuman brute fent them gruffly about their bufinefs; telling them to be off out of the place.

So it was left to this fellow to ftrip her, and to handle her, juft as he chofe. Nor can any man fay, that fhe was not ferved of him, as was the unhappy lady, whom the queen of Navarre tells of, in her *Cent Nouvelles*, of another like furious monfter. More prodigious lufts than that, have paffed through the brains of men.

As foon as he thought proper to have done with it, the body was removed into a chamber adjoining to that of the women, and there fecured, forfooth, left any fhould prefume to watch, or to pray with it! But what doubly aggravated their mifery, was, that they could plainly fee, through a chink in the door, the poor body lying, and not a thing to cover it, fave a wretched fcrap of green baize, which they had torn from her billiard table. What rafcalinefs, fpite and indignity; not to have had the decency to buy her a yard of filk, or fatin black!

And thus the poor body lay, even till it began to

corrupt, so that they were compelled, at length, to embalm it. Which they did, any how, so to speak, so chary were they of expense. After that, they placed it in a leaden coffin, and so kept it seven months; after which, it was committed to unhallowed ground, in the cathedral of Peterborough. It is true, that that church is dedicated to St. Peter, and that the queen Catherine, of Spain, was interred there, and after the rites of the catholic faith. But now it is profane, as, indeed, are all the churches in England.

Some have published and asserted, and Englishmen among them, in different versions of her death, and of the causes which provoked it, that the effects found upon the body of the queen were taken from the headsman, he being indemnified in money for the worth of her habiliments and her royal ornaments.

As much was asserted, of certain Spaniards, in the case of Francis Pizzaro, whom they, too, put to death, and as I have elsewhere spoken to.

The covering which had been spread upon the scaffold, the very boards, the flooring; everything on which her blood had fallen, was immediately either burned or scoured; for fear lest, with time, they might come to be regarded as objects of a superstitious veneration! That is to say, for fear that devout and reverential catholics might one day come to purchase them, and to behold them, with awfulness, respect and devotion; (and may there not, almost, be something prophetic, in this their apprehenfion!) even as the good old fathers of the church were in the habit of treafuring the holy reliques, and vifiting, with devotion, the refting places of the martyred dead. But this is not of yefterday; for it was ever the fame with the heretics. *Quià omnia quæ Martyrum erant, cremabant,* fays Eufebius, *et cineres in Rhodanum fpargebant, ut cum corporibus interiret eorum quoque memoria.* That is, that the reafon why they confumed every mortal thing belonging to the martyrs, throwing the afhes into the Rhone, was, fo that not only their bodies but their very memories fhould perifh. Yet defpite of all their littlenefs and their malignity, the memory of this queen will live, to lateft time, in the admiration and the praife of men.

Such was the laft of this queen, as I had it from two of her ladies, who had been prefent, and who right worthily acquitted themfelves towards their miftrefs, in the teftimony which they bore to the conftancy of her faith and of her end. They returned to France immediately after her death, for they were both of them French; one of them was daughter to Mademoifelle de Raré, whom I remember to have feen in France, about the perfon of the queen.[1] Nor did thefe two poor ladies ever fail, when on this chapter, to draw tears from the flintieft, with their paffionate and moving words.

Much alfo I learned from a book which was writ-

---

[1] See note L, at the end.

ten and publifhed, entitled, *The martyrdom of Mary, queen of Scotland, and dowager of France.* Alas, what did it all avail her to have been our queen! One would have thought, that they would have hefitated twice, ere venturing to fuch a length. It is not a fmall thing, the ire of France. And moft affuredly they would have been a little longer about it, had our king been difpofed to take the matter up. But in as much as he detefted the Guifes, his coufins, he would not put himfelf out of the way, in the matter. And what he did do, was only, apparently, out of a fenfe of decency. And where elfe, unfortunately, could the poor innocent look! and this is the account which fome have given.

Others, again, as pofitively affirm, that he ftrongly remonftrated with the Englifh queen; and, in fact, he did fend Monfieur de Bellievre to her, one of the moft confiderable, wary and able minifters in his dominion, who did not fail to carry to her all the arguments, prayers and menaces of the king; telling her, among other things, how unbecoming a fpectacle it was, for one king or fovereign to be putting another king or fovereign to death, and over whom they could neither exercife jurifdiction, by the laws of God or the laws of man.

It is even faid, that he went the length of telling her fternly, and to her face, all the ftory of Conradin, who was fimilarly difpofed of at Naples; and of predicting that a like vengeance might yet overtake her, which did the other. And in as much as it is to the point, very piteous in itſelf, and in ſome degree parallel to that of our queen; having thus touched upon it, I may as well give it at length.

* * * * *

There you have the hiſtory of Conradin, and, for the matter of which, I have heard more than one, of the more great-hearted ſort, obſerve, that the queen of England would have purchaſed to herſelf an immortality of glory, had ſhe only condeſcended to have ſhown to the queen of Scotland, a little of that forgiveneſs which was diſplayed by this good queen, Conſtance; and, farther, that by ſuch a courſe, ſhe had been ſpared all the machinations of that vengeance, which, for ever, to heaven crying, ſeldom, ſooner or later, fails to be recompenſed to the guilty.

Some ſay, that the queen of England carried herſelf politically and adviſedly in this matter; for, that not only did ſhe proceed upon the approbation, and with the conſent of her own people, but at the inſtance of many of the great proteſtant chiefs and princes, as well of Germany as of France; who all gave it for her death. True, they could get over it for ſome few qualms of conſcience; as the matter did not touch them, directly, one way or the other. Yet, for all that, in the long run, the mere countenancing redounded incredibly to their diſadvantage.

They say, too, that when the meſſenger, charged by Elizabeth, to carry to her the fatal determination, was endeavouring to convince her, how bitterly his miſtreſs lamented being driven to ſuch a courſe, and that nothing ſhort of the preſſure which her ſubjects and her counſel had brought to bear upon her, ever could have wrung ſuch a ſentence from her; she immediately rejoined, *that the queen of England was powerful enough, when it ſuited her purpoſe, to make her ſubjects' will to be her wiſh; for that there was not a prince, in Chriſtendom, more feared or revered, than ſhe was, of her people.*

For the reſt, I leave the diſcovery of the truth to time, which brings all things to light. And however it be, this queen Mary right glorioufly will live, as well in this world, as in the world to come. And doubtleſs, ere long, ſome good pope will ariſe, and at the hands of whom ſhe will be canonized, as a memorial of all the martyrdom which ſhe had undergone, in defence of the honour of God and of his law.

It is not to be queſtioned, but that, had that great, chivalrous and valiant prince, the laſt duke of Guiſe, been ſpared, the vengeance due to ſuch a death, of ſuch a queen, and his couſin, had not, at this day, been in abeyance. But enough of this ſad ſtory, which I now finiſh.

There was one that wrote her epitaph in latin verſe, and of which the ſubſtance is as follows. " Nature " having appointed this queen to be the glory of the

" univerfe, fo was fhe held in a wonderful admiration,
" as well for her beauty as for her virtues, even fo
" long as fhe lived. But England, out of the envy which
" it bore to her, expofed her upon a fcaffold, vainly
" thinking to hold her up a derifion and a fpectacle to
" all. But fuch, her malice, only ferved to render this
" queen more acceptable, in the eyes of God and in
" the eyes of man."—BRANTÔME.

SELECTIONS FROM THE

KNIGHT OF THE TOWER, HIS BOOK,

For the Inſtruction of his Daughters.

And firſt, the Prologue.

IN the beginning of April, in the year of our Lord, thirteen hundred and ſeventy one, I was in my garden, in the ſhade, all ſad and penſive; or if I was a little comforted, it was at the carolings and the chirpings of the wild young broods, with all their quainty notes; the merle, the tit, the throſtle; which were welcoming in the ſpring, ſo gay and ſprightly. Raviſhed with this gentle muſic, my ſoul was pierced; and back my memory ſtrayed to times long gone; and I began to turn with myſelf, how, in the days of my youth, I had been held in thraldom to the God of Love, and of all the miſeries which I had undergone in his ſervice, as had many another lover. But, for all my ſufferings, he more than recompenſed me, in the gift which he made me. For ſhe was practiſed to all honour and to every excellence, and her's was courtly carriage and demeanour. Of the good, ſhe was the beſt; and, as it ſeemed to me, the flower. In her was all my delight. For in thoſe days, I wrote ſongs, odes, lays, roundelays, ballads, and the beſt that I was able. But death, who harries all, took her, which coſt me many a pain and ſorrow. So that for more than twenty years I remained ſad and inconſolable. For never, with any diſtance, or with any time, can perfect love forget; but ever will paſture with the paſt.

And thus, as at the time, I was moralizing, and as I looked before me, I ſaw my daughters coming, and to whom my ſoul's deſire was, that all honour and advantage might be their's; for they were but young, and ſmall; nor, poor things, overburdened with experience. So that they would require to be early taken in hand, and to be gently broken, by happy inſtances and ſentences, after the manner of queen Prines, of Hungary, who knew ſo well to diſcipline and to train her daughters; as may be ſeen in her book. And ſo it was, as I ſaw them coming, that I bethought me of the wild young time, when I, with other mad ſparks, uſed to go caracoling about the world, in Poitou and other parts. And alſo returned to my memory, all the carryings on which they uſed to have, and tell me of, with the ladies and gentlewomen

T

whom they were for ever making up to. For never a day went over, but one or another was after them. And if they were refused by the first, they turned to the next. And met they with a good reception, or met they with a bad reception, it was all one to them. For neither sense of shame, nor of decency, had they; so brazen and barefaced were they; so plausible and ready with their tongues. For the most part, to amuse themselves was all they wanted; nor had they a thought, but how to practise upon gentlewomen, and gad about with their tales; some true, some false; and from whence came many a cruel hurt and scandal, and for which there was neither ground nor occasion. And there is not, in this world, a more detestable treason than to deceive respectable gentlewomen, or to get them into trouble; for many are imposed upon, and led on, by the horrible imprecations which are sworn to them. And often times have I argued with them, and said, "How can you go about, perjuring "yourselves, this way? for no man has any business "to swear to, or go after, more than one." But so full of disorder were they, none would take any heed. And in as much as I saw, that the time passing was but too like the time past, I bethought me that I would make a book, wherein I would have written the happy instances of admirable women, and of their carriage; so as to show, by their pattern, what was true feminacy and good conduct; and also how, by their virtues, they were held in honour and eftimation, and will continue to be fo. And alfo, in like manner, I determined to write, to point out and put in my book, the contempt which is the meed of wicked and unfeemly women, fo as to ferve as a warning, of all the mifchief which may fall on thofe who are difparaged, blamed or diffamed. And fo, for all thefe reafons which I have faid; confidering of my daughters, whom I faw fo fmall, I thought that I would make a book, wherein they might fee how to carry themfelves in the world, and have fet before them the good and the evil which had paffed in it, and thus, the better, be able to judge of the prefent. For the world is a mighty perilous thing, and envious and marvellous; for the man who will fmile on you, and take you by the hand, in your prefence, will turn his back and make a face at you. And for as much as I faw what a hard thing it was to know the world, as it now went, and for the farther reafons of which I have told you; leaving the alley, I went to another, where I knew two clerks and two chaplains, of my houfehold, to be. And I told them how I was about to enter on a book, to teach my daughters the art of converfation; and, alfo, to enable them to govern themfelves, and to diftinguifh between the right and the wrong. So I fet them all four to work, to read and to extract from the books I had, as the Bible, the Geftes of the Kings, and Chronicles of France, of Greece, of England, and many another foreign land. And all thefe books, I made them read to me; and every time that they came to any paffage, to my purpofe, I made them note it, there and then, fo as to be put into my book; which I did not turn into rhyme, but left in profe, both becaufe I thought it would be briefer, and more intelligible; and, as fo, a more acceptable token of all the love I bear my deareft children; whom I love, as a father ought to love; and whofe heart no greater joy can prove, than that they may be turned, by his labours, to the love and honour of God, and had in the delight and eftimation of their neighbours and the world. And in as much as every father and every mother, by the ordinance of God and nature, ought to inftruct their children to feek the true and right way, and to abhor the wrong; as well for the falvation of their fouls, as out of a refpect to their mortal tenements, I have made two books, one for my fons and the other for my girls, to fhow them how they are to demean themfelves. And in this labour, no enfample, that I could hear of, has been omitted, whereby they might gather, either how to feek the good or to efchew the evil. So it can fcarcely happen, that they can ever find themfelves fo fituated, but that, upon a little recollection, fomething or other will occur to them, for their guidance.

The First Chapter.

There is not a more noble, or a more delightful thing, than to hear, or to read, the chronicles of old, which have been left to us by our anceftors; whereby we were to fee, as in a glafs, the times gone by; and from them, and their notable inftances, to learn, how we, as they, may purfue the good and efchew the evil. And fo I fpoke to them, and faid, Daughters dear, feeing that I am now an old man, and that I have been longer in the world than you; it is my wifh to fhow you, a little, what it is, as far as my capacity goes, which is not much. And if I have undertaken it, it is out of the love I bear you, and the longing which I have to fee your hearts and your affections turned to the fear and love of God, and that you may be had in honour, as well in this world as in the world to come. For affuredly all true wealth and honour, virtue and fafety, to man or woman, comes of Him, and of the grace of his Holy Spirit. And it is He who gives long life or fhort, earthly and worldly goods, as pleafes him beft; for all things come of his will and ordinance. And alfo will he recompenfe the duty and the fervice, which we owe to him, an hundred-fold. And for this reafon, my dear daughters, you muft ferve fuch a Lord, who can requite an hundred-fold.

Of Two Knights who Loved Two Sisters.

In the histories of Constantinople, it is told of an emperor, who had two daughters; the youngest of whom was what daughter should be, loved God and feared him; and in all the breaches of the night, failed not to pray for the dead. And also they slept in the one bed, she and her sister. And as often as the elder would awake, and hear her sister at her prayers, she would push and jibe her; telling her, That she could not get to sleep with her noise. But what with youthhood, the ease and plenty in which they were nourished, they came to be taken with two knights, brothers, pleasing and good looking gentlemen. And so long went on their loves and their sweetness, that either came to know of the other's matters. And an appointment was made with the two knights to come to them, privily, by night. And when the one, who thought to have come in unto the younger, had drawn aside the curtains; incontinent, there appeared, all about the damsel, as it were above a thousand dead men, in their shrouds; which threw him into such a trepidation and an agony, that he was overtaken of a fever and carried to his bed. But with the other, it was not so; * * * * * *
* * * * * * * * And when the emperor heard tell, that his daughter was

with child, he had her drowned in a well, in the dark; and the knight, he had flayed alive. And so, for their crimes, they both died. But the other daughter was saved, as I told you, and am telling you. And as soon as it was day, and it was known, everywhere, that the knight was upset, and in bed, she, who was at the bottom of it, came to him, and asked him, What it was had come over him? So he told her, truly, how, when he had drawn the curtains, thinking to go in to her, he had seen, clear as noon day, as it were a cloud of dead men, all in their shrouds, round about her; and that it was this horrible and loathsome sight, which had driven him out of his wits, and that he had not yet got over his fright. And when the lady heard the truth, she marvelled, and thanked God, on her knees, who had thus saved her from perishing and from dishonour. And from that time forth, she never omitted to pray and to cry to God, all the times that she awoke in the night, and supplicated, even more earnestly than before, for the dead; carrying herself modestly, chastely and soberly. Nor was it long till a great king of Greece asked her, of her father, in marriage; who gave her. And she was ever after known as an exemplary and a sober matron. And, as such, was she spoken of, and admitted of all. But her elder sister, who was light and gamesome, came to dishonour and to her end. So, my dear daughters, take warning, by this example, how, in the watches of the night, you betake yourfelves afresh to slumber, ere, as did this emperor's daughter, you have prayed for the dead.

Here is shown, how all Women ought to Fast.

Next, my dear daughters, you ought to fast, as long as you are single, three days in the week, the better to mortify the flesh, that it wax not wanton; and you may dedicate yourselves, more chastely and holily, to the service of God, who will have you in his keeping, and repay you double. And if you cannot fast three days, at least fast on friday, in memory of the precious blood and passion of Jesu Christ, who suffered for you. And if you cannot support yourselves on bread and water, at any rate, abstain from anything which had life. For it is a marvellous propitiation, as I heard from a knight, who was at the wars between the Christians and the Sarracens. It happened that one of the Christians had had his head severed from his body with a battle axe. But the head never ceased, for a moment, to hollo, and to demand confession, till a priest had come. And when he had heard the head confess, he asked it, By what immunity it was enabled to speak, deprived of its body? And the head told him, That God never left good actions unrequited; and that he had, all his life, abstained from flesh on the wednesday, for on that day the Son of God was betrayed; and from tasting anything which had blood in it on the friday; and that, in return for this duty, God had not suffered him to be damned, or to die in his sins, before they were confessed.

Here it is shown how all Women ought to be Courteous.

Next, my lovely girls, remember to be courteous and unassuming; for there is no more beauteous virtue, nor any that will sooner gain to you the grace of God, or the love of man, than gentleness or courtesy. For gentleness will tame the most untamable and unapproachable spirit; as may be seen by the hawk, of its nature savage, but which, by kindness you may win, and bring down from the branch to perch upon your wrist; which he never would have done, had you treated him roughly or brutally. Seeing then that courtesy will dompt the savage bird, which, by nature, is devoid of reason; much more should it master and disarm the untractableness of man or woman; be they ever so haughty, fierce or forbidding. Courtesy is the only road, and unfailing passport to the hearts and affections of men. It alone can tame the untamable spirit; mitigates and kills the little angers which assail us. And, for this reason, nothing is to be desired before courteousness. I know a great lord, of these parts, who, in the time when he was able to follow the wars, wrought more knights and squires to his ends, to his pleasure, by his affability, than any of the rest of them were able to do,

by dint of money, or any other means. I mean
Meffire Pierre de Craon, who, above all the knights that
ever I knew, was the one moft deferving of praife and
honour. And I alfo know great ladies and others, of a
wonderful condefcenfion, and who, by their gracious-
nefs, have won themfelves the love of great and fmall.
So, in order to fhow yourfelves courteous to little and
infignificant people, you muft fpeak to them foftly and
patiently, and be confiderate and unaffuming in your
anfwers. They can more effectually contribute to your
fame and odour, than the great ones. For to tender
duty and refpect to the great and confiderable, is only
to give them their due, and what they are entitled to
exact. But condefcenfions which are fhown to homely
gentle folk, to poor men and poor women, come of
the heart, and of a generous natural. And in proportion as thefe poor people are conciliated, accordingly
will the honourer be honoured. For they will everywhere noife the grace of him or her. So, you fee, of
little folk come honour and advancement, and of them
are they tranfmitted. And I remember well, being in
a company of great lords and ladies, to have feen a
lady, one of the greateft there, take off her hat, and
curtfey to a common blackfmith. And when one
gentleman faid to her, " Madame, you have taken off
" your hat to a blackfmith ! " fhe anfwered him, " It
" had been a lefs reproach to have left it on to a gentle-
" man, than to have foreborne to take it off to him."

And which redounded to an incredible admiration for the lady.

How they ought to carry themselves, without twifting their heads right and left.

Again, at your prayers, or at mafs, or elfewhere, do not be like the tortoife or the crane, for women who roll their heads from fide to fide, or twift them, like a weafel, on their fhoulders, for all the world, are like thofe animals. Let your carriage be ftraight and firm, as the lymer, which is an animal that looks right before him, without regarding to one fide or the other. Keep your whole body firm and compact, and all your members in their natural pofition, and your eyes before you. And if, at any time, you have occafion to look on one fide; turn face and body together. And this will give you the reputation of being ftraightforward and to be depended upon. For thofe will ever be efteemed but light, who go twining and twifting themfelves about.

It is here told of her whom the Chevalier de La Tour dropped, through her too much Lightnefs.

Again, my lovely girls, when on this head, I will tell you what occurred to myfelf. Once, on a time, it happened that they wanted to marry me to a very beautiful and noble young lady, whofe father and mother were both in life. And fo, my lord, my father, took me to fee her ; and all forts of good cheer and entertainment was ours. And fo I took a good look at her of whom they fpoke to me ; and prefently, falling into converfation, I ftarted her on all forts of fubjects, the better to be able to judge of her. And anon we fell upon the chapter of prifoners. So I faid to her, " Mademoifelle, if a prifoner one muft be ; " methinks it were better to fuccumb to you than to " many another whom I have feen. Better to fall into " your hands than into thofe of the Englifh." To this fhe replied, looking on me, " that fhe fancied, even " now, to fee the captive fhe would care to take." I then afked her, " Suppofing fhe had taken him, would " fhe make his bondage too cruel to him ? " " Indeed, " no," faid fhe, " I would do nothing of the fort ; I " would treat him as kindly as I do my own body." " Then," faid I, " he is a happy man, who fhall have " the fortune to fall into fo noble and fo gentle a capti- " vity ! " What need I fay more ? She had plenty of wit, and plenty to fay for herfelf, and well too. Yet I clearly faw, by what fell from her, that fhe knew quite as much as fhe had any bufinefs to know ; and befides, fhe had a quick and a rolling eye. And lots of talk we had together. And at laft, when it came to parting, fhe let me fee, that fhe was ready enough, for fhe begged me, three or four times over, to manage to come and fee her, one way or another. And fhe was as familiar with me, and I with her, as if we had known each other all our days. And the young lady well knew the errand which had brought us to the house.[1] And as soon as we had parted, my lord, my father, said to me, "Well, what do you think of her, "now you have seen her? You may speak frankly." So I answered and said, "My Lord, she certainly "appears to me, to be good and good looking; but, "with your permission, she shall never be nearer to "me than she now is." And then I told him everything which had occurred to me, touching herself, her manners and her eagerness. And so I did not have her; and this, from her too much lightness, and the too much readiness that I thought to see in her. And, for which escape, I thanked God, many a time since. For hardly a year and a half had gone over, till she got herself into trouble; whether with reason, or without, I do not know. And since she died. And from this, you see, my dearest daughters, and my noble maids, how all gentlewomen, of condition, ought to be of retiring manners, self-respectful, unassuming, small talkers. They should rejoin with diffidence; nor should they be too ready to understand, or yet anxious, or allow their eyes to be seen about. For, to end the matter, no good comes of it. Many have lost their chances through too much readiness; and of whom one would have expected very different things.

[1] See note M, at the end.

Of her who eat the Eel.

I will now give you an example, upon the chapter of wives who eat the tit bits, in the abſence of their lords. There was a lady who kept a pye in a cage, which talked of everything he ſaw. And it happened that the lord of the houſe had a great eel, which he preſerved in a pond, intending one day, to have him dreſſed, as ſomething wonderful, when he would be entertaining great lords, his friends, who might be coming to ſee him. But the lady, who was gluttonous, ſaid to her houſekeeper, "We'll eat the eel." And, in faƈt, they did eat the eel. And when they had eat him, they agreed to tell their lord, that the didapper had ſwallowed him. And when the lord came home, the pye began to chaunt, "My lord, your lady eat the "eel!" So the lord went to the pond, and found his eel was gone. So he returned to the houſe, and aſked his wife, "What had become of the eel?" And when ſhe thought to ſcreen herſelf, he told her plainly, "That it was not ſo, for the pye had ſeen her eat it." On this there was a terrible rumpus and ado between them. And no ſooner was the lord gone, than the lady and the ſtorekeeper went to the pye, and plucked all the feathers from his poll; telling him, "To take "that, for having told about the eel!" And ſo the poor pye was plumed. But from that day forward, whenever any one came to the houſe with an open forehead, or pilled, the pye would as affuredly tell them, " Ha, you told about the eel ! " And from this notable example, you may learn, how no gentlewoman, unknown to her lord, fhould ever, out of mere luxury, partake of the tit bits; except, always, when called upon to entertain perfons of quality. For this poor lady never efcaped, after, to be laughed at and twitted about the eel, which the pye had told of.

Of Abftinence.

* * * * *

Wherefore, my dear girls, have a heed of this terrible vice of eating and drinking to excefs. Never eat, but at ftated hours; at dinner and at fupper-time.[1] To eat once a day is the life of an angel; twice is all that is neceffary for man, or woman: oftener than this, is the nature of a beaft. Everything hinges upon cuftom and ufage. For, to whatever habit of life you accuftom yourfelf in your youth, the fame will come pleafant to you in your after days. And, for this reafon, you muft commence, betimes, to be fober.

How perilous it is to meddle with Men of the World; and of the Lady who undertook to crofs-queftion the Marfhai de Clermont.

Fair daughters, I will give you an inftance of how dangerous a thing it is to meddle with men of the

[1] See note N, at the end.

world, and thofe who are never at a lofs for a reply. For, affuredly, to play practical jokes with them, is a lofing game. There was once a famous feaft, where were many great lords and ladies, and, among others, the Marfhal de Clermont; than whom no man was better read in the ways of the world, a weightier or a readier fpeaker, or could fhow himfelf to more advantage, in the prefence of lords and ladies. And there was alfo there a great lady, who faid to him, before them all, " Clermont, to give you my mind, you have much " to thank God for; you are allowed to be a gallant " knight, and good looking to boot; and of parts, to " admiration. And fo you would be all but perfection, " if it were not for your cantankerous and illnatured " tongue, which never will be quiet." " Well, " Madame," faid he, " is this the worft you have to " tell of me ?" " I think it is," faid fhe. " Now," faid he, " let us juft weigh this matter quietly. It would " appear to me, if rightly looked at, that I have not fo " malicious a tongue as yourfelf; and I will tell you " why. You have fpoken of me, and reproached me " with the worft that you know of me; whilft I, I " have kept to myfelf the worft that I know of you. " So, madame, what injury have I done you ? I am " not fo ready, you fee, with my tongue as you are." When the lady heard this, fhe wifhed fhe had held her peace, nor ftriven with fuch a man; and this, for reafons which I fhall not mention, but were enough commented on. And it is an old faying, that as too much impetuofity knows no discretion, it is better to hold one's peace. And this is an excellent example. For it is better, for the moft part, to keep ftill, and to carry one's felf unpretendingly, than to be too ready to pick a quarrel with thofe who have their anfwer on their tongue's tip, and will not ftick to allow more to be gathered than they care to exprefs. And, from all this, look well who it is you are about to fpeak to, and in no way incenfe them; for the ftrife of them is wonder perilous.

Of thofe who delight to go on Pilgrimages and to Tournaments.

I will give you an inftance of a good lady, who, without any real caufe, fell into difgrace, at the round table of a tournament. This good lady was young, and her heart was fet upon the world. And gladly did fhe dance and fing, fo that fhe was the delight of all the lords and knights, and good fellows generally. And fhe liked all this well, and her lord gave her plenty of liberty, and everybody accefs to her. And though it little pleafed him, yet he did it, for fear of falling into the ill graces of his neighbours, or that it fhould be faid of him, That he was jealous. So he gave her full permiffion to be prefent at all their fêtes and meetings; and no expenfe was fpared to fend her off fuitably equipped, and as became the honoured gueft of her entertainers. But fhe could very well fee, that, had it folely depended upon him, her time had been fpent at home. And, as it is the cuftom, in fummer time, when dancing is kept up till light, it happened, once upon a time, at a fête where fhe was, that the torches were fuddenly dipped; and all was hubbub and confufion. And when they had brought others, the brother of this lady's lord found her in the grip of a gentleman, who had drawn her a little on one fide. Though, in good faith, I firmly believe, there was no villainy, nor anything wrong going on. However, the brother faid, There was; and talked of it, about, till at length it got to the ears of her lord, who was fo hurt with it, that, never after, had he any confidence in her. Nor did he ever, again, find joy or pleafure in her fight, as beforetime. So that they became like cat and dog; as people out of their wits. And all their houfe and fubftance went to wrack and ruin; and all, through this miferable beginning.

I know well another fair lady, who alfo delighted in being taken to fêtes. She, too, got herfelf into trouble and difgrace with a great lord. So much fo, that fhe took to her bed, and was there fo long that there was nothing left of her but fkin and bone; fo gone was fhe as that. And when fhe was, as fhe thought, at the point of death [1], fhe fent for her friends and my

---

[1] See note O, at the end.

lord, Sir God. And then she said before them all;
"My lords and ladies, good friends all; see, to what
"I am come. You know, all of you, how once I was
"fair, and young, and plump, and ruddy; and the
"world allowed me to be handsome. See now, how
"much of all this is left. Fêtes I loved to haunt;
"justings, tilts and tournaments. But all that is past.
"I have now to return to that earth out of which I
"came. And also you know, dear friends and hearts,
"that much villainy has been talked of me and of my
"lord of Craon. But, by that God which I am about
"to receive, and upon the damnation of my soul, I say
"it; he never asked anything of me, nor did he ever
"meddle with me, more than my own father, that
"begot me. I will not deny, but that he slept with
"me, but nothing ever passed between us, either in
"thought or in deed." And though many were taken
back, on learning this, who had thought clean contrary; yet, nevertheless, the stain stuck to her, and was
ever remembered to her disadvantage. And from this
you may see, how ticklish it is for honest women to
have their hearts too much abroad upon the world;
and how little call they have to be present at feastings
and revels, when they can civilly excuse themselves.
For they are places where, without any sort of provocation, many an honest woman gets a hurt. I would
not, by this, mean to say, that it is not allowable, at
times, to stretch a point, at the requirement of your

parents or friends, and to go. But, my dear daughters, if you cannot decently decline, and do go; have a care, when night comes, and the dancing and the singing, as well for the actual danger, as for the fear of envious tongues, to be always by the fide of fome of your own people, or parents; so that if the lights come to be put out, they may be at hand, not fo much that they fhould be afraid to truft you, as to fcreen you from the fcandal of malicious tongues and eyes, which will always efpy and talk a great deal more than ever takes place; and thus more effectually guard your reputations againft the affaults of the unfcrupulous; whofe delight it ever is, to noife the evil, and to hide the good.

Of the Lady who took a Quarter of a Day to Drefs Herfelf.

There was a lady, whofe domicile was hard upon the church. But fhe took fuch a time to drefs and ready herfelf that fhe put all the clerks, the priefts and the parifh, out of patience with her. And fo it happened, one Sunday, when fhe was later than ufual, and after everybody had got tired of faying, " She will be here " prefently; " that, at length, they got to afking, " Was anything the matter ? " And as half the day was already gone, they began to be angry and fick of waiting. So, one begins to fay; " What, will my lady " never have done combing and tricking herfelf out ? "

and another, " God fend her an ugly looking glafs;
" for keeping us, this way, for ever loitering and fool-
" ing about! " And even as he fpoke, fo it pleafed
God, and to make an example of her. For, at that
very moment, as fhe was looking in the glafs, fhe faw,
in the reflection of another which the enemy was holding behind her, ———, fo ugly and ftaring, that the poor
lady went out of her mind, as one demoniac, and for a
long time was ill. But fince, God fent her health;
and, by this, fo corrected her, that, ever after, fhe
managed to do with lefs time to drefs; humbly thanking him for the leffon which he had taught her. And
from this excellent example, you may learn how wrong
it is to wafte time, yourfelves, upon fuch exercifes, or
to caufe others to wafte theirs; efpecially at the hours
of divine fervice.

Here fpeaks of Difcovering the Matters of One's Lord.

*   *   *   *   *

I fhould like you to know the ftory of the knight,
who effayed his wife, whom he faw to be young. So
he faid to her, " My life, I will tell you a moft ex-
" traordinary thing; but, for the foul of you, do not
" let it be known—I laid two eggs. Now, for God's
" fake, do not mention it." And fhe promifed him,
on her honour, That fhe would not. But fhe thought
the time would never foon enough come, that fhe

could be off, and get to one of her goſſips. And when
ſhe had got to her, ſhe began, "Ha, my deareſt friend,
"I will tell you ſomething, but it is a terrible ſecret,
"and is not to go beyond you and me." On this, the
other aſſured her, That it ſhould not. "Then," ſaid
ſhe, "may God forgive me, if a moſt horrible thing
"has not happened to my lord. For, it is as true as I
"live—he has laid three eggs." "Holy Mary!" cried
the other, "laid three eggs; how can that be. It is
"the moſt awful thing I ever heard of." So, as quick
as her legs would carry her, ſhe was off, and told another, How ſo and ſo had laid four eggs. And this laſt
told another, how five eggs had been laid of one man.
And ſo the two eggs came to be an hundred. And all
the country was full of it; ſo that, at length, it came
back to the lord. On this, he called for his wife and
ſaid to her, in the preſence of his family and friends,
"Madame, enough has been made of what I told you,
"between ourſelves. Praiſe be to God, the two eggs
"I laid have now become an hundred. You have
"told what I deſired you not." And ſo ſhe remained
without a word to ſay for herſelf, and looking like a
fool. And, from this example, learn, how no honeſt
woman ſhould divulge the ſecrets of her lord.

Of the Olden Customs.

At that time, the country was at peace, and feasts and revels abounded in the land. And all manner of knights, ladies and gentlewomen were in the habit of collecting at these fêtes, which were frequent and general; and among them came the reverend knights of those times. But if, by any chance, it happened that a lady or gentlewoman of questionable reputation, or ill spoken of in the world, sat herself above a worthy lady or gentlewoman, of untouched reputation; even though she were superior in rank, or wife to a greater lord; presently, these noble knights and champions of their virtue, would, without any sort of ceremony, come, and taking the good ones by the hand, place them above the bad ones; and tell these latter, before all, "Lady, you must not take it ill, that this lady or gen-
"tlewoman takes precedence of you. For, although
"she may neither be so nobly born, nor so rich as
"yourself, her reputation is unblemished; she is known
"to be of the good and the chaste. As much cannot
"be said for you. You displease me. Honour is only
"to be given to those to whom it is due. So you are
"not to be affronted." And in this way, the christian knights spoke; putting the virtuous ladies, and of good reputation, before the others; who thanked God, in their hearts, for how they had kept themselves safely;

for, by so doing, they had come to honour and advancement. Whilst the bad ones pulled angry faces, and hung down their heads; meeting with nothing but ridicule, jibes and contempt. And this was an excellent example to all gentlewomen. For, by the disgrace which they saw to overtake another, they, the more, feared and misgave to incur the like themselves. But, God be thanked, in our times, as much deference is paid to those who are ill spoken of, as to those who are well spoken of; which is a sorry precedent to many. For they say, " Bah, do you not see that So and so is " just as well received, and with as much worship, for " all is said of her, as such another, whom no one has " a word to say against. It is thought nothing of. " Everything passes." But, for all that, all this is specious and ill considered; to say nothing of the sinfulness. For, the truth of it is, that, although in their presence, they may be shown all outward honour and respect, as soon as their backs are turned, all the young fellows and tittle tattles begin to jabber; " Aye, there " she goes: look at her; she makes herself too cheap: " So and so and she have had many a merry bout to-" gether!" And so they reckon and place her among the contemptible. And so it comes, that the same men who will show them all outward respect and attention, to their faces, will put out their tongues at them, behind their backs. But the poor fools see nothing of all this, but rejoice in their folly; nor ever once fufpect their fhame or wickednefs to be known. So, you fee, the times are changed from what they ufed to be; and, as it feems to me, for the worfe. And it appears to me, that it would be better, plainly, to all, and before all, to tell them their follies and their faults, as they did in the good old time, I tell you of. And I will tell you yet more; what I have heard of old knights, who lived with Meffire Geffry de Lugres and others; and who have ridden and travelled with them about the world; how, when in the fields, one of them would afk, " Whofe caftle or house is yon ? " and it was told him, " It is fuch a lady's ; " if the lady happened to be of an ill reputation, or her honour to be doubted of, he would go a quarter of a league out of his way, fooner than pafs her door. And when he got there, he would * * * ; and then he would take a piece of chalk, which he always carried in his fatchel, and he would write on the gate, or the pofts, A f——, A f——; and then he would fet his name to it, and be off. But if, on the contrary, he happened to be paffing before the hotel of a good lady, or gentlewoman, he would make for it, with all the hafte he could, and he would defcend, and knock, and enter, and fay, " My " good friend," or, " My dear lady, I pray God to " continue you the grace to be accounted as you are; " for, madam, you are greatly to be honoured and " refpected." And, by this means, the good were kept in an holy fear, and to the mark; nor daring to venture on what might hazard their honour and reputation. And, for my part, I wifh we could fee thofe times again; for never, do I believe, were there fo many deferving of blame, as at this prefent.

Le Livre du Chevalier de La Tour Landry.

A LAMENT, OR LILT;

Written by Richard Cœur de Lion, in his Captivity.

NDIGNATION in the soul, the captive, beft, is fired to eloquence. But to while away one's forrow; one can weave a song.

For all the largefs Richard dealt; how poor return he now receives! Ought they not to blufh, for very fhame, thus to leave me, two years unranfomed, to languifh and to perifh in a dungeon?

Know, my barons; Angles, Norman, Gafcon, Poitevin; the pooreft knight among ye, had I freed. I mean no reproach to any man; but I am ftill in prifon.

It is a true faying, *Nor kith, nor kin, dead man hath*; or why am I thus here, a beggar, and alone?

Of my proper fufferings, I fpeak not. It is the fate of war. It is of the ingratitude of my fubjects that I would complain. What a reproach will it be to them, fhould I perifh in this hideous den!

That I fhould be inconfolable; it is but natural.[1] The King, my lord, I know it well, is harrying my realm, defpite the oath was fworn to, between us, for the common weal. This alone nerves me. No; ere long, thefe fhackles will I burft.

Bards, my friends, Chail and Penfavin; whom I have loved, and yet do love, proclaim, How little have mine enemies to vaunt, in thus attacking me — that ne'er was found in Richard, perfidious heart or falfe — that it is the part of cowards and of fcoundrels, to levy war upon a pinioned man!

Countefs Soir;[2] God be the watcher of your fovereign worth; with his Holy Mother, and him, for whofe caufe I am now in bonds!

Hiftoire littéraire des Troubadours.

[1] See note P, at the end.
[2] See note Q, at the end.

BAYARD MEETS WITH HIS FIRST LOVE.

PON the departure of the King, the French garrisons, which remained in Lombardy, (the enemy being no longer in the field,) abandoned themselves to all sorts of festivities; among others, tournaments, which were the prevailing ones of the age. Bayard, turning this respite to advantage, went to see his friends, in Savoy; where, at the court of the duke, he had been brought up, a page. Charles I., his old master, and whose memory he cherished, by this, was dead. His widow, Blanche Paleologus, heiress of Montferrat, (daughter of William IV., and of Elizabeth Sforza,) was then living at Carignan, in Piedmont; which had been settled upon her, as her dower. She was a mighty worthy and a virtuous lady, and one who had no less esteem for Bayard, than had had the late duke, her husband. Her court was as brilliant as was any other in Europe, and

strangers were entertained at it with even a royal magnificence. She had then, for chamberlain of her houfehold, the lord de Fluxas, whofe wife, before her marriage, had been, and ftill remained, the favourite of the princefs. This lady had lived with her, in the quality of maid of honour, at the fame time that Bayard, in the capacity of page, had been about the duke. And this was, now, fome ten years gone. She had been, from the firft, a lovely, a gifted and a virtuous woman, and was come of a noble houfe. Bayard, on his fide, was no lefs advantageoufly endowed; a conformity that quickly begat in them a liking, which no lefs quickly ripened into paffion. So that, had it fimply depended upon themfelves, they certainly had married. But the voyage which the duke made to Lyons, with the entrance of Bayard into the fervice of the French King, were the means of feparating them. So that, up to the time of which we are fpeaking, excepting by letter, they had entirely loft fight of one another. In this interval, the beauty and the worth of the lady, albeit fhe was portionlefs, had procured to her the alliance of the lord de Fluxas, a rich and powerful baron. And when fhe faw the knight, at the court of the duke, fhe met him with all the tendernefs and fympathy, which, by the conventionalities of fociety, it were admiffible to evidence, in fuch a cafe. She told him, with what pleafure fhe had heard of all the occafions on which he had diftinguifhed himfelf;

as at the tournament of the lord de Vaudrey, that of
Aire ; with all the others where he had been ; efpecially of the day, at Fournoie, where the king, himfelf,
had deigned to notice him ; and the fame of which
had been blazed abroad, all over France and Italy.
She congratulated him on all the happy fortune and
fuccefs that had overtaken him, fince laft they had
parted, young people ; and each delighted in recalling
to the other, all the fondnefs which had been between
them. At length fhe faid, " Seeing you find fo much
" pleafure and honour in tournaments ; fuppofing you
" were to give one, for the entertainment of the prin-
" cefs in whofe fervice you firft won your maiden
" fpurs ? " " Madam," faid Bayard, " you know well
" that you were the firft I ever loved, and that I have
" always carried myfelf toward you with reverence and
" humility ; and that I have not been, nor am I, lefs
" touched with all the fenfe of the honour of your at-
" tachment, than with that of the duchefs herfelf. You
" have, Madam, but to require what may be for your
" pleafure, for hers, and for that of all the court."
" Seeing it be fo," faid the lady Fluxas, " then, dear
" knight, you will infinitely oblige the princefs and
" myfelf, by giving us a tournament. So many of your
" gallant countrymen are in the garrifons, about, that
" it can hardly fail to be a noble one." " I promife
" you," faid Bayard, " that you fhall have it, and in a
" few days. And feeing that you are the woman, of

"all the world, whose love and whose honour are dearest and most precious unto me, I hold you in too infinite a respect, to ask of you other favour, than that you will give me your hand to kiss, and from your arm, a bracelet only." The lady gave it to him, and he took it from her hand, without, however, telling her of the purpose to which it was to be dedicated. And when the hour of supper was come, he had the honour to sit at the table of the duchess, where, when a lad, he had waited as a page. And after supper, they danced. And this good old lady did him again the honour to express to him all the pleasure with which she had watched his walk in life, and made him to tell her, over again, everything that had befallen him, since last they were together.

Bayard, now home for the night, could think of nothing but his tournament. To him, it was something more than a mere gratification. It became a passion. The whole night was spent in drawing up the programme. And, with the light, he despatched a trumpet to all the neighbouring towns and garrisons, to announce to all the officers and gentlemen, who might be disposed to appear in complete armour, that, the fourth day from thence, which would be a Sunday, Sir Pierre du Terrail, otherwise Bayard, knight, would give a tournament, in the town of Carignan; of which the prize would be a lady's bracelet, and a ruby of the value of an hundred ducats; which should be presented by him, to the knight who might beſt perform, at three courſes with the lance, and twelve ſweeps with the ſword.

The trumpet made the proclamation, and brought back the names of fifteen gentlemen, who undertook to be preſent. The ducheſs was enchanted to hear of the gallantry of Bayard, and ordered that the ſtands ſhould be ready, in the tilt yard, by the time appointed.

The day come, our knight was on the ground, betimes, accompanied by the Lord de Mondragon, and two others, armed *cap à pied;* and, within a little, the other combatants began to make their appearance. The firſt who entered the liſts, were Bayard and the lord de Rouaſtre, a ſtout and hardy gentleman, and ſtandard bearer to the duke. He made his début with a magnificent charge, ſhivering his lance into four pieces. But Bayard, in revenge, broke his likewiſe, into half a dozen ſplinters, having firſt driven it clean through the ſhield of his competitor. They than ran a ſecond courſe, with no leſs ſpirit than the firſt; Bayard so violently aſſailing the vizard of the lord, that creſt and plumage were carried away upon the point of his lance; cauſing him, at the ſame time, to reel in his ſaddle; without, however, unſeating him. At the third encounter, Rouaſtre managed to raiſe his lance adroitly, whilſt that of Bayard was again broken to pieces. The next who entered the liſt, were the lords de Mondragon and de Chevron, who acquitted themselves to the admiration of all. The other combatants appeared, in their turn, and all did wonders.

The encounters with the lance over, those with the sword began. At the second blow, Bayard sent that of his adversary flying; breaking, at the same time, his own. Successively, the others took their turn. All were declared to have performed nobly, and the tournament closed with the day. On this, the duchess desired the lord de Fluxas, to invite all the gentlemen to sup with her. And as she was magnificent in everything which she undertook, the reception was worthy of her and of her guests. After the repast, and before the amusements and the dance began, the clamour of the hautboys and the trumpets announced, that the prizes were about to be given to those to whom they might be decerned. The lords de Grammont and de Fluxas, as umpires of the field, having first entertained the vote of the princess, proceeded, successively, to collect those of the company present, the ladies, and competitors themselves; and which were found to be unanimously for the knight. So it was to him that the judges presented it. But holding down his head, he only blushed, and refused to receive it. Finding however, that there was no escape, and that he must take it; he told them, "that it was not to him, but to the lady

"Fluxas that any honour which there were, should be attributed; that, as it was she who had condescended to gratify him with the bracelet, it was for her, also, to present him with the same." The lord, satisfied as well of the virtue and the honour of his wife, as with Bayard, allowed, without either taking, or evidencing any sort of umbrage, to the reasonableness of what he said; and turning, with the lord de Grammont, to the lady, the latter addressed her thus; "Madame, my lord of Bayard, to whom, unanimously, the prize of the tournament has been adjudged, avows, that it is you, solely, who are entitled to the bracelet; for that it was through the virtue of it that he was enabled to acquire it. And so, Madame, he adds, it is for you to dispose of it; for which end, I now present it to you." The lady accepted this new gallantry, on the part of the knight, with her accustomed grace, and thanked him for all the honour which he had done her. "Since you tell me," says she, "that it is through my poor bracelet that you have won, I will, for your sake, and as a testimony of the love I bear you, treasure it, to my dying day. But as to the ruby, seeing that you will not accept of it, I think it should be given to the lord de Mondragon, who, after you, numbered most voices." The ruby was then given, and the decision was generally approved. After this, the ball commenced, after the manner of that court, where gaiety was the order of the day. Out of compliment to the prefence of the French nobility, the fêtes were kept up for five or fix days; thefe over, each one returned to his garrifon.

No words could exprefs the delight of the duchefs, thus to fee her old page fo loved, honoured and refpected, that very jealoufy, itfelf, was difarmed. Bayard went to take leave of her; affuring her, " that next to " the prince, whofe fervant he was, there was no one " in the world who fhould command him, before her- " felf; and that, to his lateft day, he would be willing " and prepared to oblige her." From the apartment of the duchefs, he went to that of his firft love, the lady Fluxas, of whom he took his laft farewell; the lady, as himfelf, diffolved in tears. Nor was this generous attachment ever interrupted between them, till death, for ever, feparated them. Nor was the reputation of either fo much as canvaffed or fufpected. And yearly, while they lived, it was their practice to fend to each other, one little trifling memento or another.

And, on his departure, for many a long day, there was nothing talked of, at the court of the princefs, but the virtues of the knight, Bayard, and his noble qualities. Two notorious marks of his gratitude, in him, a mafter paffion, he left behind him. One, in the cafe of Pifon de Chenas, who has already been fpoken of;

and the other toward the fquire, under whom, as a lad, he had learned to ride. He made to the firft, a prefent of a noble horfe; and fent, to the fecond, to Montcailler, where he was married, and had settled, a beautiful mule.

BERVILLE—Hiſtoire de Bayard.

TITLE AND INTRODUCTION TO PERCEFOREST.

Title.

THE Right passing, Ornate, Delightful Mellifluous, and most pleasing History of the very noble, victorious, and superl:tive King Perceforest, King of Great Britain,[1] founder of the open hall, and of the Temple of the Sovereign god. With the marvellous emprises feats and adventures of the most warlike Gadifer, King of Scotland. Whom the emperor Alexander the great crowned Kings under his obedience. In which history the reader may see the fountain and Accomplishment of all Chivalry, the right Culture of true Nobility, Prowess, conquests without end, achieved since the times of Julius Cæsar. With many Prophecies, Relations, stratagems, and the divers fortunes of the same.

Newly imprinted at Paris, mil. v. cēs. xxxi.

[1] See note R, at the end.

Introduction.

To the moſt worthy, warlike, infuperable and invincible heroes of the French nation — all honour, health, prowefs, victory and triumph!

I know not, O moſt magnanimous lords, if it may not appear ſtrange to your heroical magnificence, that I ſhould have undertaken to addreſs myſelf to your univerſal monarchy; ſeeing that my poor parts are ſcarce capable of a ſtyle anſwerable to be entertained of the meaneſt of your graces. In very ſooth, lords, thus hardily to approach ſo many clear and piercing ſpirits, may well be thought by you to be preſumptuous. And even aſſuming that of your gracious condeſcenſions, you would deign to commend and to accept my pains, yet would the envious and diſparagers too eaſily catch on wherewithal to decry and to defame them. Truly, noble lords, I am right well aware, how little capacitated is my poor filly ingyne to any one thing worthy to be ſubmitted to your moſt judicious underſtandings. Yet, neverthelefs, I would not wiſh it to be ſuſpected by your Excellencies, that I could, for a moment, be wanting in that honeſt deſire which I have ever poſſeſſed, to illuſtrate, transmit and extol the imperiſhable renown of your highneſſes; for, verily, it merits all the praiſe which tongue can give. And ſeeing that ſuch praiſe is no more than is due, it is incumbent of every gentle ſoul to dedicate, unweariedly to lend itſelf to your praiſe;

to honour you, to collaud, and to dwell upon and magnify your everlasting fames. And certes, lords, your right generous naturals, admirers of the feats of virtue, could not better than be bent to such a study; for they will there find the spacious ocean of all noblenefs, the right ample domains of virtue ; the sumptuous manfions of all honour, the arcs triumphal of imperifhable achievements; and finally, the only summary of all faith, honour, fealty, prowefs, integrity — the ensample refident in your moft invincible and moft noble hearts; there ingraffed of the ever memorable antecedents of your ever bleffed predeceffors, and, by you, laborioufly cultivated, improved on and furpaffed. Alfo would they there find the right clear fountain of Parnaffean dew, where the Pegafean nymphs, accompanied of the heavenly Apollo, fuck all their eloquence divine, and all their gorgeous infpiration. So that it is for all thofe to whom the gods, propitious, have lent a ray of their divinity, leaving all other matters, to betake themfelves to the confecration and celebration of your immortal deeds; the more fo, as by fo doing, they would conquer to themfelves, no lefs, a never-dying fame. In this right famous ocean, in this pale of virtue, in this honourable manfion, and on thefe arcs triumphant, will you find feated, and in dominion, the eloquent Gaguin, the hardy Argenton ; that fource of knowledge, Bude; the eloquent orator, Emille ; that illuftrious magiftrate, the urbane Collin ; the counfellor, Brochet ; the maronian Marot; with so many other excelling spirits, who have acquired unto themselves fame and reputation. Yet have your merits surpassed every tribute which has been advanced of them, or of others. Nor is this all; for not only have those of a common origin with yourselves, but all nations, renouncing the meed and matter of their own princes, abandoned themselves to the magnifying of the high achievements of the French nobles. There is no country which has not sung the praises of the magnanimous Pepin; the conqueror and Augustus, Charlemagne; the chivalrous paladins, under them flourishing. So that books, without number, and in every tongue, are for ever resounding of their triumphs and of their prowess. If then every soul, thereto capable, has given itself up to the blazoning of your honour, and of your praise; it is but meet that I, to the utmost of my poor might, should follow in so commendable a precedent: more especially, consideration had to how kindly I have been received and treated in France; and to how much more flatteringly my poor labours have been entertained, than, from any merit of theirs, they could have ever hoped for. All which considered, as it appears to me, I should rather fall under the suspicion of ingratitude toward you, by refraining from, than of presumption, in submitting to your lordships some such slight performance, as well in keeping, at once, with my temerity and insignificance. Alas, my most illustrious lords, in what a ſtrait am I ? If I am to be filent, I am ungrateful. If I proceed, there is no flight of mine can ever attain, but at the riſk of falling, to the very leaſt of your eminencies. Needs muſt I then ſteer clear, if that be poſſible, of theſe two extremes. To which end, having nothing of my own to offer to you, I will preſent you with ſomewhat which is of another. There is now fallen into my hands, the moſt pleaſant hiſtory of the moſt noble king, Perceforeſt; and by ſo much the more worthy to be dedicated unto you, as you yourſelves, lords, ſurpaſs all other nobles in nobility. For it is the true inſtitution and emporium of chivalry, the open hall of adventure, the temple to the ſovereign god, the ſchool and diſcipline of valour, and the fountain of true magnanimity. You will there ſee, O magnificent lords, the valiant Perceforeſt, and the noble Gadifer, his brother, inſtated to be Kings, by the conqueror, Alexander the great; the one of Great Britain, and the other of Scotland. You will ſee all the ordinance of the open hall; to which, nor baſe nor craven ſoul, or ever yet had acceſs. You will ſee twelve knights, all ſons of kings, deſcending from their high eſtate, and concealing themſelves under the maſk of a private condition, the better to be at liberty to follow chivalry. You will ſee twelve vows vowed, the leaſt of which were more arduous to perform than the twelve labours of the great Hercules. You will ſee thoſe vows accompliſhed, and carried through. You will see twelve triumphant tournaments, where every one of them carries off the prize; and that the very one for which his vow had been made. You will there see the princely entertainments, the inestimable jewels and the favours. You will see the first source, and the continuance of many a passion; the cruel martyrdoms and the agonies of lovers and of the ladies of their love. You will see the incredible virtues and force of the enchantments with which the false Darnant enveloped and preserved himself in his forests. You will see him trampled underfoot, and done to death, of the victorious Perceforest. You will see the admirable dexterity of the queen of the Fairies, and also of Morgane. You will see Bruyant, the faithless, enemy to the knights of open hall, oft and oft to deceive them. Yet, at the length, you will see him overcome, and done to death, of Passelyon, an infant of a year old; and infant though he were, knight. You will see Betides, son to Perceforest, and contrary to all which his father could urge, take up with the Roman traitress, Circes. You will see by what artifices she gained the affections of Perceforest, and of the queen, his wife: how, by her contrivance, Luces, Roman also, her former lover, ingratiated himself into favour; and by what means they conspired the destruction of Great Britain. You will see Julius Cæsar to descend, and the furious and terrible battle, wherein the champions of the open hall were discomfited. You will see, later, the stock of Gadifer, king of Scotland, to reflourish, and restore the whole country. You will see the gentle spirit, Zephyr, play a thousand tricks, and, again, requite as many favours to the knights. You will see, at last, the valiant Gallafer to win the blood-red sword, and the shield of the sign of the cross. You will see marvellous visions in the temple of the sovereign god, and how all the evil spirits and enchantments were banished out of the kingdoms of England and of Scotland. In a word, you will see, and without end, surpassing undertakings, wars, tournaments, adventures, doleful instances, prophecies, delightful passages, chivalric precepts and admirable ensamples. And know, noble lords, that the mighty Gallafer, with the blood-red sword, which is the word of God; and the shield of the cross, which is the shield of faith, is emblematic of our Saviour, Jesus Christ, who, at the sovereign temple of the God of heaven, is armed of his father with his precious cross; and who, with the breath of his word, has chased away our capital and mortal foe; the infernal enemy of this universal Christendom; of which you, most worthy lords, have conquered by your virtues, and those of your ancestors, the ever christian crown. Accept, then, surpassing lords, this history, comprised in five volumes; each in right ornate and mellifluous language. Read and reread the imperishable exploits, therein contained; arousing every noble breast to imitation and to adulation. Take to you the shield of faith, wherewith to oppofe the enemies of the fame. Brandifh the fword of the word of God againft the perverters of the true and faving faith. Follow on the footfteps of thofe gallant knights, the memory of whofe achievements is as the fpur to prick the generous foul to emulation. And, pardon me, lords, if, feeing it were beyond my power to fubmit to you anything of my own, I have, at leaft, prefented to you that which it were becoming, on your parts, to accept, and not the reverfe. And if the everlafting God, of his divine grace, will but vouchfafe to me the might to blazon, as is called for, your immortal deeds, the lighteft particle of that might fhall be dedicated and be referved unto that blazon. And to that eternal God, I now pray, that he will yet more and more exalt you; and to the higheft pitch of all profperity, felicity and honour.

The fervant. ii.
Perceforeft.

A ROYAL AIRING IN THE SIXTEENTH CENTURY.

Fragment of a letter from Brantôme to his Nephew.

MY lord Francis de Bourdeille, then, your grand-father, was the fon of the illuftrious father and mother of whom I have fpoken. As foon as he was well grown, and of an age fufficient, his father prefented him to the queen of France, Anne, duchefs of Brittany; in whofe fervice he remained eight years; having the honour of being her firft page, (and, confequently, the one whom fhe always addreffed,) and to mount upon the mule which immediately preceded that of the queen. And it was a great diftinction, in thofe times, for the pages of queens and of great princeffes, to be, in fuch a manner, preferred above the others. And it was the good man, the late Monfieur d'Eftrées, Grand-mafter of the artillery, and who was fo in every way worthy of the charge, that rode the one behind, as he has often affured me ; adding, that many a time have the two of them been whipped, to keep each other in countenance. For your grand-father was always getting into one fcrape or another; for he was naturally giddy-pated, and full of all forts of roguery, tricks and contrivances ; but his chiefeft delight ufed to be to fet his mule at a trot, at times when it was his bufinefs to walk. And as foon as ever he would fet off, the poor queen would holloa after him, *Bourdeille, Bourdeille, I will have you whipped; that I will; I give you my honour; and your mate, too; both of you.* But fhe might as well have talked to the winds ; for each of them would put it off on the other. The one before infifting, that the fault was none of his, if the other would come driving on, in fuch a manner, upon the top of him ; and the one behind, that he had only been endeavouring to keep up with the one before. And fo, between them, they would get right well whipped for their pains, in fpite of all their excufes. But Monfieur d'Eftrées affured me that the fault was invariably on the fide of your grand-father, who was fure to be the one to begin.

BRANTÔME.

AN UNADMIRABLE CRICHTON.

OWARDS the beginning of June, I set out by way of Calais, whence I was to embark; having with me a suite of upwards of two hundred gentlemen, or, at least, persons calling themselves such; and of whom, in fact, many were parties of the first distinction. The aged Servin came to present his son to me; at the same time entreating me, if it were possible, to make an honest man of him; adding, that it was a result which he rather hoped for than expected; not, however, said he, that I can find in him any want of stuff or parts, but on account of his incurable propensity to vice of every sort. And he had reason enough for what he said. Curious, from all he told me of him, to see the young man, I determined to sift him closely for myself. I saw at once before me, a miracle and a monster of nature, for really I can think of no one word, which,

in itself, would convey an adequate idea of this strange assemblage of the rarest gifts of nature with vices the most irreconcileable. Fancy to yourself a spirit, so comprehensive that there was hardly anything which could be known, which it did not know; a perception so swift that it took in whatever was presented to it, at a glance; and a memory so prodigious, that nothing escaped it. He was acquainted with every department of philosophy; and in that of mathematics, more particularly with fortification and drawing. He had all knowledge, even to theology, of which he was so much master, that he could be, when he would, an excellent preacher, and an able controversialist; for, or against the reformed religion, was all one. He had acquired not only the Greek and the Hebrew, with all the languages which we commonly call, the learned, but all sorts of patois and jargons. He could catch, so happily, every manner of intonation and accent, that that, joined to the readiness with which he could assume the air and manners, as well of the different European nations, as of the provincial French, enabled him to pass, at all times, and in all places, for a native. He had turned this faculty to so good an account, that he had personated every type of character, and to the life. In fact, he was the most inimitable mimic; and as good a comedian as an age will produce. He was a tolerable poet. He played on all sorts of instruments; was well acquainted with the principles of music, and sung as pleasingly as correctly. He would say mass; for he was determined to do, as well as know all things. His person was, in every way, in keeping with his mind. He was clean made, nimble, active; constituted to all sorts of exercises. He was a fair horseman, and whether dancing, wrestling or leaping, he was equally a proficient. There was no out-of-door pastime in which he did not excel; and, to boot, he was a first rate mechanic, and handy at all kinds of knackery. Reverse the medal; he was a liar, double-faced, treacherous, cruel, cowardly, a cheat, a drunkard, a glutton, a pot companion, a master in every species of debauchery; a blasphemer, an atheist. In a word, every vice was to be found in him, whether contrary to nature, piety, honour, society or morals. And such he showed himself, even till the last: for he perished in the flower of his prime, in a brothel; his flesh rotted on him by debauchery; a bottle in his hand; cursing and denying God. — *Mémoires de Sully*.

MARRIAGE,[1]

alias

THE FARCE OR INTERLUDE OF

ADAM, THE HUNCHBACK OF ARRAS.

GOOD people, all; do you know how I came to change my coat? The laſt time you ſaw me, I was a married man. I am now a clerk; hot from Paris; and am now come to bid you all adieu. Fact. It is not for nothing that Paris is ſo vaunted. It is all that is ſaid of it. There are not wanting fair ones there, who already aſpire to my attentions. Impatient, they attend me. Brief; I am off. My time, you ſee, was not altogether thrown away.

Coxcomb! What is it thou art about? Doſt thou flatter thyſelf, in thy vain heart, that thou haſt but to ſhow thyſelf, and all Paris to come forth to meet thee?

[1] See note S, at the end.

No; never did man of mark come out of Arras! Adam, announce thyself as thou wilt; oblivion is thine everlasting meed.

God has given me parts; I know it: they shall be turned to account. The men of Arras are but fools: a tongue in the cheek is all the applause my verses ever yet got out of them. By my faith, I am thrown away upon them; and, between ourselves, I have seen enough already of the fair adorables of Paris, to reconcile me to the loss of those of Arras.—And goody Manoie; what is to become of her? My wife, too, whom I am leaving with her father? Leaving dost thou say? surely thou knowest, in thy fond heart, she will be after thee.—And you yourself, rascal, would'st thou have the wickedness, the hardheartedness, to put asunder that which mother church hath tied together?— Must I out with it? Well, then, to tell you the honest truth; I made a slight mistake. When I married, I was young, and I was in too big a hurry. I was at that period of a man's life, when his reason is in leading strings, his heart is tinder; and a lass, a spark: in a word, I was soft. You all know what it is, to see a balmy, pleasant spring; heaven serene, birds singing, leaves springing, grass growing, calves skipping, lambs bleating, streams purling, zephyrs sighing. And, friends, you also know, how pretty considerably four or five months modify all this. In two words, the moral is before you. God, Sirs, my wife, the first

time I faw her, why, I took her to be fair as the lily; ruddy as the rofe. The lark fcarce feemed to me more merry; fhe had the waift of a midge, and the eye of a dove. Alas, my friends, time; time that fpareth nothing, too early robbed her of her charms. Her white, now white no more, was yellow; her red, black; her temper, the devil; her eyes, blazes. It is all a miftake: She is the fame fhe ever was. It is you yourfelf, Sir, that are changed, and I know the wherefore. There is an old proverb; " *   *   *
" *   *   *   *   *   ." You underftand me. The thing is common enough.

Such, my friends, is the ufual fport of love. It diftorts and magnifies everything it lays its eyes on; and of the homelieft face will make a gypfey queen. The locks of my charmer, which now, too plain, I fee to be but black and lanky, I then took to be golden, wavy, curled. Her eyes, which now I perceive to be little, red and piggy, I then fancied to be open, blue, and laughing. No mortal could abide that amorous glance, fhot from beneath thofe heavenly vaulted brows; arched as with the fineft pencil of the mafter. On her glowing and her burfting cheeks, each time fhe fmiled, you might behold two bewitching little dimples to retreat; for all the world refembling to the beauteous faucers of the rofe. In a word, fhe was nature's mafter-piece; perfection. What with her pretty little foot, her jimpy waift, her taper limbs, her pouting little lips, her teeth so white and pearly, she completely turned my head. And well she knew it, the arrant little baggage. It was " O no," and, " O " don't ; " and what with her airs and her prudery, she did with me exactly what she had a mind to. She hooked me on by throwing me off. Jealousy, love, hate, rage ; each, in their turn, the little vixen brought to play. No battery but was turned to account. And the deeper I floundered, the bigger fool I. At length, I could hold out no longer, so I married her. So you all know, now, how I came to be victimized. But seeing that I have not found my lord, Cupido, all he promised for, and that he has thought proper to break his word with me, I intend to take the liberty of doing as much with him. So then, my friends, whilst there is yet time, and before I am made a daddy of, or any other little unforeseen domestic felicity shall have turned up to interfere with my arrangements, I have made up my mind to leave things as they were. Brief ; I am off : of matrimony, I have had *satis* and to spare. Adieu. *Fabliaux où Contes du xii et xiii Siècle.*

THE CRUSADES,

alias

THE CONTROVERSY BETWEEN

THE KNIGHT OF THE CROSS AND THE UNCROSSED KNIGHT.

 WAS fauntering, the other day, upon my horfe, (it was near Saint-Remi,) and I was in miferable fpirits at the time, for I could not get out of my head, our poor chriftians who were at Acre, abandoned of their countrymen, and whom the enemy were fo hotly preffing. This wretched imagination fo fadly abforbed me, that, unconfcioufly, I loft my way. Coming, at length, to myfelf again, as I was looking around for fomeone to direct me, I chanced to fee two knights, who, after their fupper, were apparently paffing abroad to enjoy the evening air. They feemed to be difputing with much vehemence. Anon they fat down by the fide of an

hedge. As there was nothing but the hedge between us, (and my curiosity being now sufficiently aroused,) I crept quietly along it, till I had gotten opposite, so as to be able to overhear all which passed. One of them, it appeared, had just assumed the cross, and was busy exhorting his companion to follow his example. "No man knows better," said he, "than yourself, that God has given you a reasonable soul; capable to discern the right from the wrong, and that he has promised to all those who follow his precepts, a great and a glorious reward. The opportunity is now given to you to merit that salvation. You cannot but know the condition in which the Holy Land now lies. The kingdom of God is a prey to the infidels. Are we not craven knights, thus tamely to stand by, and look on, untouched, at any such profanation? How could we fitter dedicate, than to his glory, the life and the means which his mercy has vouchsafed to commit to our keeping?"

"Humph!" said the other; "if I understand you rightly, what you are wanting me to do, is this; to be off, and at the price of my blood, to participate in the conquest of an outlandish country, not one foot of which ever can be mine, even supposing that we do conquer it: to turn out of my house, and to entrust the charge of my lands, my wife, my children, my all, to the keeping of the hounds in my kennel. I have often heard the old saw; *What you have, keep:* a saying which, to my mind, smacks wonderfully of good, com mon fenfe. Among other things, it tells me, that it were little fhort of madnefs to give up one hundred fous in cafh, for forty upon paper. God has nowhere told us to fow any fuch like chaff; and he that does, ten to one but he will come to be a beggar for his pains."

Knight of the Crofs. Sir, you came naked from the bowels of your mother, yet has not that prevented you from finding yourfelf, this day, well grown, well filled and well clad. Providence has anticipated your every want. Befides, you are forgetting, that He will recompenfe, an hundred-fold, that which is lent to him. Alfo you cannot but know, that there are conditions impofed to the award of his paradife.

The uncroffed Knight. Friend, I fee, every day, perfons who have been toiling their lives away, and sweating blood and water, to get to themfelves fomething of the fort. I fee them packed off, for their redemption, to Rome, the Afturies, or goodnefs only knows where. What becomes of them when there, I can form no fort of conception; but this I do know, that they return, to a man, naked; without a fou, and without a fervant. A man can as faithfully ferve his God, in France as at Rome; and, truft me, paradife may be reached by a cut lefs roundabout, than *via* Acre. You think, do you, for the like of that, that I am to crofs the feas; but I, I think differently, and that it were the height of folly to go all that way, and all to be the slave of another; whilst a man can, quite as well, remain at home, and purchase heaven in his own proper house.

The Knight of the Cross. Sir, what you have just uttered, scarce merits the courtesy of a civil reply. You fancy, as it seems to me, that you are to be saved without a thought, or without an effort; an expiation which has cost to martyrs their blood. Not a day of your life but you may see penitents renouncing their all, and burying themselves up, alive, in their monasteries; never esteeming any sacrifice of their's to be sufficient to entitle them to the recompense on which their souls were set.

The uncrossed Knight. On my honour, Sir, your arguments are not to be resisted. But, why, Sir, might I ask, do you not rather address yourself to our rich abbots, our fat deans, our prelates; whose profession it is to serve God. What, are they to be possessed of all his wealth, below, and we to be told, that it is for us to turn out and fight his battles! You must allow, the thing is not reasonable. Alas, small care is it to them, the hail or the snow. Though they doze their lives away, their teinds come not the less to hand. By my faith, if that is the way to get to paradise, they would be blockheads to follow any other; for the like of it, it would be a job to find.

The Knight of the Cross. That is none of your affair. Let be, the prelates and the parsons. What you have to look to is the King of France, who, confiding his children to the hands of God, is about, for the falvation of his immortal foul, to imperil his mortal body. To fay the leaft of it, he has as much at ftake as you have. Yet, you fee, he allows nothing to ftand in his way.

The uncroffed Knight. My friend, every night of my life, I fleep in peace. I hurt no man living. I am on good terms with all my neighbours; and, by St. Peter, if this fort of life is preferable to yon other, beyond the feas, and where I muft be at the beck of another, I would not mind prolonging it a little longer. And you, Sir, whofe heart feems bent to deeds of bold emprife and chivalry, off with you : it is for you, not me, to dompt your haughty Signor of a fultan. You may tell him, with my compliments, that I cannot but laugh at his projects and defiance : that if he comes to difturb me, in my hall, I will let him fee that I know how to defend myfelf; but that as long as he choofes to remain quietly at home, he need have nothing to fear on my account : I fhall certainly be the laft to moleft him.

The Knight of the Crofs. You have not a thought in your head, but peace and tranquillity ! Hey, Sir, do you think, then, that you are to live for ever? Who knows, but this very night you may be hurried away? Eat, drink and be merry; yet, who knows, if to-morrow the game is to be renewed? death is stalking around, among us. His mace is in his hand. Young, old; all comers alike; the first he meets, he knocks upon the head. Wait till your turn be come, and with what agony, reproach, remorse, will you not then look back on this hour!

The uncrossed Knight. Sir crusader, there are some things which I can never sufficiently admire. I see all sorts of persons, great and small; the best among us, and the least exceptional, leaving for those countries. That they conduct themselves there as becomes christians, I cannot for a moment allow myself to doubt; nor can I, any more, that their souls are refreshed and purified thereby. Yet, for all that, (and how it comes about, I cannot, for the soul of me, conceive), but, to a man, they invariably return, bandits; the pests and scourges of society. And, again, I say, if God is everywhere, he is as much here as there; nor is it likely that he is going to hide himself, on purpose, from me. Besides, I will tell you a bit of a secret, in your ear; that though I would cross a brook as readily as another, there is a little too much water, according to my notions of things, 'twixt here and Acre; and what is more, it is so deep, that if once, by any hap, I got into it, I have some misgivings as to whether I should ever scramble out again.

The Knight of the Cross. There again; you have not one thought but of your life! Will you never remember, that you have to die. I pray you think,

How will you ſtand prepared, when that hour arrives ? Will you be as ſenſeleſs as the beaſt in your ſtall; of which, pitched upon a dunghill, one ſees the laſt? Ah, my friend, bethink thee that there is an hell; and that he who would ſave his ſoul in life to come, muſt begin by renouncing children, wife, poſſeſſions, in the life which is.

The uncroſſed Knight. Sir, you have convinced me. Your overwelming eloquence is not to be oppoſed. From this day, I make a ſacrifice to God of my pleaſures and my blood. In the name of the King of Glory, who, for our redemption, made for himſelf, of his creature, a mother, I am reſolved, this day, as you, to take the croſs, and thus to merit heaven, and heaven's glories. For it is but meet, that he who will not be at the pains to come to the feaſt, in the wedding garment, be compelled to remain at the door.

Fabliaux ou Contes du xii et xiii Siècle.

THE SEVENTH, EIGHTH, TENTH, ELEVENTH,
TWELFTH AND THIRTEENTH CHAPTERS
OF THE SIXTH BOOK OF THE MEMOIRS
OF DE COMMINES.

CHAPTER 7.

How King Louis, by a diſtemper, loſt the uſe of his ſenſes and his ſpeech; alternately recovering and relapſing; and of how he carried himſelf in his chateau of Pleſſis les Tours.

AND at this ſeaſon; the year of our Lord fourteen hundred and ſeventy nine, was there truce between the aforeſaid parties. And peace the king wanted, eſpecially in the quarter of which I ſpeak, but only on the conditions, it was to be, in all points, to his advantage, as I have ſaid. And he was already beginning to age and to fail. And ſo it fell, as he was ſitting at his meat, at Forges, near Chynon, that he was overtaken of a paralyfis, and at the fame moment, he loft his fpeech. At once he was taken from the table, and placed before a fire. The windows were made faft, and notwithftanding he ufed every effort as though he would make for them, he was prevented by thofe that were about him. And this was done for the beft. And it was in the year fourteen hundred and eighty, in the month of March, that all this befell him. And of fenfe, fpeech, or memory he had not. Things, you will remember, were in this ftage, when you, my lord of Vienne, who, at that time, were his phyfician, arrived. Incontinent a clyfter was prefcribed; you had the windows to be opened, that he might breathe; on which, there and then, voice and fenfe, in fome degree, returned; he got upon his horfe and made for Forges, for the attack had been on him in a little parifh, diftant fome quarter of a league thence, and where he had been to hear mafs.

The faid lord was well heeded for, and foon began by figns to exprefs his wants. Among other things, he called for the official of Tours, that he might confefs himfelf; fhowing them by his manner that he was to be fent for. He alfo made them underftand that I was to be gone for; for I was away, at Argenton, fome ten leagues off. When I arrived, I found him at table, and about him were mafter Adam Fumée, who formerly had been phyfician to the late King Charles, and at the fame time I am fpeaking of, was Mafter of the requefts ; also another phyfician, called mafter Claude. Of what was faid to him, he feemed to take in little or nothing; but in fuffering he was not. He made me gather, by figns, that I was to fleep in his chamber. His words he could hardly put together. I waited on him, for fifteen days, as well at table as about his clofet, as *valet de chambre*; which I took to be a great honour; and I was handfomely provided for. And at the end of two days, his fpeech began to return, and with it came his underftanding. And it feemed to him that no one could fo well catch, or interpret his meaning as myfelf, fo that he would never allow me from his fide. And his confeffion was made to the faid official, I prefent, or otherwife they never could have underftood oneanother. It was but little he had to fay, as, but a few days before, he had already difburdened himfelf. For whenever the kings of France are about to touch for the "King's evil," they fail not to confefs ; and this, he never omitted to do, once by the week. And if others neglect to do as much, they are a great deal to blame ; for of infected, there is ftore, and at all times. And as foon as he had come a little to, he began by inquiring, Who thofe had been, that had ftood between him and the air? It was told him, and, then and there, he chafed them from his prefence. From fome of them, their offices were taken, nor would he ever fee them more. Of other fome, as my lord de Segre, and Gilbert de

Graffay, lord of Champeroufe, he took nothing; however, he sent them away. The moft part were taken back at this vindictivenefs; blaming fuch a way of acting, and faying, It had all been done for the beft. And they faid rightly. But the imaginations of princes are infcrutable, nor are they to be fathomed of every man who thinks to found them. For, the truth of it was, that there was nothing of which he lived in fo perfect an horror, as to be deprived of his authority, which was very terrible; or that he fhould ever come to be challenged in any matter whatfoever. Nor had he forgotten, how the King Charles, his father, when on his deathbed, had got it into his head, that they were determined to poifon him, and at the inftigation of his fon; fo much fo, that they could not get him to eat; and yet how, for all that, it was decided on, after weighty deliberation, by his phyfician and his chiefeft minifters, to compel him to do fo; and which was done, broths being forced down his throat; foon after which affront, the faid King Charles died. The faid King Louis, who, all his days, had fhown his abhorrence of the like meafures, was, beyond all expreffion, wounded to find that he had been fubjected to a like indignity. And much as he may have felt it at heart, he forced himfelf, even more, to refent it before the world. For the real and hidden fear that moved him was, an apprehenfion left they fhould take it into their heads to depofe him, under pretext that his parts were no longer what they ufed to be, or equal to the guidance of the ftate.

As foon as he had let fall this thunder clap among thofe whom I have named, he began to call for the affairs in hand; wanting to fee the difpatches that had been made during the ten or twelve days he had been ill; and with the drawing up of which, the Bifhop of Alby, his brother, the governor of Burgundy, the marfhal de Gié, and the lord de Lude, had been charged. For it was they who were about him when the malady came on; and they were all quartered right underneath his bedroom, in two little clofets. And he would needs fee the letters and difpatches which, daily and hourly, were coming to hand. The chiefeft were placed before him, and I read them to him. He made a fhow as though he were attending; taking them in his hands, pretending, all the time, to be reading them; whilft, in reality, he had not any conception of what they were about. Prefently, he would ftutter out fomething, or, by figns, give us to collect what was to be done. However, we made but few expeditions, tarrying the upfhot of the malady; for he was a mafter with whom it well behoved fervants to be wary. And this malady was on him fome fifteen days; when, fenfe and fpeech reftored, he was again in his ufual ftate: yet ftill, terribly fhaken, and in a wonderful apprehenfion of falling anew into his former helpleffnefs; for by temperament, he was but little difpofed to put his faith in the confolations of his phyficians. And as foon as he found himfelf to be pretty much as he was wont, he releafed the Cardinal Bellue, whom, for fourteen years, he had retained a prifoner, though he had often been interceded for, as well by the Apoftolic See as by divers others. It ended by his receiving abfolution, in a brief which was fent to him, at his own folicitation, by our Holy Father, the Pope.

When this vifitation firft came over him, thofe who were about, taking him to be as good as dead, proceeded to remit a cruel, and, beyond meafure, unconfcionable tax which he had lately impofed, at the inftigation of my lord des Cordes, his lieutenant in Picardy, for the fupport of, and to keep on foot, ten thoufand infantry, and two thoufand, five hundred pioniers. And this levy was called, The encampment. And with them he joined fifteen hundred men at arms, moftly veterans, and who were to fight on foot or horfe, as occafion called for. And in addition to this, he caufed to be prepared a vaft number of tents, with all the neceffary ammunition, and waggons to carry the whole. And this camp, which was, in all things, after the model of that of Burgundy, coft him well fifteen thoufand francs the year. And when all this hoft was affembled, he went to fee it, where it was pitched, in a little valley, hard by Pont-de l'Arche, in Normandy. And the fix thoufand Switzers, of whom I fpoke, were with them. And but once did he fee this hoft; and prefently he returned to Tours, where again the malady came on him, and with it went his voice. And for fome two hours we took him to be dead; and he was in a gallery, lying on a paillasse, and many were about him. My lord de Bouchage and I, we recommended him to my lord, Saint-Claude. Thofe who were with us recommended him alfo. And incontinent his fpeech came to him, and he rofe, and walked, withal, about the houfe; but yet very feebly. And it was in the year fourteen hundred and eighty one that this fecond attack was. And he went about the kingdom as was his wont. And he came to me, at Argenton, (where, for a month, he was laid up.) Thence he went to Tours, where he was again overtaken. From that he made his way to the fhrine of my lord, Saint-Claude; to whom, as you have heard, he had been devoted. As he was leaving Tours, he had fent me into Savoy, againft the lords de la Chambre, de Miolent, and de Breffe, while, all the time, he in reality countenanced them underhand, in as much as they had feized on the lord de Lins, of Dauphiny, whom he had put about the government of the duke Philip, his nephew. And after me he hurried a ftrong body of gens-d'armes; and I led them to Mafcon, as againft the faid lord de Breffe. However, he and I were at one, in fecret, and he took the faid lord de la Chambre, as he was lying in his bed at Turin, in Piedmont, where he was, and the faid duke alſo. And he let me know of it. And with that I withdrew the gens-d'armes; for he carried the duke of Savoy to Grenoble, where my lord, the marſhal de Bourgoyne, the marquis of Rothelin and I, went to his encounter. The King then ſent for me to Beaujeu, in Beaujolois, where I was horrified to find him ſo gone and changed; and much I marvelled how he could get about, as he did: but it was his great heart ſupported him. At the ſaid Beaujeu, letters came to hand, appriſing him how the ducheſs of Auſtria had died of a fall from her horſe; for ſhe had been riding on a fiery little cob that had thrown her, falling on a log. Another verſion was, that this was not the immediate cauſe of her death, but that ſhe had died of a fever. However this be, ſhe was dead within a few days after the ſaid fall, to the irreparable damage of her ſubjects and alliance; for never after had they peace or ſafety. For ſhe was held in a much greater reverence, of thoſe of Gand, and the other towns, than was her huſband, in as much as ſhe was their ſovereign lady. And this fell out in the year fourteen hundred and eighty two. The ſaid lord made me liſten to all this news, being in much glee; and he farther told me, how the two children were in the hands of the Gandois, whom he knew to be ripe for any miſchief, and wavering in their allegiance to the houſe of Burgundy. And the thing, he ſeemed to think, had fallen out in a lucky moment for him; for the duke of Auſtria was young, and his father yet living. In addition to this, he was in apprehenſion on every hand; a foreigner beſides, and but ill ſupported. For the emperor, his father, was by much too niggardly; on which account, as was natural, he was leſs conſidered.

So, there and then, the King began to ſound and tamper with the chiefeſt of the Gandois, through the intermediary of my lord des Cordes; and to bring upon the ſtage the marriage of my lord, the Dolphin, with the daughter of the ſaid duke, our preſent queen Margaret. And the ſaid lord brought this about by means of none more than an old penſionary of the ſaid town, called William Rive, a dark and crafty man, and another, one Coppinel, a clerk of the town, who was beſides a ſhoemaker by trade, and a great man among them. For theſe are the claſs of perſons muſt be turned to account, when a multitude difaffected, or ripe and ready for revolt, is to be dealt with. The King, by this, had returned to Tours, where he ſhut himſelf up ſo cloſe that but few ever ſaw him; entering into a moſt marvellous fuſpicion of everybody, and living in a perpetual dread of an attempt on his authority or prerogative. He put away from about him all thoſe who had been habitually attendant on him; without, however, depriving them of their offices. He ſimply ſent them to their houſes, or their poſts. However, this did not hold long; as he lived but little after. And all forts of unaccountable things he did; fo much fo, that all who faw him, took him to be poffeffed, or out of his wits: but little did they know him. As to his being fufpicious; all great princes are fo; efpecially the more warier, and thofe who have made for themfelves an hoft of enemies, and incenfed many, as this one had done. And befides, he knew well, how little he was loved of the great ones of the realm; or, indeed, for that matter, of the fmall. For he had taxed the people more than ever prince did; and although it may have been his purpofe to have relieved them, as I have faid, this fhould have been attended to fooner. The King, Charles the seventh, was the firft who, with the connivance of certain ftout and hardy knights that were about him, and who had feconded and aided him in the recovery of Normandy and of Guyenne, then held by the Englifh; attempted and carried through this precedent; namely, the practice of levying taxes, at his pleafure, and independently of the co-operation of the States-General. And true it is, incredible amounts were called for, as well to garrifon the recovered territories, as to break up and difband the companies of freebooters with which they were infefted. So to this the lords of France confented, in return for certain penfions that he fecured to them, in confideration of the taxes which were to be levied on their lands. Had this King been longer fpared, with thofe of his counfel, who thought and acted with him, he had never halted where he did. But as it is, seeing all which has since fallen out, and must yet fall out, he has sufficiently burdened his own soul, and those of his successors, for in that he gave a cruel wound to the vitals of this kingdom, and which long must bleed. For it was he who instituted this terrible onus of a standing army, which he affected after the manner of the Italian courts. The said King Charles the seventh levied, at the time of his death, in one way or another, eighteen hundred thousand francs, upon his kingdom; and retained some seventeen hundred men at arms for all gendarmerie. And these were only employed to the ends for which they were raised; namely, the defence of the various provinces. And for a long time before his death, there was no more free quarter, or wandering abroad about the country; which was a wonderful respite to the people. Yet at the death of the King, our master, he was raising forty-seven hundred thousand francs, and had on foot some four or five thousand men at arms; and of footmen, as well for the camp, as garrison pensioners, upwards of twenty-five thousand. So it is little to be wondered at, if he had sundry misgivings and qualms of conscience; or that he could understand himself to be misliked. But if, on the one hand, he was filled with these alarms; on the other, he was reassured in the devotion of certain whom he had brought up, and who were under obligations to him. Of these there were many, and who, on their lives, had not been wanting to him. In addition to this, scarce a soul ever set foot within the gates of Plessis, (where he had shut himself up,) excepting his immediate servants, with the archers, of whom there were four hundred; and who, day and night, kept watch upon the gates, or paced, in companies, the walls. No lord, or other considerable personage was allowed to live in it, and but two or three, even of the greatest, were permitted to enter at a time. No one was in the habit of going to it, but my lord of Beaujeu, now Duke of Bourbon, who was his son-in-law. And all around the lying of the said Plessis, he had had planted a stout iron fence or rail; and inside the walls, a sort of *chevaux de frise*. The same was also at all the points by which the ditches of the said Plessis were accessible. Moreover, he had at the corners, four dovecot sort of towers made, of iron, wondrous thick, in which were loopholes pierced, whence his artillery could easily be discharged. And it was a marvellous sight for a man to look on, and it cost him more than twenty thousand francs. And, to crown all, he put forty crossbowmen, who, day and night, were in the ditches, and had orders to draw on every man who should approach by night, or before the gates were opened in the morning. For he had got it into his head, that his subjects were getting a little unmanageable; and that if they could only see their way, they might be disposed to attempt on his authority. And it is unqueftionable, that there was fome underhand talk, on the part of certain, of feizing on the fortrefs, and taking matters into their own hands; alleging that everything was at a ftandftill. But of fuch extremities, they ftopped fhort. And in this, they did wifely; for he had amply provided for their reception. He kept inceffantly changing his valets-de-chambre, with his other fervants; faying, that nature delighted in diverfity. For all fociety, he had about him two or three poor wretches, men of no condition, and of but equivocal reputation, and who, hence, could eafily divine, if they had any fenfe, that, with him would all their earthly profpects ceafe; and as much fell out. Nor did thefe people ever lay before him anything that was directed to him, let the import be what it might, faving only what went for the fafety and prefervation of the ftate; for, of any other matter, he now took thought no more. All he wanted, was to be left in peace, or in truce with all. To his phyfician he gave ten thoufand efcus the month; and even as much as fifty-four thoufand in five. Of lands, he made large donations to the church; but of thefe, none were allowed to hold; befides, they had enough and too much already.

Chapter 8.

How the King sent from Tours for one known as the Holy man of Calabria, thinking he would cure him; and of the unheard-of things which the said King did, during his malady, for the retention of his power.

Among others, the more known in their time, for their sanctity, the King sent into Calabria for one Brother Robert. The King called him, *The man of God*, in consideration of his holy life; and in his honour, the King, that now is, caused a monastery to be raised, at Plessis-du-parc, to replace the chapel, near Plessis, by the butting of the bridge. And the said hermit, when but eleven years of age, had betaken himself to a cave, and there he had remained till his forty-third year, or thereabouts; that is, till our King sent to him one of his stewards, who went, accompanied by the prince of Tarente, son to the King of Naples; for, without the consent of the Pope and his natural prince, he refused to go. And this, in so simple a man, showed much wariness. He had built two churches in the neighbourhood of where he lived; nor had he ever once tasted, from the time he took to this solitary kind of life, either fish, or flesh, or egg, or milk, or cheese, or butter; nor do I think I ever saw man alive who led so holy a life, or from whose lips the Holy Ghost did rather seem to speak. For he was neither a clerk nor lettered; nor had he ever learned anything. It may be, his Italian dialect helped a little to countenance the wonder. The said hermit passed through Naples, honoured and waited on, as though he had been some great Legate Apostolic, as well by the King, as his family. And he discoursed with them as a man would do, well versed in courts. Thence he took the road to Rome, where he was visited by all the cardinals. He had three several audiences of the Pope; they two alone. And at each time he was seated close by him, in a chair of state, and for three or four hours together, (which was a wonderful honour for so inconsiderable a person,) expressing himself, the while, with so much propriety, that there was no one who could choose but wonder. And our Holy Father allowed him to found an order called, The hermits of St. Francis. From Rome he continued toward our King, who received him as if he had been the Pope himself; casting himself on his knees before him, beseeching him, that it might please him to have his days prolonged. His reply was such as it became a considerate man to make. I have many a time heard him speak in the presence of our King, that now is, and of his court; and over a space of two months, and it really seemed as though he were inspired of God, such were the things that he urged and remonstrated; for, otherwise, he never could have uttered what he did. He is yet alive; and seeing no man can divine what way matters may yet fall out; I will say no more about them. Many thought it a good joke, the coming of this hermit, called, The holy man; but they little knew the inmost thoughts of this sagacious King, nor did they divine the ends he had in view.

Our King, then, was in this Plessis, but few being about him, saving only archers; racked with all these wretched suspicions of which I have spoken. But he had taken his measures; for no man was allowed to harbour, either in the field or in the town, of whom he had any sort of misgiving; but he had him removed, or ordered off by his archers. None but affairs of the last importance, did any one venture to broach. To look on him, one had rather taken him to be dead than alive; to see him was something almost beyond conception, such a skeleton was he. For all that, he was richly dressed; even more so than he had ever been in his better days, or than was his wont. He would be clad in nothing less than robes of crimson satin, lined with the choicest martin. He was ready enough with his purse, and without any sort of solicitation; for none had dared to ask anything of him, or indeed, to open their lips to him. Of more than one, he made sharp examples, and this, to keep himself feared, and lest he might come to have his power disputed; and as much, he told me himself. He dismissed his household, replaced them, broke gens-d'armes, docked pensions, and carried out all sorts of changes. He confessed to me, himself, some few days before his death, that his whole time was spent in nothing else than in making and in unmaking. He had himself more talked about, far and near, than ever king was; and this he did that the world should not fancy him to be dead. For, as I have said, few could say to themselves, they saw him; but when every body could see and hear for himself, of his carryings on, it was as much as they would do, to credit him to be but ill. Abroad, he had his emissaries on every hand; in England, to reconcile and smooth down to them the marriage; and he failed not to remit regularly what was there owing, as well to the king as to private parties. To Spain, he was all tact, amity, conciliation, and presents were lavished on every hand. He would have a good stout horse, or mule bought, let the figure be what it might. But it was principally with an eye to his own people, and not foreigners, that all this was done. Dogs were sent for, right and left; to Spain for a sort of mastiff; Brittany, for little jimpy greyhound bitches, hounds and spaniels, for which any price was given. From Valentia, he had brought little velvet coated dogs, and which he paid for at a higher figure than the owners even cared to ask. To Sicily, he would send for any well known mule, especially if the owner was some public officer, and he would make him take the double of its worth. From Naples, he had horses; and all sorts of wild and unheard of beasts kept coming from every quarter. From Barbary, came

The Death and Character of Louis XI. 351

a fort of little tiny lion, no bigger than a fox; and they called them, *Adits*. To Sweden and to Denmark, he fent after two kinds of creatures; one were elks, not unlike the ftag, and big as the buffalo, with fhort and thick horns. The others were called reindeers, and are fomething of the build and colour of the fallow deer; however, with larger horns. In fact, I have feen them with fo many as fifty-four branches. And for every of thefe beafts, he gave the merchants four thoufand five hundred German florins. Yet when they came to be brought before him, it was as much as he did, if he even faw them; nor, for the moft part, did he put any queftions to their keepers or their bringers. And, in fact, he was always doing fomething of the like, in order to continue himfelf even more feared, as well of his neighbours, as of his own fubjects, than hitherto he had ever been. And this was his drift, and to this end were all thefe things done.

Chapter 9.

How the marriage of my lord, the Dolphin, was concluded with Margaret of Flanders, and fhe conducted into France; at the vexation of which, King Edward, of England, died.

[This chapter, ranging a little wide of the object in view, which is fimply to reproduce the character of Louis XI., is purpofely omitted.]

CHAPTER 10.

How the King carried himself, as well toward his neighbours, as his subjects, during his malady; and of all was sent to him, from divers quarters, for his recovery.

Thus was this Flanders match confummated, which the King had had fo much at heart; and the Flemings were now at his difpofition. With Brittany, which, from his heart, he detefted, he was at peace; keeping them, however, in a perpetual ftate of alarm, owing to the body of troops that he continued on their frontier. Spain was alfo at peace with him; nor did the king and queen of that country afk any better than to continue fo. Befides, he kept hanging over them, as a perpetual fource of anxiety and coft, the affair of the county of Rouffillon, which he held of the houfe of Arragon, and had been made over to him by King John, of Arragon, father of the King of Caftille, who now is, as fecurity for certain conditions which were not yet complied with. Touching the Italian powers, he wifhed to be on terms with them. Some fort of half treaty there was with them, and embaffies he often had going and coming. In Germany, the Switzers were as much his fubjects as his own people; the Kings of Scotland and of Portugal were his allies. A part of Navarre was at his bidding. His fubjects trembled before him. What he willed, that inftant was carried out; without a word or without a murmur. There was nothing that could be thought of toward his recovery, which was not sent to him from every corner of the globe. The Pope, Sixtus, the laſt dead, hearing that the King deſired to be poſſeſſed of the corporal, or veſt, in which my lord, St. Peter had officiated, at once diſpatched it, together with other relics, and which afterwards were returned. The holy vial, which is at Rheims, and never yet had been removed of its place, was brought into his bedchamber, at Pleſsis, and was ſtanding on his cupboard at the time of his death. He was intending to have himſelf anointed with it, like as he had been at his coronation; though ſome ſay, he was to have had his whole body ſo, which is ſcarce likely, for the ſaid holy vial is very ſmall, and holds but little. I ſaw it then, and alſo when they were putting the ſaid lord into his grave, at our Lady of Clery. The Turk, the ſame that at preſent reigns, ſent him an embaſſage, which got as far as Rheims, in Provence; but the ſaid lord refuſed to accredit it, or to allow it to approach him any nearer. The ſaid ambaſſador brought with him a great quantity of relics, which had fallen, at Conſtantinople, into the hands of the ſaid Turk. All theſe he offered to the King, together with a conſiderable ſum of money, provided the ſaid lord would undertake to keep in France the brother of the ſaid Turk, who was then there, in the hands of the Knights of Rhodes;

and is now at Rome, in thofe of the Pope. By all this is to be feen the greatnefs and importance of our King, and by how much he was confidered and honoured of the world, and how everything which either religion, piety, wealth or grandeur could think of, or afford, were placed at his difpofition, and for the prolonging of his days. However, it was all to no avail. He had to pafs by that gate where all have paffed before him. One grace did God vouchfafe to him. For even as he had created him more wife, more liberal, more virtuous, in every way, than any, the princes of his time, and who were his adverfaries, and his neighbours; fo did he permit him alfo to outlive them and furpafs them in length of days. However, this was but with fome of them. For the duke of Burgundy, Charles; the duchefs, his daughter; King Edward; Galeas, duke of Milan, with King John of Arragon, were all dead fome few years before. As for the duchefs of Auftria, King Edward and himfelf; there was no difference between them worth fpeaking of. In every one of them, was there of good and of evil; for they were but men and mortal. Yet, without any fort of prepoffeffions, I may fafely fay, that all the attributes becoming the ftate of a king and a prince were evidenced of him, in a higher degree, than of any of the others. I have feen them almoft all, and know perfectly of what they were capable; fo I fpeak not lightly.

Chapter II.

How King Louis, on his deathbed, had his son, Charles, sent for; of the ordinances and injunctions with which he charged, as well him as others.

In this year, fourteen hundred and eighty-three, the King was moved to send for my lord, the Dolphin, his son, whom now, for many years, he had not seen. For he was unwilling he should be permitted abroad, as well on account of the great tenderness of his constitution, as out of a dread lest he should come to be laid hands on, and that, under colour of his name, trouble might be stirred up in the state. For as much had been practised against the king, his father, in his own case, when a child of no more than eleven years, by certain great lords of the realm. And this war was called, *The Praguerie*. But it came to nothing, and was no more than the passing disaffection of a court.

Above all things, he recommended to his son, my lord, the Dolphin, certain of his people, and expressly charged him, on no pretext whatsoever, to remove this or that officer; giving him as his reason, that when the King Charles the seventh, his father, was called to God, he had dismissed all the more sufficient and famous knights of the realm, who had served and seconded his said father, in the recovery of Normandy and Guienne, and in driving the English out of the country; and had helped him to restore peace and order, and leave it rich and powerful, (as it came to him,) and for all which, his miftake, he after paid dearly; for it brought on the war known as, *For the public weal*, (of which I have fpoken elfewhere,) and which had gone well nigh to coft him his crown.

And foon after that the King had left off to talk with my lord, the Dolphin, and the marriage had been confummated, (as I faid,) the malady, (and of which he trefpaffed,) came upon him, on a Monday, lying on him till the Saturday following, the laft day but one of Auguft, fourteen hundred and eighty-three. And I was about him till the laft; for which reafon I will fay fomething of it. And as foon as the attack was on him, he loft his fpeech, as had been the cafe in the preceding one. And when it came back, it was to find him more feeble than he had ever yet been; although he had already been fo weak, that fcarce could he carry his hand to his mouth. And now fo ghaftly and fhrunken was he, that it was very piteous to us all to look on him. The faid lord, now giving himfelf up for dead, difpatched incontinent for my lord de Beaujeu, his fon-in-law, at prefent duke of Bourbon, commanding him to go to the king, (for fo he called him,) his fon, who was at Amboife, and to commend him to him, as alfo all thofe who had ferved him. And he put into his hands the entire charge and government of the faid king; enjoining him, that certain parties were not to be allowed to be about him, and for which he gave him weighty and ample reasons. And if the said lord de Beaujeu had only carried out his orders; or, at the least, a part of them, (for there was something of so high a nature, or so contradictory, it was not to be gone through with,) and if, in general, he had kept closer to his counsel, I think it had been better, as well for himself, as for the state; seeing all that has since fallen out. After him he sent to the king, the chancellor and seals, with all pertaining to his office. He dispatched to him also a portion of the Archers of his Guard, their captains with them. And after went his kennels, his hawks, and all belonging thereto, with everything of the sort. And all who came to him, he sent them on to Amboise, to the king, for so he called him, entreating them to be faithful to him. And of each was some injunction carried; especially by Stephen de Vers, in whose charge the young king had been brought up, and who had been his principal valet-de-chambre. And our King had already made him bailly of Meaux. His utterance never again left him from the time it returned, nor yet his senses; nor, indeed, had he ever them so clear; for incessantly he kept purging, which drew from him all the vapours of the brain. Nor ever once, in all his sufferings, did he complain, as all conditions of people do, when they find themselves unwell. At least I am one of that sort; and I know many more who are the same. Besides, it is generally held, that it is a relief to complain.

Chapter 12.

A comparison of all the miseries and sufferings undergone of King Louis, with those which he inflicted on many others; with a continuation of all he did, and had done to him, up to the time of his end.

And still he continued to make himself understood. And this, his malady, hung on him, (as I have said,) from the Monday till the Saturday, at night. And if I am about to make a comparison of the miseries and the tortures which he inflicted upon others, with those that he himself was called on to endure at his death, it is not without the hope, that they may have been the means of translating him direct to Paradise; and that God may have been pleased to accept them in the place of Purgatory. And if they may neither have been so grievous, nor so protracted as those which he imposed upon others; again, he was of another and more considerable standing among men than they had been. And if we will remember, that all his days, he had never known restraint, but, contrary, been so feared that Europe seemed to have been created but to do him reverence, then must we allow, that that little, so contrary to the grain and temper of the man, must have also been no less direful to him to submit to. And still he pinned his faith in this good father, who was now at Plessis, and had been brought from

Calabria; and he was for ever sending to him, telling him, how he well knew, that if he only would, he could easily prolong his days. For despite all the ordinances and powers he had delegated, by those about him, to my lord, the Dolphin, his son; he never lost heart, but still had hopes to come round. And, beyond a doubt, had it so fallen out, he had made short work with the new court that he had sent to Amboise, to be about the young king. And seeing the infatuation with which he clung to the said hermit, it was concluded by a certain ecclesiastic, together with others, that he was to be plainly told, how he was only deluding himself, and that he had nothing now to look to but God, and his mercy. And when this was to be broken to him, Master Jacques Coctier, his physician, was to be present; for all his hope was in him; and he gave him, every month, ten thousand ecus, in the hope to prevail upon him to lengthen out his days. And this was ordered of Master Oliver, so that all his thoughts might now be dedicated to the discharge of his conscience, and he should no longer place his reliance either in the holy man, in whom he trusted, or in the said Master Jacques, his physician. And even as he had, in pure caprice, and without any sort of trial, probation, advanced the said Master Oliver and his fellows to a dignity other than were befitting to any such persons; so also took they upon themselves, without any sort of diffidence, or circumlocution, to break to such a prince, a sentence which it but ill sorted with any such messengers to carry. For there was none of that becoming reverence, or consideration shown that the circumstances called for, or which would have been of those who, all their lives, had been about him; yet who, out of pure waywardness, he had, a little before, dismissed from his attendance. [1] For, even as in the case of two famous persons, the duke de Nemours and the count de St. Pol, whom, in his day, he had put to death, (and of one of which verdicts, on his death-bed, he confessed the wickedness, and repented him; the other, not;) having their sentence carried to them by a commission encharged with the same, and which commission, in two or three words, announced to them their fate; handing them over to a confessor, for the discharge of their consciences, in that little moment which was remaining to them: so, likewise, did the aforesaid open to our King, this fearful doom, in terms, brutal, barbarous and unfeeling. For they told him, in half a word, " Sir, we must do our duty by you; you need not be running after the holy man, or any other man. It is all up with you. You must think about your soul; for nothing now can save you." And this they all stuck to, and confirmed. But all he told them was, " I still hope God will bring me round; peradventure, I am not so bad as you may suppose."

What a shock must it have been to him to hear

[1] See note T, at the end.

such a message, and so announced! for never was there man who more feared death, or more passionately wearied heaven and earth to avert his hour, than he. And, all his life, he had enjoined his servants, and me among the rest, that if ever we should come to see him in the article of death, on no account was he to be told of it; but we were simply to say to him, that, perhaps, it would be as well to confess himself. But never was that cruel word, *death*, to escape us, for he did not believe he should ever survive it, or have the heart to abide so terrible an enunciation. However, he submitted to it, calmly, as did he to all his other sufferings, to the very last; and even more resignedly than any man I have ever seen die. To his son, whom he now styled, King, he sent repeated instructions. His confession was devoutly made; and his prayers he reiterated almost uninterruptedly; being such as the occasion called for, or were enjoined of the sacraments, which, of his own accord, he received. And, as I have said, he spoke as clearly as though nothing had been upon him; thinking of nought save what might be for the advantage of the King, his son; signifying, how he wished the lord des Cordes to be about his son for another six months, and how they were to divert him from any thoughts of attempting Calais, or any other place; alleging, that though he may have been disposed, himself, to make such experiments, and for the advantage of the king and kingdom, yet still they were hazardous; more especially any attack on Calais, which would assuredly bring the English on him. And he desired, above all things, that the kingdom should be left in peace, for five or six years, which was more than he had ever allowed it to be in, in his lifetime. And to be honest, it wanted it sadly. For, albeit, it was vast and full of resources, so also was it poor and miserable; and this, chiefly, through the incessant to and fro of gens-d'armes; wandering from one country to another. He forbade them to get into any trouble with Brittany; but told them, that duke Francis was to be left in peace, and no way provoked. And as much he enjoined toward all the neighbour states; so that the king and kingdom might remain in quiet till such time as the king were grown, and of age to act upon his own discretion.

And thus indiscreetly, as you have heard, was his end announced. And this I have the rather dwelt upon, in as much as in a preceding paragraph, I had begun to draw a comparison of all the miseries which he had inflicted upon others, who were at his mercy, and under him, with those that he underwent, himself, at his death; so that it may be seen, that, albeit, they were neither so grievous nor so long, (as I have stated in the said paragraph,) yet, nevertheless, they were considerable; remembering his natural disposition, which called more imperatively for compliance than did that of any man of his time. Nor had any had more of it; fo that ever fo fmall a flight or incompliance was a very terrible vifitation. Some five or fix months before this death, he entered into a marvellous fufpicion of all forts of men; but, more efpecially, fuch as might naturally look for power. Of his very fon he ftood in awe; and he had him clofely guarded, nor was any man permitted accefs to him; either to fee him, or to fpeak with him, fave with his licenfe. And at the laft he came to be jealous of his own daughter, and his fon-in-law, the now duke of Bourbon; and he would alfo know who and how many were with them, when they came to Pleffis. And at length he quafhed a board which the faid duke prefided over at Pleffis, and by his own orders. And at the time his faid fon-in-law and the count de Dunois returned, with the deputation which had been prefent at the nuptials of the king, his fon, and the queen, at Amboife; and as they were about, with their train, to enter the faid chateau; the faid lord, who was wondrous guardful of the gates, looking from a window that gave upon the court, and feeing them enter, called to him a captain of his guard, and bade him go and flide his fingers gently over the perfons of the following of the faid lords, fo as to afcertain whether they had piftols concealed beneath their robes; but that he was to do it warily, as though frolicking with them, fo that they might not fufpect him! Now, fee by this, if, all his life, he had made men to live in the fear and the dread of him, it was not now returned to him in his own coin. And where was that man to place his confidence, whose heart misgave him of his own son, son-in-law and daughter? And this I say, not of him only, but of all other lords, who rule by hate and not by love, that never, till their old age, do they meet with their recompense. By a just retribution, the man who feared them, they live to fear. And what a hell on earth was it to this king to be such a prey to all these alarms and passions?

He had for his physician, as I have said, one Master Jacques Coctier, to whom he gave the bishopric of Amiens for his nephew, and other offices and lands for himself or his friends, over and above his stated stipend. And the said physician comported himself so shamefully by him, that one would not so much as think of speaking to his valet in the infamous and insulting manner he did to his king. Yet in such a fear of him did the said lord live, that he dare not give him his discharge. And of this rudeness he bitterly complained to those about him, yet he never could muster up the courage to dismiss him. For, once, when he approached it, the said physician had told him, impudently, and to his face, "I know well you will send me packing, one of "these fine days, as you have done all the rest of "them; but (and here he confirmed it with a thun- "dering oath), if you do, you will be dead before the "week is out." The shock of this he never recovered; nor did he ever after give over to fawn on him and to bribe him; which, assuredly, was little short of Purgatory, on this side the grave, considering the observance in which he had been held of the highest and the greatest among men.

It is not to be denied, that he had had very grievous prisons, or rather, cages, made; some of iron, others of wood; lined, as well within as without, with plates of metal, and faced with open bars. They were of eight feet square, and of the height of a man, and rather better. The first who ever invented such things, was the bishop of Verdun, who was also the first to try how they fitted. For he was put into the first, as soon as ever it was finished, and in it he lay fourteen years. Many is the one who has cursed them since, and I among the rest; for, under the present king, I had a taste of them for eight months. Besides these, he had procured, from Germany, chains, very terrible and massive, for the feet. And to one end was a ring attached, to hold the ankle, something like the locket of a necklace, and to the other, a great ball of iron; out of all conscience, weighty. And these were called, *The King's little collars or bracelets*. Yet, for all that, I have seen many prisoners of distinction with these shackles on their feet, who came, later, to be advanced, and owe their all to him. And among the rest, a son of my lord de la Gruture, in Flanders, who was taken in a battle, and whom the said lord married, making him his chamberlain and seneschal of Anjou, and giving him one hundred lances; alfo the lord de Siennes, another prifoner of war; and the lord de Verger; to both of whom he affigned gens-d'armes, and each became either chamberlain to him, or to his fon, and held other great offices. As much he did for my lord de Rochefort, brother of the conftable, and one named Roquebertin, a Catalan, and also a prifoner of war, to whom he did many kindneffes, as to fundry others, whom it would be too long to name, and of divers nations. But all this is foreign to the matter in hand. So I will revert to what I have already faid; that, if in his time, he had been the contriver of thefe miferable and heartlefs boxes; fo, likewife, before his end, came he to find himfelf in fimilar, albeit lefs ftrait, as alfo to fuffer a more mortal agony, than any he had ever caufed to another. And this I take to have been a great grace, godfend, for him; and to have been a part of his purgatory. And I have told it all, too, to fhow how no man, let him be who or what he will, but fuffers, either in fecret or notorioufly; but more efpecially thofe who have made others fo to do.

The faid lord, towards the clofe of his days, caufed, as I have faid, his chateau of Pleffis to be environed with a ftout iron fence. And the walls he had fpiked or ftudded with iron nails, with jagged heads, and as thick as they could ftand. He was well aware that this fortification would never withftand the affault of a regular army, or yet a fiege; but this was not what he dreaded. What he was in apprehenfion of, was merely this — that fome lord or lords, either by ftratagem, or connivance of thofe within, might come to be mafters of the place; and that then they would take the government into their own hands, fetting him afide, as a man now out of his wits, and no longer fit to be in authority. The gate of Pleffis was never opened till eight of the clock; nor was the drawbridge lowered till that hour; at which time the officers entered, and the captains placed the ordinary fentinels. After this, the Archer guard was pofted, as well at the gate as about the court, as it might be in the ftricteft frontier town. And no one entered but by the wicket, nor then, fave to the knowledge of the faid lord; excepting, always, the maiftres-d'hôtel and perfons of that condition, whofe bufinefs could not be with him. Now, would it be even poffible to retain a king, to keep him more rigoroufly, religioufly, or in a clofer prifon, than this king kept himfelf? The cages in which he had confined the others, it is true, were but of eight feet fquare : yet had he, fo great a prince, but a little court yard in which to turn himfelf; and even into that he ventured but feldom; reftricting himfelf to a gallery, fcarce leaving it but for this room or that. And he could get to his chapel without croffing the faid court. After this, will any one venture to fay, that this king did not fuffer as much as the reft? he, who thus buried himfelf alive, had himfelf guarded; who was in a constant apprehension of his own children, and of his nearest blood; who chopped and changed, daily, the servants whom, from children, he had seen around him, all whose honour, health and substance was of him; who, in no living soul could put his confidence, but that he must shut himself up with all these hideous bolts and bars and gates? And if the prison was more considerable than the ordinary run of prisons, so was the prisoner more considerable than the ordinary run of prisoners. It may be said, there have been spirits more suspicious than his own. If so, they were not of his time; and, peradventure, were they neither so sagacious as he, nor had they such subservient subjects. And, mayhap, they have been cruel and tyrants, but this man was cruel to none but to those who had first provoked him. I have not thus dwelt on what is said above, in order merely to show the natural jealousy of our King, but to signify, that the resignation with which he bowed to all his trials, so like to those that he inflicted upon others, was, in my opinion, so much punishment which our Lord would commute to him in the world to come. I speak as well of all those indignities to which, in his extremity, he was subjected, as of all those sicknesses, sore and terrible to him, and that he trembled at the very thoughts of, or ever they were on him. And all this I enlarge on, that all those who come after him, may have some little more bowels toward their subjects than he had, and be some little lefs ready to punifh than he was. However, I do not wifh to deal too hardly with him, nor can I fay, I have ever feen a better prince. And if he oppreffed his people, this is alfo to be faid, no other was fuffered to do it; ftranger, or of his own country.

And now, after all his agonies, his fufferings, his fufpicions, it pleafed our Lord to work a miracle on him; for he reftored him, as well in body as in mind; as is ever his way, in effecting his miracles. For he removed him out of this miferable world, in a wonderful relapfe, no lefs of health than of underftanding; his memory clear and vigorous to the laft. All the sacraments were received; nor could we perceive him to be in any kind of fuffering. And he was inceffantly repeating to himfelf his *Pater nofter*, and his laft words were about his sepulture. And thofe who were to follow his corpfe were named. And he told to thofe who were about him, how he yet hoped to be fpared to a faturday; a grace he had entreated our Lady to procure him, in whofe interpofition was all his hope and fiance. And even as he had prayed, fo it fell; for he trefpaffed on a faturday, the laft day but one of Auguft; in the year of our Lord fourteen hundred and eighty three; at eight of the clock, in his chateau of Pleffis; where the faid malady had firft come on him, the Monday preceding. And may our Saviour have mercy on his foul; and have it received into his kingdom of Paradife!

CHAPTER 13.

A diverſion on all the miſeries of the ſtate of man; more eſpecially of princes; as ſhown in thoſe who lived in the times of the author; and firſtly of King Louis.

Little need the poor and the miſerable of this world build their hopes, or put their faith in the profit thereof, when ſo great a king as this, after having ſo much ſuffered in it, ſo much laboured, was compelled, at laſt, to abandon all; unable, by an hour, to prolong his days, though heaven and earth were wearied thereto. I have known him, and I was with him, for I was his ſervant, in his beſt days; and I have beheld him at the height of his proſperity, yet never did I know him vacant to ſorrow and to care. Above all diverſions, he loved that of the chaſe; hawking alſo in its ſeaſon; yet he never took the ſame delight in birds he did in hunting. With women, he never meddled; at leaſt, ſo long as I was about him. For it was toward the time I firſt came to him, that he had loſt a ſon, which had wonderfully arreſted him; ſo much ſo, that, there and then, he made a vow to heaven, in my preſence, that, ſaving the queen, his wife, he never again would touch any woman. And although this is no more than is enjoined on us all, of Holy Church, it was certainly a wonderful inſtance of ſelfdenial on the part of one who had ſo many at his diſpoſition, thus religiouſly to abide by his oath : the more fo, as the queen, however refpectable a lady, was not altogether the one in whom a man would naturally look to find the moft delight.

And of all this hunting came well nigh as much vexation as delight. For his whole foul was in it ; fo much fo, that he would force the ftags, as one poffeffed. He would rife before the day, go any diftance, nor would he leave off for any fort of weather. So, as often as not, by the time he got back, he was dead beat, and wafpifh, and out of humour with everything and everybody. For this is not the kind of fport that will always accommodate itfelf to the fantafy of thofe who are given to it. However, he was more an adept in it than any prince of his time; and this, by the allowance of all. And at this work he would always be, lodging about in the villages, till fuch time as there came word of war; for, fcarce a fummer would go over, but fome account or other had to be fettled between himfelf and duke Charles of Burgundy. And in the winter there would be truces. He was alfo often in trouble about the county of Rouffillon, with John, the King of Arragon, father to Peter of Caftille, at prefent King of Spain. And the one and the other of them were poor, and already in difficulties with their fubjects in Barcelona and elfewhere. And though the fon had nothing, or yet anything to look forward to, farther than the fucceffion of the King, don Frederic of Caftille, his wife's brother, (and which fince came to him,) yet they managed to give the king a great deal of annoyance; for, at heart, they were attached to their own country and laws. And all this coſt our king and kingdom dear; for then there fell or was taken, many a brave man; and no end of money was ſpent, for the war laſted long. So that the time which he allowed himſelf for amuſement, was but a very ſlender portion of the year; and he was always in ſome travail or other, as I have ſaid. And even when his body was at reſt, his ſpirits were at work; for he had occupation on every hand. And he was invariably interfering in the affairs of his neighbours, or in thoſe of his own ſubjects. He had ſpies in their courts and camps; and ſowed diviſion on every hand. When he was at war, nothing was prayed for but peace or truce; when at peace, or during truce, it was as much as ever he could do to ſupport them. With all ſorts of little peddling things, he mixed himſelf up, and which it had been more prudent and dignified for him to have left alone. But ſuch was the man's nature, and thus was it. With all this, he had a memory ſo prodigious, that nothing eſcaped it; and he knew everybody, as well within his own kingdom, as abroad.

In very truth, he ſeemed rather to have been born to regiment a globe, a world, than a ſimple empire.

Of his extreme youth, I ſpeak not; for I was not about him. As ſoon as he was grown, he was married to a daughter of Scotland, and againſt his inclination;

nor took he any delight in her, so long as she lived. After her death, to be out of the way of the factions and troubles of the King, his father's court, he withdrew to Dauphiny, (which was his own,) and where he was resorted to of many considerable persons; in fact, more than he had the means to retain. And now being in Dauphiny, he married a daughter of the duke of Savoy, which he had no sooner done than he fell out with his father-in-law; and terrible wars they had between them. The King Charles, his father, coming to see him with so menacing a following, and so large a body of gens-d'armes to be at his disposition, determined to put himself at the head of a large army, and to drive him out of the kingdom. To this end, he got under way; and at length, after an infinity of trouble, he succeeded in detaching a good many of his adherents, having enjoined them, in their character of subjects, and under the accustomed penalties, to leave his son and come over to him. And if they submitted, it was to the intense indignation of the King, our master; who, though still in a condition to hold his own, well considering the aroused choler of the King, his father, thought better to withdraw before him, and leave him master of the country. Thence he went, and some few with him, to the court of the duke of Burgundy; who received him in a manner becoming his rank, disparting of his means to him and to his principal attendants, as the count de Comminges, the lord de

Montaubon and others, in the form of penſion, and at a rate of ſo much by the year. In addition to this, during all the time of their ſtay, he was in the habit of making occaſional gratuities to his ſervants. Yet, ſuch was the charge to which he was put for the ſupport of ſo large a body of retainers, that he was often in want of money, which was an unfailing ſource of anxiety and vexation; ſo much ſo, that he was compelled either to borrow it, or to beg it, which was a ſore humiliation to a prince who, all his life, had rather been uſed to lend and to give. Nor was it all ſmooth ſailing in this court of Bourgogne; for he was under the neceſſity of conciliating and cringing to the duke and his principal governors, or elſe they would have grumbled by reaſon of his too long ſtay; for he was among them ſix years; and all this while, the King, his father, kept plying them with embaſſies, urging that he ſhould either be expelled, or given up to him. And from all this you may eaſily think, that he did not exactly eat the bread of idleneſs, or that he was exempted from his trials and ſolicitudes. When then was the time in which he can be ſaid to have taſted of either pleaſure or repoſe? all theſe things well conſidered. I do verily believe, from the day of his birth till the day of his death, never did he know but of travail and of care. And I think, were all the days ſummed up in which he proved more of diſtraction and of joy than of labour and of ſorrow, they would be found to make a very little figure.

Methinks there would be told one day of pleasure and of ease of heart, for twenty of bitterness and of despair.

He lived about sixty-one years. Curiously, he had got it into his head, that he was not to pass his sixtieth year; alleging, that now, for very many generations, no king of France had: some say, since the time of Charlemagne. However, the King, our master, was well on in his sixty-first year.

* * * * *
* * * * *

Conclusion of the Author.

Thus have we seen the ends of all these great men, and in this little time; and who had, one and all, all their days, been toiling and striving after power and glory; with all the travails, sorrows, cares they underwent: how, their days they shortened; and how, peradventure, their souls they jeopardized. And here, I speak not of the Turk; his account, I take to be settled by this, and that he is now lodged where all his predecessors have gone before him. Of our King, I am not without the hope, (as I have already said,) that our Lord has had mercy on him: as much will he have on the others, if good it seemeth to him. But, to speak more humanly, (as a man who, though he may have but little learning, has yet had some little conversance with this world, and the ways thereof), had it not been wiser in them, and would it not be wiser in all princes; nor only in them, but in those of the middling sort, who are their subjects, to follow a more medium course, in all these matters? that is to say, to be less careful, less painful, more moderate in their desires, to have fewer things in hand; to hold their God in a greater reverence; to be less intolerant toward their neighbours, less oppressive toward their people; less the tyrants which I have, in my book, shown them to be; and instead, more to take their pleasure and their ease? For, by this would their lives be more long; old age, death and infirmity would later come upon them; and when death did come, it would leave them more unfeignedly, and more generally regretted; whilst fewer would be gaping or longing for it; and less, too, would they apprehend that death.

Could one possibly find more telling instances whereby to be convinced, how poor a thing is man; what a very nothing, and how miserable is his life; and that there is no help for it, for the great, or for the small, but that, incontinent they be dead, they must be held in the loathing and the horror of the living? Nor is this all. For needs must the soul, when it doth doff its mortal cerement, attend, and before the Almighty, his judgment seat. And this is a truth; that, no sooner hath the soul the body left, than, in that instant, is the sentence given, and according to the deeds, which of it were done in the flesh. And this judgment is called, *The judgment singular.*

PHILIPE DE COMMINES.

A PLEASANT TALE OF LOUIS XI.

MONG sundry other pretty little tricks, artifices, contrivances, gallantries, perpetrated by this good King, in his day, was this, that, in a civil way, he managed to get shut of his brother, the duke de Guyenne, and at a time, too, when the poor gentleman looked for nothing less than such a mark of his attachment, seeing the many, less considerable, which, every day, were heaped upon him. In fact, so happily did the King play his part, (for the decease, he most passionately deplored,) that no one would ever have suspected anything about the matter, had it not been for a fool that had belonged to his said brother, but whom, after his death, he took into his service. As the story is a pleasant one, I will give it.

One day, at Clery, being on his knees, at his precious prayers and devotions, before the great altar and our Lady, whom he called, *His guardian angel;* no one near him, excepting this fool, and of whom he made no account, taking him to be too big an ass to make head or tail out of what might come from him, he begins, *Ha, my good Lady, my little love, my pricele/s friend, in whom has ever been my confolation and my joy; you muft pray to God for me, and be my interceffor with him, and get him to forgive me the death of my brother, whom I had poifoned by that rafcally abbot of St. John.* (Obferve, although the fellow had done no more than he ordered him, how he calls him, *rafcally;* and, in truth, it is no more than he, and all the like of him, deferve to be called.) *It is to you that I confefs myfelf, as to my good patronefs and miftrefs. And, after all, what elfe could I have done? He would perfift in troubling the kingdom. Get me pardoned, then, dear Lady, and I know of fomething nice that I have for you.* I fuppofe by this he muft have meant fome offering or other; for, every year, it was his cuftom to make great and coftly prefents to the Church. But, as it turned out, the fool had neither been fo far off, nor fo bereft of his ears or his wits, but he had managed to fuck in this moft rich piece of confidence, and not only that, but to carry it about with him till dinner time, when, feeing the King at table, he gave him the benefit of a fecond edition, aloud, and before all the company; telling him, over and over again, to his face, that he had made away with his brother. Who was amazed, if it was not the King? (One cannot be too much on their guard with thefe fools; for, fometimes, they are a match for the fhrewdeft. They out with everything they fee or hear, or, by that ſtrange, unaccountable fort of inſtinct, or divination they manage to come by.) After this, this fool was but little feen about; for he fent him packing by the felfsame road his brother went, and which fo many had gone before; and this for fear, left, by ſticking to his ſtory, the fcandal might come to ſtick to himſelf.

I remember, now more than fifty years ago, when a lad, at College, in Paris, having heard this ſtory from an old canon, who was well on to eighty years of age. And this ſtory has been handed down to this day, from canon to canon, and been confirmed to me by others fince. In the *Annals of Bouchet* may be feen the wickedneſs, with the miferable end and the remorfes of this wretched abbot.

BRANTÔME.

SELECTIONS FROM MONTAIGNE.

That to philosophize, is to learn to die.

*   *   *   *

THE end of all our ways is death [1]; the goal to be for ever in our sight. Let it affright us, and how is another step to be taken but in trembling and in fear! True; there is the remedy of the vulgar sort; not so much as to think on it. But from what a very blockishness must this miserable impassibility proceed: needs must they bridle the ass by the stern.

It is no great wonder [2] so many are let into the trap. Let but slip, as of unawares, the name of death among them, and straight are they in a sweat, and nigh to a man will they cross themselves, as though it had been the devil himself. And in as much as he, death, must get into their testaments; catch a man of them setting his fist to one, till his physician shall have given him his quietus! And then, what between

---

[1] See note U, at the end.
[2] See note V, at the end.

the agony of his mind and the agony of his body, God knows what a pretty kettle of fish he makes of it. And in as much as death was a word, which, roundly averred, grated somewhat too harshly upon the Roman ear, as though carrying with it a certain unhappy augury, that people had fallen upon a periphrastic manner of imparting its equivalent, when occasion necessitated an allusion to the same. For, instead of flatly telling you, *that So and so was dead*, they would say, *Were he now alive, he would be here, or doing this, or that*; preferring, rather, to touch upon life though past, than death though present. It is from them that has come down to us the expression, *The late Mr. So and so*.

The old saw is to the point; " A long loan is as " good as a gift." I was born between eleven and twelve of the clock, on the last day of February, fifteen hundred and thirty three; reckoning by our present computation ; the year beginning with the first of January. So it is precisely a fortnight since I completed my thirty ninth year: clearly I have a right to as many again. Would it not be very folly in me to begin, thus early in the day, to busy and to flurry myself about matters so palpably removed ? But ho, friend ; whither away : young and old are hurried from the scene alike ; and where the man but makes his exit, as though that instant he were entering upon the stage ? Of what avail to preach, to moralize, so long as the pattern of Methusaleh is before us, never a foul of us, nay, though one foot be already in the grave, but will take himfelf to have twenty years of marrow in his bones. Befides, poor fool that thou art, who hath foretold to thee the number of thy days? Is it upon the pleafant cozenage of a phyfician that thy hopes are built? Better look about thee; upon things as they are, as experience fhoweth them to be. According to the ordinary run of life, you have to be thankful that you are yet among the living. You have already outlived the accuftomed limits. And that it is fo, you have but to reckon up, of all whom you have known, how many more are they, in comparifon, who have been called away, ere they have arrived unto your years, than after. And even of thofe who have achieved unto themfelves renown with pofterity, count them up, and I will pledge myfelf to fhow you a rounder total who have departed before, than after, their thirty fifth year. It is confonant to reafon, as to piety, that we fhould accept, as the meafure of our humanity, the precedent of our Lord and Saviour, Jefus Chrift; thirty years. No more was reached of Alexander the great; the greateft man, being merely man, who ever lived.

By how many avenues will death furprife us! Fevers, agues, maladies, with all their train, e'en docked from the account. Who would have ever thought to have feen a duke of Britainy ftifled to death, as one of them was, in a crowd, at the entry of

Pope Clement, my countryman, into Lyons? Have we not feen one of our kings to be killed, really, in the frolic and the femblance of a fight? and of his progenitors, another to perifh, miferably, of the joftling of an hog? Of what avail was it to Æfchylus, a crumbling roof about his ears, to feek his fhelter neath the cope of heaven? lo, an eagle cracks a tortoife on his pate! Died there not another of the choking of the kernel of a grape? an emperor, as he was combing himfelf, of the tooth of a rack: Æmylius Lepidus to have tripped on the fill of a door; Aufidius of the flamming of another, as he was entering to his hall of counfell? In the arms of a woman, gave they not up the ghoft, Cornelius Gallus, prætor; Tigillinus, captain of the watch, at Rome; Ludovic, the fon of Guy de Gonfagne, of Mantua the marquis; and, more terrible yet to be told, Speufippus, the Platonician, with one of our own popes? See poor Bebius, in his hall of judgment, remitting to a week the fentence of a caufe, or ever the week were gone, hurried away himfelf to his account: Caius Julius, the phyfician, as he would open the eyes of another; behold, his own for ever clofed in death! And if I might mingle with all this, inftances which have come under mine own knowledge, I could tell of an own brother, the captain St. Martin, who, though but three and twenty, had already given ample earneft of his coming prime. For he, playing at tennis, and having received a blow from the ball, at the back of the ear, and to all appearance, a very nothing, abated no jot his sport; yet in five or six hours, he was a dead man; and of an apoplexy, caused by that very blow. With such examples and warnings as these before our eyes; of such daily and hourly recurrence, how were it even possible to drive away the thoughts of death from our minds; or that at every turn, we should not look to find ourselves face to face with him? But what matters all this, you will say, so long as we do not trouble our heads about it? Your philosophy is also mine; and in what manner soever I could see a chance of preserving myself from such assaults, though it were under the hide of a calf, I am not the man to be above it. All I want, and pray for, is, to be enabled to pass my days in ease: the best entertainment I can procure to myself, I take, how little pretentious, or exemplary soever it may appear in the eyes of the world.

But it is madness to suppose such a game is to be carried on for ever. They go, they come, they trot, they dance, but never a word of death. All this is very fine, so long as it lasts. But when death does come, as come it will; or in an hour they look not for, to them, their wives, their friends, their children; what sighs, what moans, what tears, what lamentations, do we not see? Can any one thing be pictured, more broken, confounded, distracted, or amazed! These matters must be sooner looked to: forewarned is forearmed.

And as for that beaftly infenfibility of the commoner
fort, even fuppofing, by any poffibility, it might once
come to be harboured of any reflecting breaft, (and
which, I am confident, it never could), on fuch conditions, one had better, far, be without it. If he were an
adverfary from whom our heels would carry us, I would
have every man of us to take to them. But feeing that
all fuch thoughts are vain; that he will collar you as
well in the retreat, as in the field; and in as much
as there is no armour proof to his affault, let us learn,
betimes, to abide his fhock, firm and undaunted. And
firft and foremoft, to defpoil him of that great advantage
wherein he lordeth it over us, let us take a clean contrary method to that of the common. Let us take
away from him all his ftrangenefs; let us touch him, and
let us handle him; let him be of our familiars. Let
nothing be fo ever prefent to us as the thoughts of death;
under every afpect, and under every form. At the
ftumbling of an horfe, the falling of a tile, but the
pricking of a pin; let us fuddenly retire into, bethink
ourfelves, What, and if this were death! and withal
fteel and nerve ourfelves to the encounter. In our
cups and in our feafts, let it be the ever burden of our
thoughts — the utter fragility of all things mortal.
Never muft pleafure fo far be allowed to ufurp the
maftery over us, but that, ever and anon, we may be
recalled to the wholefome memory of in how many ways,
our very fports may become, themfelves, the fport of

On Death.

death; and of all the many doors by which he may surprise us. And so did the Egyptians; for in the height of their mirth, and in the midst of their riot, they would bid to their board, the convive of a dead man's bones, that, by the beholding of him, they might be remembered of their mortality.

Seeing, then, it is uncertain where or when death is to find us, let us e'en be beforehand with him; attend him at every moment and in every place. To premeditate of death is to premeditate of liberty. He who hath learnt to die hath unlearnt to be a slave. There is no evil, in this life, to him who hath well digested this; that the deprivation of life is not, in itself, a loss. To know how to die, at once emancipates us from every thraldom and from all constraint. Paulus Æmilius when that wretched king of Macedon, his prisoner, had sent to him, entreating him to be spared the indignity of being carried, a spectacle, at his triumph; for all reply sent him, *Let him make his prayer to himself.*

Truly, in whatever direction it may be, if nature does not lend an helping hand, it is but little head either art or industry will make. Constitutionally, I am not melancholy, but rather dreamy; nor is there any thing with which, from a child, I have been more possessed, than the imagination of death. It was the same in the heat and licentiousness of my prime. In the company of ladies, at cards, or at dice, when such an one had sworn, to look at me, that something wrong was being stomached; that I was jealous of this or that young spark, or that I were praying for a double six, an ace; God, he knows, I was turning with myself, how, but the other day, So and so had found himself at a feast, as I was, all hale and hearty, and how, from it, he had retired, his belly full of victuals, and his head of love; to sicken and to die. And still, as I thought, methought, What, and if it had been I !

"Jam fuerit, neque post unquam revocare licebit."
" Let a man once be gone, and no power again can recall him."

This is not the thought to wrinkle my brow, any more than another. It cannot but be, coming first to entertain ourselves with such reflections, that they will torment us and distract us. But by persisting to pass and to repass them before our eyes, we arrive, in the long run, to be reconciled to them. Were it not so, I, for one, should be living in a perpetual state of frenzy and affright; for never was there man who counted so little upon to-morrow, or promised himself less, from the duration of life than myself. And neither does that surprising health, which, almost uninterruptedly, till this day I have enjoyed, any more wheedle me into the hope of length of days, than doth disease into the despair. Not a tick of the clock, but methinks I am off; and as my *pater*, I am for ever muttering to myself,

"That which may be done another day; better this." And truly, the chances are a very nothing, that hazard and expofure will anticipate or divert our end. And if we will but ponder with ourfelves, how many thoufand cafualties, independently of that one which moft we fear, are for ever hanging over our heads, we fhall find that, fick or heal, on fea or on land, in the fray or in the tent, death is everywhere, and equally at hand. *Nemo altero fragilior eft : nemo in craftinum fui certior.* (No one man is more frail than another; nor is any more certain of to-morrow.) To delay, but for an hour, to do the thing that muft be done, or ever I am off, to me is long. It was but the other day that fome one, raking in my pocket book, happened to ftumble on a memorandum of fomething which I wifhed to be attended to, in the event of my deceafe. And I told him, and it was no more than the truth, that though, when it occurred to me, I was but at a league from my own door, in health and life, I had, neverthelefs, jotted it down, there and then, as I had no reafonable affurance that I was ever to live to reach it. By force of continually brooding over and foftering fuch thoughts, they have become, with me, a fecond nature. I am, alike, at every moment, prepared for what I may be called upon to become ; nor will there be anything of which it will be in the power of death, come he when he will, to remind me. We muft ever be booted and ready, fo far as may be, at a moment's notice, to turn out. We muft have shaken hands with the world, closed our every account but with ourselves. At home we shall have enough to look to, without wandering, in such an hour, abroad. It is not so much the having to die which troubles such an one, as to find himself cut off, the shouts of triumph in his ear; or this other, as that he must decamp, ere he can have disposed of his daughter, named tutors to his children, executors to his estate. One is wild to leave a wife, another a son, as elements even vital to the very essence of their being. For myself, I thank my God, I am prepared, at this moment, or when it seemeth good to him, to depart, without a pang, and without a thought. I have detached myself from every human tie; I have taken leave of all, save only of myself. Never did any man more amply or deliberately prepare himself to leave the world than I; or lay himself out to take a more advised farewell of it, than I am proposing to do.

[1] Most dead is best dead.

"Miser, ô miser, (aiunt) omnia ademit
Una dies infesta mihi tot præmia vitæ."

("O wretched, wretched man, that I am," will they cry, "one single hour is to rob me of all this wealth, and felicity of life.")

And he who builds,

"Manent (says he) opera interrupta, minæque
Murorum ingentes."

("See, my gardens, halls, my walls; all must I leave unfinished.")

---

[1] See Note W, at the end.

Nothing muſt too paſſionately be taken in hand, of which we may not reaſonably hope to ſee the fulfilment; or if it be, it muſt be taken with the proviſo, not too much to reckon to look upon the end. But as life is made for action, I would have every man to be buſy; ſo long as he can, to ſpin out the offices of life. For my part, when death comes for me, I would like him to find me watering my cabbages, and rather put about to have to leave my beds unweeded than at being compelled to attend to his ſummons. I remember to have ſeen one, on his laſt legs, bewailing himſelf, what a hard thing it was that he muſt go, leaving a then hiſtory, which he had in hand, no lower carried than to the fifteenth or ſixteenth of our kings.

> "Illud in his rebus non addunt, nec tibi earum
> Jam deſiderium rerum ſuper inſidet una."

("But they quite forget to add, that with death dies likewiſe the regret of all theſe things.")

We muſt diveſt ourſelves of all theſe miſerable and baneful hankerings. And even as our cemeteries are planted nigh neighbour to the temples, the highways and the halls, in order, ſays Lycurgus, that the common ſort, the women and the children, by the perpetual apprehenſion of the ſame, might the leſs diſtractedly be brought to look upon their end; that, by this continual beholding of theſe wretched charnel-houſes of our humanity, theſe endleſs files of hearſes, of corpſes, of mourners and of mutes, we should be for ever recollected of our mortality; and like as the Egyptians, in the height of their abandon, would bid to their halls, and as their gueſt, the dead man, anatomic, who, from his chapleſs lips was to tell them, *to eat, to drink, and to be merry; for that, dead, even as he was, would they be,* ſo, no leſs, have I taught myſelf to have not only the imagination of death for ever preſent to my mind, but his name continually in my mouth. There is nothing of which I more willingly inform myſelf, than of the deaths of men; their dying words; with what countenance, what face they have confronted it; nor is there any one page, in hiſtory, to which I more greedily turn. From my propenſity to ſtuff in, and expatiate on ſuch like matters, it may be ſeen how paſſionately my heart is ſet on them. Were I any hand at bookmaking, I would have a ſort of regiſter compiled, notes and commentaries to boot, of all the different poſſibilities of death. He who would teach mankind to die, would teach them, as well, to live. Dichearchus made one with ſome ſuch title, but with other and leſs eminent ends in view.

To all this, it will be oppoſed, that the reality is ſo different a thing from the experience, that, let us have our leſſon ever ſo well by heart, when we come to have to repeat it, it is odds but the half will have eſcaped us. Let them ſay what they like; to have familiarized ourfelves with him is half the battle. And what; is it nothing to have gotten thus far upon our journey, without a thought and without a fear? And befides all this, nature herfelf is ever on our fide, leading us gently by the hand. For, fuppofing our death be fhort and violent, then have we not fo much as time to be aghafted, languifhing, and I clearly perceive, that, in proportion as I become more and more involved, lefs and lefs account I make of life. I find it a much harder job to digeft the thoughts of death, in my faddle than in my bed. And precifely as I do let, one by one, the commodities of life efcape me; verily, becaufe they are no longer commodities to me, do I find myfelf more and more reconciled to the inevitable change. All this encourages me to hope, that the farther I recede from the one, and the nearer I approach to the other, the lefs reluctantly fhall I come, at laft, to crofs the barrier, and to change fides.

As I have found, in many another matter, the force of that faying of Cæfar's, *that things, for the moft part, appear to us more formidable at a diftance than at hand;* fo have I in this; that in health, ficknefs has invariably feemed to me a much more terrible affair than when I came to be ftruck down by it. The jollinefs in which I find myfelf, the content, the eafe, the happinefs; all, together, confpire to make their oppofites appear fo difmal, that in imagination they are already doubled, and, in my mind, I become perfuaded that they are much more unendurable than they ever prove, when really upon me. In the article of death, I hope to experience as much.

Let us now fee, by thofe ordinary gradations and declenfions to which we are fubjected, how nature imperceptibly beguiles us from the fenfe of our diminution and decay. How much, to the old man, remains, of the ftrength and vigour of his prime? Cæfar, to an old foldier, broken and decrepid, who came to him with the requeft to be allowed to make away with himfelf, pleafantly looking on him, replied, *Friend, art thou fure thou art alive?* To be ftricken down, on a fudden; I do not think that we are, by nature, conftituted to bear any fuch blow. But in gently leading us by the hand; as it were on an imperceptible decline, by flow degrees, I find that nature invariably bowls us into this wretched predicament, and fo happily accommodates us to it, that, at no one moment, is there any perceptible fhock to tell us, that there and then our youth was departed. For the lofs of youth is, beyond a doubt, a more lamentable death, as well in effence as in verity, than is that of a languifhing, protracted life, or of old age; inafmuch as the tranfition is not fo regretable from ill-being to nil-being, as it is from a ftate of jollity and hope to one of fuffering and of defpair.

Even as a body wafted and infirm is unequal to its charge, fo is it with the foul. We muft fortify and arm her againft the affaults of fuch an adverfary. For as it is impossible for the citadel to be, at the same time, in repose and in alarm; let her once have arrived to this mastery, and she may vaunt, (and what were in itself almost surpassing human compass,) that it were no longer in the power of either hope, fear, torment or anxiety, to find any sort of access unto her. She is now ruler, triumphant in her breast; mistress of her every passion, every lust; can face, alike undauntedly, temptation, penury, reproach, affront, with all the ills and wrongs of fortune and of fate. Let him, who can, get to himself this privilege. This is the only true and sovereign liberty. This alone it is which can enable us to make a mock at injuries, indignities, of powers; to laugh at the prisons, the shackles and the bars!

Nor has our holy religion had any more grounded assurance, humanly speaking, than the contempt of life. Farther, the very rudiments of reason might have taught us as much. For why should we fear the loss of that which, once gone, it is no longer in our power to miss? And seeing, again, in what an infinity of ways we are menaced of death, is it not a greater penance, to be for ever living in the apprehension of an hundred, than boldly once to go through with one? What can it matter when that overtakes us, which, sooner or later, inevitably must? Socrates, to one who told him, that the thirty tyrants had condemned him to death, had merely to rejoin, *and nature them.* What madness to be shivering and shuddering on the brink of a releafe which muft for ever waft us from our every woe? And even as our birth was to us the birth of all which is beneath the fun; fo, of all things, our death will be the death. So that it were about as fenfelefs to be bewailing ourfelves, that we fhall not be alive one hundred years hence, as it would be, that we had not been fo, an hundred gone. Death is but the birth of another life. Even fo did we weep, and with like apprehenfion were we torn from the womb; fo did we caft off our former man, as we burfted into this. What can be but once, can be nothing terrible. Is it common fenfe, to fear fo long, a fpurt fo fhort? Of long time and of fhort time, death is the equalizer. Neither long nor fhort are the properties of that which is no more. Hear Ariftotle, and he will tell you, that by the waters of the Hypanis do there float of little beafts, the whole duration of whofe days is but a day. And he among them that dieth with the cock, is hurried away, e'en in the vigour of his youth, whilft he who tarrieth to the evening dew, 'tis but to be referved to a miferable old age, and to decrepitude. Who is he who would not laugh, to fplit himfelf, to fee thefe midges of an hour difcourfing of the rights, the wrongs; felicities and infelicities of life? No lefs with ourfelves; the longer or the fhorter, as compared, not to fay with everlaftingnefs, but with the lifetime of mountains, rivers, trees, the firmament, nay, more than one animal, is but a very nothing.

[1] But nature, herſelf, is for ever harping as much in our ears. " It is your buſineſs," ſays ſhe, " even as " you came, to go. The ſame road you followed, from " death to life, fearleſs and paſſionleſs; by the ſame " return from life to death. Your death is a link in " the chain of the order of the univerſe: a member " of the life of all things."

> " Inter ſe mortales mutua vivant,
> Et, quaſi curſores, vitæ lampada tradunt."
>
> (" Eternity to none is given. Life to the coming times we hand, as in the ſacred games, the torch, the runner to the next tranſmits.")

" Am I, for you, to alter all this admirable adjuſt-
" ment of the univerſe? Know it is the very compact
" of your being. Death is a part of your life. It
" is your proper ſelves that you would away with.
" Death has an equal property with life, in every
" breath you draw. The day you begin to live,
" you begin, no leſs, to die. Every day you live,
" it is ſo much gone of life, of her capital, of her
" expenſe. Nay, the whole occupation of your life
" is but to heap up unto yourſelves death. Alive, you
" are very dead; for dead you are to ſo much of your
" life as is already paſt. Or, if this will ſuit you better,
" you are at once dead and dying: dead to ſo much as

---

[1] See Note X, at the end.

" is paſt; dying to ſo much as is to come. Now, the
" death which is to come touches you infinitely more
" ſenſibly, and to the quick, than does that which is
" already paſt. If you have had your fair ſhare of life
" and its enjoyments, it is your buſineſs to be ſatisfied:
" be up and be off. If you had not the wit to make
" the moſt of it, or if you were ſcurvily uſed of it;
" what are you to loſe in loſing it? to what end would
" you cling to it? Life, in itſelf, is neither a good nor
" an ill: it is the place where good and ill is to be
" found: the finding thereof depends upon yourſelf.
" And he who hath seen one day hath ſeen all days.
" For yeſterday was even as this day, and to-morrow
" will be as a thouſand gone. There is no other light,
" nor is there any other darkneſs. This ſun, this
" moon, theſe ever wandering ſtars; this beauteous
" firmament on high; they are the ſame to which your
" fathers' father turned; it is the ſame in which your
" children's children will rejoice. And even at
" the beſt, and at the moſt, a twelvemonth ſees the
" round of all the ſcenes, of all the acts of this, my
" comedy. For if you will but look upon it; what
" are the revolutions of the ſeaſons, other than the
" youthhood, fervour, manhood, decrepitude of na-
" ture? She has had her day; nor does ſhe know
" any better, or any other trick, than afreſh to com-
" mence where ſhe left off. And ſo will it be to the
" end of the chapter. I have other things to attend to,

" than to be contriving for you, this or that fresh pas-
" time. Make way for the coming batch, as the last
" made way for you. Impartiality is the first rudiment
" of equity. Who can complain, where all, alike, are
" comprised? And though you live till domesday,
" you will be no whit the longer, or the shorter, dead.
" 'Tis for eternity; and as long will you be in that state
" which you are fleeing, as though, from the womb,
" you had given up the ghost. Nor will you any more
" know displeasure, or memory of that loss, the thought
" of which, now, you cannot abide. Nay, less than a
" very nothing, is death to be feared; that is, if any-
" thing less than nothing can there be. Neither living
" nor dead, does it in any way concern you. Living,
" because you are so; dead, because you are no more so.
" Nor did ever any man die before his time. For so
" much time as you leave behind you, can no more be
" said to be yours, than can that which evolved or ever
" you were born. You have no more to do with the
" one than with the other. Let it stop short where it
" will, there and then is the sum total. The profit of
" life consisteth not in length of days, but in the account
" to which those days are turned. Many is the one
" has attained to a good old age, whose years have been
" but few. It depends upon how you have lived, not
" how long, that you have sufficiently lived."

" Again, think you never to arrive, whilst every day
" you must be nearing? Was there ever lane but butted

"somewhere? And if company you muſt have to
"diſtract you by the road; is not all creation trudging,
"lumbering he ſelf-ſame way? Is there the thing in
"life, which is not, equally with yourſelf, haſting and
"withering away? A thouſand men, a thouſand
"women, a thouſand children, a thouſand cattle of the
"field, in the ſelf-ſame moment with yourſelf, no leſs
"give up their mortal breath. To what purpoſe is it to
"retreat, if retreating place there is none? You have
"ſeen what a providence it was to thouſands to be taken
"away, thereby to be ſpared the miſeries which awaited
"them. Yet the one who would have changed the
"change, where did you ever ſee? So it is downright
"ſottiſhneſs to miſgive the thing of which you literally
"know nothing, either of your own proper experience,
"or that of another. Why ſhould you turn round upon
"myſelf and deſtiny? What is it that we have done
"to you? Is it for you to dictate to us, or we to you?
"And even admitting that your years may have been
"ſhort; your life was not. Five feet is as much a man
"as ſix feet-ſix: neither is a man, nor are his days, to
"be meaſured with a ſtrap. Chiron would not ſo much
"as look on immortality, having come well to under-
"ſtand its nature, and of which he was appriſed of his
"own father, Saturn, himſelf the God of time and
"of duration. Diſpaſſionately aſk yourſelf, How much
"more inſupportable had been immortality to man, than
"is the means to which I have conſtituted him? If

" you had no longer death to look forward to, you
" would be for ever curfing me for having deprived you
" of it. It is wittingly that I have dafhed this cup
" with fome little bitternefs, left, coming to fee its
" commodity, too greedily you might run to it, and fup
" it up. To temper you to that moderation, fo as
" neither to flee that life which I have given you, nor
" that death which I require of you, I have mingled
" the one and the other, with the fweet and with the
" bitter. It was I who taught Thales, the firft of your
" fages, that to live and to die were indifferent; and by
" which, my knowledge, he replied, right fagely, to one
" who afked him, 'If fo, why then did he not die?'
" *For life and death are one.* Earth, air, water, fire, not
" a member of this, my univerfe, any more tends to
" retain you in life, than to deprive you of the fame.
" Why, above all days, your laft day fhould you dread?
" It is no more anfwerable for your death, than the one
" which preceded it. It is not the laft ftretch that
" knocks you up: it is the one in which you are
" knocked up. All your days you are journeying to
" death: the laft you touch it." And thefe are the
advertifements which our good mother, nature, gives us.

I have often mufed with myfelf of how it came,
that, in times of war, the affaults of death, whether
upon ourfelves or others, are fo infinitely lefs formidable
in the field than in the city. And fortunate is it for us
that it is fo; elfe what were an army, fave an hoft of

blubberers, night watchers, and of doctors? Again, seeing that death can be but death, I have no lefs marvelled to perceive how much more fteadily it will be encountered of a groom, or a cottager, than of his mafter or a lord. I do verily believe, that it is rather all the appalling apparatus with which we furround it, that really affrights us, than is it the thing itfelf: this piteous departure from all our wonted mode of life: thefe cries, thefe tears; thefe howling women; thefe thunderftrucken and aghafted vifitants; thefe broken valets and thefe blanched maids; the darkened chamber and the difmal lamp: confeffors at your head, phyficians at your feet; brief, the chamber and the court of horrors and of death! What is this but to bury a man alive?

Even as the child will whine to fee, but in a mafk, the fportive face that fcares it; fo, no lefs, are we amazed at death. The mafk muft be torn, as well from the faces of things as of perfons. Off let it be, and behind it we will but find to be enfconced, that fame poor filly death, which, an hour ago, an hind, or a chambermaid fubmitted to, without a pang and without a thought. Happy is that death which precludes to us the pomp of any fuch conclufion!

Apology for Raymond de la Sebonde.

* * * * *

* * * [1]About this time, the doctrines of Luther began to be noifed abroad, making formidable inroads on our ancient faith. Where all this was tending, he (his father,) was well aware; clearly forefeeing, *par difcours de raifon*, by inference of reafon, that this *commencement de maladie*, beginning of leprofy, would naturally degenerate into an execrable atheifm. In as much as the common people, incapable of arriving at conclufions of their own; abandoning all things to fortune and appearances; once given the initiative to call in queftion the defcent of traditions, fuch as thofe of the myfteries of their faith, and which had ever been held as facred in their eyes, would never halt till they had fhaken all authority, the very earth, to its centre — till they had trampled on, as the yoke of tyranny and of oppreffion, all thofe convictions which they had received, whether from the majefty of the law, or the reverence of eftablifhed cuftom; determining, that henceforth, nought fhould be recognized to which it had not interpofed its fanction, or lent the countenance of its implicit approbation.

* * * * *

It was the darknefs of paganifm, and never to have

[1] See note Y, at the end.

heard of our holy faith, which caused that mighty soul of Plato, though mighty only of a mortal mightiness, to fall into yet this neighbour scandal; that, of all others, the young and the old are the most naturally disposed to religion; as though its force were our weakness. The bond which should arrest our will, our affection; win our souls and tie them to our Maker; it should be an infusion taking its ground, not from our passions, our impressions, our convictions, our infirmities, but from a compulsion, divine and superhuman; knowing but one form, one visage, one brightness—the authority of God and his grace. Now, the heart and the soul, once broken and subdued unto faith, it is but meet that they should bring over to the cause of righteousness our every member; each in his several faculty. Nor is it to be imagined that there is any page of this great book, on which is not graven the name of its Author; or that there is any portion of his handiwork which announceth not the hand that made it. He hath imprinted on these, his high workings, the impress of his divinity; nor have we to thank, but our own imbecility, that we are incapable to attain to the superscription. It is no more than he himself has told us, "That things invisible are made manifest by the "visible." This is the worthy end to which Sebonde laboured; and he has shown us, how there is no one portion of this universe which belies its Author. It were injurious to the divine goodness to suppose, that the univerſe were not a party, conſenting to our faith. The heavens, the earth, the air, the ſeas; our bodies, ſouls; all; all things that are, alike atteſt it. The words are there, if we are but capable to read them. For this great globe is an holy temple, wherein the Creator hath placed his creature, to contemplate, not ſtatues reared by mortal hands, but thoſe of the immortal Spirit faſhioned; this ſun, this moon, theſe ſtars; theſe waters and this earth; that, in the beholding of them, we might no leſs behold the hand that made them. "For the inviſible things of him," ſays St. Paul, "from the creation of the world, are clearly "ſeen, being underſtood by thoſe that are made." Now, all our wretched reaſonings and glimmerings are but the unlicked and the lifeleſs clay; the grace of God, it is the faſhion and the form: it alone can give them all their virtue, all their price. And even as all they tell us of a Socrates, a Plato, was but ſtillborn, vain and profitleſs, not to have been impregnated of that grace; nor to have owed its actuation to a love and an obedience toward the Maker of all things; to their having never heard of him; ſo is it with our imaginations, our concluſions. Subſtance they may have; but it is faſhionleſs and void; unquickened of the faith, the knowledge and the grace of God. Coming to be enviſaged and fortified by the light and acceſs of faith, the arguments of Sebonde aſſume weight and ſolidity. They may be ſerviceable to the apprentice, to put him on the track of this knowledge. They will drefs, and in fome fort render him fufceptible of the divine grace; by the means of which, later, his faith is to be perfected and to be maintained.

* * * * *

What is it the Word is propofing, when it tells us " that we are to beware of worldly philofophy;" when it is for ever preaching, " the wifdom of man is but " folly before God; that, of all things vain, man is " the vaineft: that he who thinketh he knoweth, hath " yet to learn what to know is; that man, who is " a very nothing, if he would think to be anything, " doth deceive and impofe upon himfelf." Thefe pencillings of the Holy Ghoft do, in fo lively and fo clear a manner, fupport what I would maintain, that I would not afk to myfelf any other weapons, wherewith to confound thofe who, in all humility and unfeignednefs, would fubmit themfelves to his authority. But needs muft they be fcourged with a rod of their own graffing; they will have reafon to be combated but by itfelf.

Now, let us, a moment, view this man, alone, as he is, armed only with his own proper arms; unreplenifhed of the grace of God, which is all his advancement, all his ftrength, and all the foundation of his being. Let us fee him, I fay, in all this fine equipment! Let him give to me to underftand, and by the force of his reafon, where and what be the foundations upon which he hath built to himſelf this mighty pre-eminence which he taketh to poſſeſs upon his fellow beaſts? Who hath told to him that this glorious circling of the heaven's vault; theſe ever blazing lights, ſo fiercely rolling themſelves aloft, over our heads; the eternal compact of the mighty deep, for his commodity and uſufruct, alone, were created and foreordained? Is it poſſible to conceive anything ſo ridiculous, as that this wretched and this beggarly creature, not ſo much as maſter of himſelf; the ſport of fortune and the elements; a prey to every ſort of miſery, aſſault, ſhould be ſetting himſelf up to be lord and emperor of the univerſe; ſo much as to underſtand the lighteſt part of which is beyond his power, much leſs to direct the whole? And this ſufficiency which he arrogateth to himſelf, to be, alone, of earth's tenants, him, by nature, capacitated to riſe to the appreciation of the beauty and contrivance of the whole; the only one, who, to the great architect, can return him thanks for all his bounties; who, of the world, can regiſter the incomings and the outgoings, the wear and the tear; who hath conveyed to him this noble privilege? Let him ſhow to us his charters, his title deeds to this, ſo glorious an inveſtiture! Or have they been granted but in favour of the wiſe? Then touch they but a few. Are fools and knaves entitled to any ſuch preference? they, the moſt abject of the creation, are they to be placed in an eminence above the reſt? And is this one to be believed? Hear him. "On whofe account, "then, are we to conclude the world to have been "made? For thofe, affuredly, who have the gift of "reafon; thefe, at once, are gods and men, than "which there is nothing more worthy." But we will never fufficiently have fpit upon the impudency of fuch conjunctions. Ah, man, poor man, wherein doft thou account thyfelf! [1] When we confider this heaven, which fadeth not away; thefe funs, thefe ftars; their beauty and their fearfulnefs; their filent, pathlefs, folemn, and their ftately march; when we reflect on all the influences which they exert, not merely on our actions, fortunes, but our very inclinations, thoughts, refolves, which, as reafon compels us to allow, are at the mercy of their every change—when we fee, that not only is a man, though that man a king, but all which is beneath the fun, even to principalities and powers, are fhaken and overthrown, but at their lighteft perturbation—if our virtues, our vices, our fufficiency, our fcience, all, aye, even to this very difcourfe which we are now making of them, is by them, and through them, as fane reafon teacheth—if, I fay, it is to the difpenfation of the heavens that we owe this modicum of reafon which we have, how are we to enliken it, or compare it unto them? how defer, to our fcience, their effence and their conditions? Everything about them diftracts us and amazes us. Why fhould we go about to deprive them of foul, of being,

---

[1] See note Z, at the end.

and of speech? What have we ever seen in them to argue a dumpish and a leaden insensibility; we, too, who can know no more of them than what they may impart to us? And even allowing that we have never perceived in any other creature save man, evidence of a reasonable soul; what then? Hath the sun a fellow: doth he the less cease to be, for that we have never seen his like; or is his march to be gainsayed, till we have found whereunto for to liken it? If nothing is to be, but what we have seen, verily, our knowledge may be small packed. Is it not very toys of the human fancy, to be making of the moon, an earth, as our own; to map it out into mountains and valleys, as did Anaxagoras; to plant in it cities and provinces; to lay out colonies in it, for our occupation, as did Seneca and Plutarch; to make of our dusky earth a burnished and a glistering star? "Among other discommodities of our mortality this is "one, that the darkness which encompasseth us, spring- "eth not so much of an inevitable necessity, as of a "love of error."—" The corruptible body doth over- "lay the soul; the fleshy tenement, the spirit, which "is ever set to muse of heavenly things."

Presumption is our original and inherent failing. The most lamentable and helpless of all God's creatures is man, and withal the most scornful and disdainful. And though he sees and knows himself to be planted here below, mid all the filth and refuse of the world, fast chained and tethered to the most wretched, stagnant, and unconsidered corner of the universe; stuck in the lowest chamber of the house, the farthest removed from the heights of heaven's majesty — of all that fly, that float, that crawl, with the most grovelling; yet will he not cease to be lodging himself, in his imagination, above the circles of the moon, and to be trampling the very heavens beneath his feet. It is upon the same presumptuous sufficiency with which he equalleth himself unto God, adjudgeth to himself divine conditions, that he withdraweth and separateth himself from the herd; dispenseth this or that faculty to his fellow beasts and companions; distributeth to them so much of understanding as good him seems. How can he discover, by the mere force of his intelligence, the interne and the secret workings of the brutes that be? On what grounds will he undertake to establish that imbecility which he assigneth unto them? When I play with my cat; who knows but she maketh as light of me as I of her? We are entertained, alike, with our mutual buffoonery. If I have my hour to begin and to leave off, has not she hers? Plato, in his picture of the golden age, under Saturn, numbers among the principal advantages possessed of the world, in those times, the intercourse which was common with the beasts. For, by this means, men, coming to see into, and understand their several natures, were permitted to arrive to an unlooked-for and an admirable sagacity, and so to be capable of a more incomparable felicity, than, since, has been suffered. Could there be any stronger testimony than this, of the impudency of our pretended superiority, as touching beasts? This great man was of opinion, that nature, for the most part, in their organization, had an eye to the prognostications which, in his age, were drawn from their vitals, motions. This want of a common medium betwixt them and us; why is it not as much, or as likely, in ourselves as in them? It is yet to divine where the misunderstanding lies; for they can no more comprehend us, than we them. And with as much reason may they dub us asses, beasts, as we them. It is but little marvel that we can make nothing of them, when neither can we of a Basque or a Troglodyte.

* * * * *

All which I have said is of purpose to maintain the analogy of things human; to recover and recall us to the crowd. Neither are we above nor below the rest. All that is beneath the sun, saith the sage, runneth like fortune, incurreth one law. Difference of degree, there may be; order, rank; still, under one aspect, face of nature. We must brave this man, and hustle him again into the bounds which he hath broken. The miserable has outstepped the pale. Of his nature he is circumscribed and bound, subjected to similar conditions with other animals of his kind. He is of a like limited scope; without ny sort of real prerogative, or ascendency; unchallenged or essential. That which he arrogateth to himself, in opinion and in fantasy, existeth not, either in sense or in reason. But even granted that it does; that in him, alone, of all the animals, resides this capacity to perception, this licentiousness of imagination, whereby to know that which is and that which is not; what he will and what he nill; the true from the false; it is a privilege somewhat dearly bought, and of which he hath small cause to glorify himself. For from it comes the troop of ills and wrongs to which our flesh is heir; sin, suffering, sorrow, irresolution, despair. I say, then, to return to where I was, there is no colour of reason to suppose that the animals perform, by an unaccountable instinct and agency, those very functions, which, in ourselves, are the result of deliberation and of free will. Contrary; from like effects, we should conclude like operations; from nobler effects, nobler operations; and consequently allow, that by this very reasoning faculty, this self-same process of operation, by which we arrive at our ends; by a like, where not a readier, do the animals at theirs. Why should we condemn them to this, I know not what inevitable necessity; we, who in ourselves, know no such violence? And farther than this, it is a more honourable prerogative to be directed, unfalteringly, upon our way; to be kept right by an harmonious and a natural adaptation; it is a nearer touch of the divinity, than to be conforming, advisedly, to the prescriptions of a wit, rash and changeling. Better truft to nature than to our own hands, the reins that guide us. The vanity of our prefumption makes, that we would rather be indebted to our own fufficiency than to her providence. We frankly abandon to the other animals the better half; award to them the gifts of nature; honouring and ennobling ourfelves with capabilities acquired. A miferable compofition, as it feems to me! For I would very much prefer thofe poffeffions which were intimately and inherently mine, before thofe that I was compelled to beat about to come at, or to purchafe by a tedious apprenticefhip. It is not in the difpofition of things to be tendered any higher countenance, than to be led by the hand of nature and of God.

* * * * *
* * * * * [1] Human reafon can but perceive of things by the inftruments at its difpofition; and never will we recollect the downfall of that wretched Phaeton, for having attempted, with a mortal hand, to hold the reins, to guide the horfes of the chariot of his father. Into a like abyfs is our own prefumption precipitated; fhattered and confounded, no lefs, with its own proper temerity.

—They are all but toys, day dreams, and fantaftic follies. Would it but pleafe our mother nature, one day, to open to us her fanctum; to fhow to us the arcana of her treafure-houfe; her myfteries, her work-

[1] See note A A, at the end.

ings; to fit our wretched eyes to the beholding of the same—O good God, what imposition, what misconception would be laid bare to us: how shrunken a thing would all our knowledge prove! I do very much misgive me, if one single position is exactly as, or in the place, we take it to be; and when I die, I shall go hence more ignorant of everything than of mine own proper ignorance.

Have I not seen in Plato this divine admission—that nature is nothing else than a sort of poetical enigma? pretty much as if one would say, a landscape read by night of the evanishing and the flashing of the cloud. "*Latent ista omnia crassis occultata et circumfusa tenebris; ut nulla acies humani ingenii tanta sit, quæ penetrare in cœlum, terram intrare possit.*" "All those matters lie hidden and involved in so impenetrable an obscurity, that no wit of man can scale the things of heaven, or dive to those of earth." And certainly philosophy is little other than a kind of sophisticated poesy. Whence do the older worthies draw all their philosophy, if not from the poets? Nay, they were poets themselves, and treated their art as such. Plato is but a loose poet. Timon captiously calls him, A huge forger of miracles. Through all the sciences, alike, there runs a sort of poetic licence. Even as women, when the teeth which nature gave them, fail them, take to those of ivory; and when their natural colour has forsaken them, o'erlay their checks and necks with powders and with paint; and as they make to themselves trunk-sleeves of wire and whalebone bodies, backs of laths, and stiff bombasted verdugals; and in the open face of day, trick and set themselves off with counterfeit and artificial advantages; so it is with science. And our very laws are said by some, to be founded, in part, upon certain legal fictions; yet these be the root of justice. She gives us as current cash and as an earnest, those very things which she herself alloweth to be but mere inventions. For these *epicycles, concentrics, eccentrics,* which astrology has had to call in to enable her to keep herself abreast the times; she simply gives them to us as the most likely way she can hit on to account for the phenomena presented of the heavenly bodies. The same with the rest. Philosophy offers to us, not that which is, or even she believes, but that which she can fashion, having in it most likelihood and plausibility. Plato, in his treatise upon the condition of man and of the beasts, warns his hearers, " What we now give you, were it confirmed to us by an oracle, we would likewise confirm to you; but, seeing it is not, we have only offered it as the most probable thing to be truth that we could think on."

Nor is it to heaven alone that they have sent their cordages, their pullies, their axles and their wheels. Let us just consider a little, what they have told us of ourselves and of our own mechanism. Positively there is no greater retrogration, trepidation, augmentation, recoiling, perturbation in the ſtars and heaven's ſyſtem, than they have feigned to find in this poor, ſilly little *corpus* of a man. Verily, it was with reaſon that they did call it, *Microcoſmos, A little world,* ſo diverſe the materials they have uſed to build it and to ſtock it. To account for, to reconcile, the properties that they ſee in man; the various functions and faculties which they perceive to be in us; into how many fragments have they ſplit our ſouls; into how many holes and corners have they hunted it? Into how many degrees and ranks have they graduated this poor creature, man, over and above the natural and perceptible? to how many offices, ends, vocations, have they aſſigned him? A ſort of public anatomy do they make of him. He is the ſubject on which they expatiate, dilate, and harangue. And though they have had every facility to turn him, to handle him, to twiſt him, to rip him, to ſtuff him, to take him to pieces, to put him together again; every man of them after his own notion; yet are they as far as ever from making either head or tail of him. Not only not in fact, but not even in fancy, can they turn him out ſo creditably but that there will be ſome hitch, ſome ſcrew looſe; ſomething wanting to their tailoring, all licentious as it is; mended and patched up with a thouſand ſhreds and tatters. Nor is there any ſort of excuſe for them. For when a painter would give us the heavens, a ſpire, trees, mountains, clouds; objects removed from his attainment, we merely require, at his hands, some sort of rude, approximate resemblance. But when he would undertake to draw ourselves, or any other subject with which he is familiar, we look to see a perfect likeness; nor will we be satisfied with less; and if he miss it, we despise him.

Commend me to the Milesian lass; who, seeing Thales, the philosopher, to be for ever in a brown study; his eyes incessantly poking on the stars, laid a saucepan in his way, to trip him over; and thereby to warn him and teach him, how it would be time enough, when he had well looked to what was going on under his nose, to send his eyes aloft to the rummaging of the skies. For, as saith Democritus, by the mouth of Cicero,

> Quod est ante pedes, nemo spectat;
> Cœli scrutantur plagas.

("What is before him no man inquires; all their care is to seek and grope the regions of the sky.")

But such are the terms of our humanity, that the knowledge which we have of that which encompasseth us, is as much removed from us, as high above our heads, as is that of the sun and of the stars. As much says Socrates, in Plato, when he applies to those who meddle with philosophy, the taunt which the Milesian woman threw to Thales, namely, *that what was under his eyes he could not see.* For never was there yet philosopher who could account for what his fellow does, nay, nor for that matter, for what he himself does; nor even can he tell, whether the one, or the other, be man or be beast.

These sort of people, who find the reasonings of Sebonde too timid; who are ignorant of nothing; the lights of the world; who know everything; have they ever chanced to found among their books, their cogitations, how hard a matter it is to know their individual selves? We see clearly enough, that our finger moves, our foot moves; that certain parts have a will of their own, follow their own minds, without ever once asking our pleasure, our licence; that a certain character of alarm will raise a blush, a certain other induce a deadly paleness; such an imagination will act upon the milt alone, such another but upon the brain. One thing will force us to laugh, another to cry; again, a third will amaze, and stagnate and petrify the blood. The presentation of certain objects will make the gorge to rise; of others again, certain other members. But as to how an essence, purely spiritual, worketh all these operations in a body given and determinate; and the nature, method and contrivance of all these admirable instruments, agencies; that, no man hath ever known. *Omnia incerta ratione, et in naturæ majestate abdita*, says Pliny, "Things are but to be divined of by reason; "being wrapped and concealed in the majesty of "nature." And St. Augustin, *Modus, quo corporibus adhærent spiritus . . omnino mirus est, nec comprehendi ab homine potest; et hoc ipse homo est:* "The sympathy "by which the soul doth cleave to the body is wonder- "ful, nor is it conceived of man; yet such is man." Yet never a doubt is there made about the matter. For the conclusions of men are swallowed on the strength of faith and tradition, on authority and credit; as if it were matter of religion and of law. We receive, as we do any other jargon, that which is commonly held; we adopt this precious truth, with all its shoulderings, its scaffoldings of arguments and proofs, as though it were an edifice, based, firm, unassailable, unshakable. Nor is there a man of us will pick at it; but, contrary, it is who best can tinker, and cobble up this faith received, with all the little wit he has; in itself, a commodity wondrous plastic, pliable, contortious. And hence it comes, that the whole world is overrun with folly, with madness and with lies. The reason why so few things are misgiven of, is this; that vulgarly received impressions never once are brought to the test. The root is never groped for, where all the rottenness lies; they fumble but among the branches. They do not ask, What Galen said, had it reason in it? but, Did Galen express himself thus and thus? Verily, it was in keeping that this bridle, this holdfast upon the freedom of our thought, should be extended to the schools, to science, to the arts. The god of scholastical learning is Aristotle. It is as much matter of religion to discourse of his ordinances, as it was of those of Lycurgus at Sparta. His doctrines are to us a sort of canon law, though peradventure, as false and unfounded as another. I do not see why I should not as readily adopt Plato, his ideas; or the atoms of Epicurus, or the fulness and the emptiness of Leucippus and Democritus, or the water of Thales, or the infinity of nature of Anaximander, or the air of Diogenes, or the numbers and symmetry of Pythagoras, or the endlessness of Parmenides, or the unity of Musæus, or the water and the fire of Apollodorus, or the similar parts of Anaxagoras, or the discord and concord of Empedocles, or the fire of Heraclitus, or any other opinion from among all this infinite confusion of imaginations and conclusions arrived at of this poor human reason, in its infinite wisdom and farsightedness, in whatsoever it meddles with; as I should that of Aristotle upon this matter of the principles of natural things; which principles he attributes to three elements —matter, form, privation. And can anything be more idle, than to make inanity itself, the contriver and begetter of substance? Privation is a negative. With what conscience, what face, can he pretend it to be the author and architect of things that be? Yet is not this to be doubted of, for that would be to grant to us the use of our reason. All their endeavour and argumentation goes, not, to sift the truth, but to shield the founder of their school from strange assaults. His dictum is the *ne plus ultra* beyond which no man is to be permitted to inquire.

Certain principles once granted, a man may draw exactly what conclusions he pleases from them; for, according to the law and ordinance of this conceffion, the reft will naturally follow, without any fort of let, or unreafonablenefs. By this, we come to find our principles well grounded, and all the fuperftructure to follow, as a matter of courfe. For our mafters, at firft go off, and beforehand, manage to get fuch a footing in our minds, that, after, they can convince us of exactly what they lift; juft as do the mathematicians, with their axioms given. The data, reliance and confidence which we concede to them, give them the means to draw us to the right hand and to the left; to work us precifely as they pleafe. To whomfoever we grant thefe firft principles, then is he our mafter and our God; and fo wide will he lay his foundations, that, have he a mind, he will carry his edifice to the clouds. In all this bufinefs and altercation of the fciences, we have taken for gofpel the faying of Pythagoras, "That every mafter "is to be allowed in his own art." The logician goes to the grammarian for the meaning of his words; the orator borrows of the logician his common-place of argument; the poet from the mufician, his harmony, his cadence; the geometrician from the arithmetician, his proportions. The metaphyficians take, as the bafis of their inveftigation, the conjectures of the phyfician;

for every science has its forestalling principles; so that, on every hand, the human reason is bridled, stifled and suppressed. But if once you attempt to rally, or attack the head and front of all this credulity, and wherein the error lies, straight you are shut up with, "No; "there is no disputing with those who deny principles." Now, as for principles, there can be no such things among men, if God do not think proper to reveal them. So, the whole affair, beginning, middle and end, is but moonshine, day dreams, vanity and smoke! And as for those who would fight us with "given "principles;" we have but to encounter them with given the clean contrary. For, one presumption, one theory, has no more authority than has another presumption, theory, if reason make not the difference. So, the whole of them must be put to the proof; and, first and foremost, these first principles, for it is they that do tyrannize and war upon the rest. An overweening certitude is the surest evidence of folly and of extreme uncertainty; nor are there any who more consummately impose upon themselves, or are less worthy to be called philosophers, than the Philodoxes of Plato.

In matter of physics, what we have to know, is this; Is fire really hot, is snow really white; if matter be, in very truth, hard and soft? And as for those retorts, which, as old wives' tales, have come down to us, how, to one who misdoubted of heat, it was told, "to get into the brick-kiln, and fee for himself;" and to another, who denied cold to be inherent to ice, "He had better put a bit in his pocket;" they were unworthy of, and disgraceful to the pretensions of a philosopher. Had they but been content to leave us in our natural state; allowed us to receive the impressions from without, as they conveyed themselves to us, through our senses; enjoined to our appetites their free and natural play and exercise; the use of them as nature intended them to be used; such replies had been rational enough. But they come with a very poor grace from those who have been preaching up to us, " that the mind of man is the controller-general of all which is above and below the vault of heaven; that it embraces all things; that it is capable of all things; and that by means of it is everything known and brought to light." Such like answers would be to the point enough, among the savages, who manage to procure for themselves length of days, peace, and tranquillity; and that, too, all heedless of the precepts of Aristotle; whose name, peradventure, they never so much as heard of; and who are indebted to nature for a far greater fortitude than they ever could have attained from their reason or invention. The very brutes were no less capable than ourselves of such replies as these; as were any others who might yet be living in obedience to the pure and simple laws of nature. But they have renounced to all such follies. It will not do, to tell me, " It is so, for you see and feel that it is so." What they have to do is, to tell me, If what I think I feel, I, in reality, do feel. And, after that they must explain to me, if I do feel it, the why, and the how, and the what. Let them name to me the name, the home, the comings and the goings of the heat and of the cold; the nature of that which acts, and of that which is acted on; or let them renounce to their pretensions—neither to allow or to accede to anything, but with the consent of reason. It is their touchstone for their every matter of essay; but, assuredly, it is one full of falsehood, of error, and of doubleness.

Where can her science be put to a fairer test, than in the case of her own proper self? If we are not to believe her, speaking of her own self, how is she to be credited, speaking of that which is above, beyond, without? Surely, if she knew anything, it would be her own nature, her own domicile. That domicile is the soul; of which reason is a part or an emanation. But as for that only, true and perfect reason, (the title of which we have usurped to our poor, silly, shallow cogitations, imaginations;) it is enshrined in the heart of God. There is her home, and there is her retreat; and it is thence that it parteth, when it pleaseth Him to reveal to us a ray of his divinity; even as Pallas sprung, all armed, from the brain of Jove, to communicate and to impart herself to the world.

Now, let us, a moment, see what this human reason

has taught us of herfelf, and of the foul: not of that great foul of the world, of which almoſt all philofophy holds the heavenly bodies and firſt elements to be participators; nor yet of that which Thales attributed even to things inanimate, drawn thereto from a confideration of the magnet; but of that foul which is within us and which beſt we ſhould know.

* * * * *

The firſt law which God impofed on man was one of pure obedience. It was a commandment fole and fimple; farther, he was neither to know, nor to inquire; inafmuch as to obey is the natural return of a reafonable foul, allowing of an all bounteous and omnipotent Superior. From obedience and from fubmiffion fpring every other virtue; contrariwife, from prefumption doth all fin. And of this waywardnefs came the firſt temptation to which our nature was expofed, on the part of the devil. The firſt poifon that he ever inſtilled into our fouls, was the promife which he made to us of fcience and of knowledge: " Ye ſhall be as gods; " knowing good and evil." And the fyrens, in Homer, when they would enfnare Ulyffes, encompafs him in their ruinous and inextricable toils, could think of no likelier bait to tender to him, than fufficiency. Curiofity is the peſt and fcourge of man. And this is why ignorance is for ever preached to us, by our holy religion,

as an article indifpenfable to our faith and obedience :
" Beware left any man fpoil' you through philofophy
" and vain deceit, after the traditions of men, after the
" rudiments of the world."

All the philofophy of all the fects is of accord in this;
that the fovereign good confifts in the tranquillity of the
body and of the foul. But where is it to be found ?
In very truth, it would feem to me, that nature, to put
us in conceit with this, our miferable and beggarly predicament, has given us, as a fet-off, prefumption. As
much was allowed of Epictetus : " Opinion," fays
he, " is all that man can properly call his own." A
very whiff and a fmoke is our portion. The gods,
faith philofophy, are poffeffed of health in effence, forrow in intellection : man, on the contrary, poffeffes his
good but in imagination, his ill in reality. We do well
to deify the powers of our imagination, for all our
wealth is no more than day-dreams. Liften to the
ravings of this calamitous and this miserable being !
" There is nothing," fays Cicero, " fo delightful as
" the purfuit of letters ; I mean of thofe which open
" up to us the immenfity of nature ; reveal to us the
" heights of heaven's majefty ; lay before us, as in a
" map, the earth, the feas, and all that in them is. It
" is they which have taught unto us religion, equity,
" difcipline, fortitude ; difpelled the fhades of darknefs ;
" that which was hid, declared ; above, below, on this
" hand and on that. It is by them that we are taught

Apology for De la Sebonde.

" to well live and happily live ; to pafs away our days,
" void, alike, of difpleafure, of pain, and of offence !"
Would not one think, to hear him thus declaim, that it
was of the Almighty himfelf, the everlafting and the
omnipotent God, that he were haranguing? — As for
the effect, a thoufand poor applewomen have paffed,
in their villages, a life more equable, more undifturbed,
and more affured, than ever did Cicero.

> Deus ille fuit, deus, inclyte Memmi,
> Qui princeps vitæ rationem invenit eam, quæ
> Nunc appellatur fapientia ; quique per artem
> Fluctibus è tantis vitam, tantifque tenebris,
> In tam tranquilla et tam clara luce locavit.

(" Beyond a doubt he was a god, great Memmus, prince of life;
who firft that reafon broached, which now we wifdom call ;
who, by his art, the ftorms of life allayed ; black night difpelled, and broke to glorious day.")

Here are fine words and noble fentences ; yet did a
bit of a mifhap reduce the underftanding of this fame
man to a more degraded condition than that of any
half-witted dizzard, and this, defpite his God of a pre-
ceptor, and all this divine fagacity. [1] With no lefs im-
pudence does Democritus preface his work : " I am
" about to fpeak of all things !" And on a par, is
that prepofterous title which Ariftotle gives us, of
" mortal gods," with the conclufion of Chrysippus

---

[1] See note B B, at the end.

"that Dion was as virtuous as God." And even my Seneca tells us, "That though he may be beholden to "God for his being, he is, to himſelf, for his well-"being;" a ſaying in keeping with this other, "It is "juſtifiable to value ourſelves upon our virtues, which "it were idle to do, if we owed them to God and not "to ourſelves." This alſo is of Seneca: "That the "wiſe man hath a fortitude like unto God's; but ſeeing "that it is lodged in a mortal frailneſs, therein doth he "ſurpaſs him."

There is nothing more common than to meet with ſallies of a like temerity. There is not a man of us who will ſo much bluſh to find himſelf compared unto God, as he will be offended to ſee himſelf depreſſed to the rank of other animals; ſo much more jealous are we of our own ſtanding than of that of our Creator!

But we muſt trample under foot theſe prepoſterous pretentions; we muſt ſhake, to the very foundations, the ridiculous aſſumptions upon which theſe untenable imaginations are baſed. As long as he ſhall think to have any proper and inherent force, independence, never will man conſent to recognize, as he ought, his Maker. His geeſe will ever be ſwans, as the ſaying is: we muſt ſtrip him to his ſkin.   *   *   *   *
*   *   *   And even admitting ſcience, knowledge, to be capable of all they ſay; of blunting, of mitigating the misfortunes which beſet us; what can it be alleged to do, which downright ſtockiſhneſs will

not accomplish in half the time, and much more effectually? Pyrrho, the philosopher, in a storm, as his quantum of consolation, had but to lay his finger on an hog, snoring, at full length, on the deck. It is to the trick of a teamster, or an athlete, that philosophy, as the wind-up of all its talk, is forced to send us; in whom, commonly, we shall perceive a lesser dread of death, a greater aptitude to suffering and privation, more invincible endurance than mere theory will ever enable any among ourselves to attain, if not, in some measure, analogously constituted, or early inured unto hardship. How is it that we can so much more readily perform the most sickening operations on an infant or an animal, than on our grown-up selves; if not by their superior unapprehensiveness? How many, by the mere force of imagination, have been thrown into violent distempers? Do we not, every day, see them blooded, purged and pilled, for remedy to ills which nowhere are to be found, save in their own imaginations? When real calamities are wanting, we eke them out with the help of those of fancy. " This colour, this hue; sure " certainly there is rheum impending:" " so hot a " season, it is impossible but fevers will be abroad:" " something is hanging over you; it is written in the " crossing of the life-line of your palm!" And as if this were not enough, we go, point blank, to the assault of life itself: " This is not the kind of health to last; " the man is bursting with health; blood must be let, "the fyftem lowered, or nature will go pop." Compare the life of fuch a man, tormented with his vapours, his crotchets and his fpleen, with that of a poor one, leaving nature to mind her own bufinefs; taking things as he finds them, without any fort of mifgiving or prognoftication; who is ill when he is on the flat of his back, and not before. I fay, compare with fuch an one, this other, who, as common as not, has the gravel in his brains or ever it has gotten to his bladder. As if it was not time enough to have it there, when it got there, he muft anticipate it in imagination, and make an hafte to its approach. What I have faid of medicine; as much might be afferted of knowledge, generally. * * * In the very beafts we may fee how much the agitation of the fpirits will tend to the impairment of the fyftem. What is told of thofe of Brazil, its natives, how no other death is known among them, fave that of old age; which fome would fain attribute to the ferenity and tranquillity of the air, I would rather place to the ferenity and tranquillity of their fouls; difcharged of all paffion, imagination, occupation, purfuit, wafting or difpleafant; as people paffing their days in an admirable fimplicity and ignorance; ftrangers, alike, to laws, letters, kings, rulers; religion, philofophy. * * * *

* * * * Of what is this moft fubtle folly weaved, but of the moft fubtle wifdom? As of the moft paffionate attachments come the moft paffionate eftrangements; of the moft untroubled health, the

moſt confounding maladies; ſo, of the moſt rare and exquiſite emotions of the ſoul come the moſt tranſcendent follies, and the moſt erratic. There is not the parting of an hair betwixt them. We have but to look upon the lunatic to perceive how ſympathetically folly will lend itſelf to the moſt inordinate operations of the ſoul. Who is there that doth not know, how difficult is it to draw the line between half-hazarded ſcintillations of a free and a witty thinker, and the outburſts of a divine and a ſupernatural enthuſiaſm? Plato tells us, the melancholy are, of all others, the moſt excellent, the eaſieſt to be tamed unto diſcipline; yet are there none of ſo natural a propenſion unto folly. What an infinity of ſpirits have their own proper vehemence, facility, loſt and overthrown! What a declenſion, and all from the very intenſity and exaltation of his temperament, have we not lately ſeen in one of the moſt ingenious and judicious poets of the age; the one who the neareſt approached to the antique and primitive, of any Italian who hath yet appeared? Hath he not now wherewithal to thank himſelf for all this murderous vivacity; this light which hath blinded him; this nice and adapted ſuſceptibility to reaſon which hath deprived him of reaſon; this ſcrupulous and laborious reſearch after knowledge, which hath landed him in imbecility; this extraordinary comprehenſiveneſs of ſoul which hath robbed him of all ſoul; that reſtleſſneſs which now, for ever, is at reſt? It was rather with indignation than commiseration that I saw him, at Florence, in this humiliating condition, surviving his very self; unconscious of himself and of his works; which, unknown to him, yet under his very eyes, had been put to the press, all scribbled and unformed.

Would you see a man in his natural condition; as he ought to be; in a fixed, sure and immoveable firmness? Smother him up in fat, in apathy; bid him be idle and be gross. To be wise, to be men, we must be beasts again; we must be blind or ever we can see. And if it is objected to me, that this stupifying of the spirits, this deadening to care, to sorrow and assault, draws with it this necessary consequence, that it also renders us less susceptible to the endearments, the delights of life; I deny it not. But the misery of our lot is this, that we have not so much to enjoy as to elude; that we are not so much gratified with the highest pleasure, as we are distracted with the lightest pain: the highest health does not so much arrest us, as the lightest trouble. To be well is simply not to be ill. And this is why that sect, which the most deified voluptuousness, came to place supreme felicity in supreme indolence. To be exempted from ill is all the well we have any call to look for below.

* * * * *

Of all others, Christians have a right to know by how much curiosity is the inherent failing and original sin of man. The determination to get to himself wisdom and knowledge, was the firſt downfall of our ſpecies; precipitated it into the abyſs of eternal damnation. Pride is his loſs and his perverſion. It is pride which draws him out of the beaten track; which makes him haſte to, and faſten on newfanglednefs; preferring, rather, to be the leader of a loſt and an erring troop; a wanderer on the road to ruin; to be a teacher, a domine, of madneſs and of lies, than a diſciple in the ſchool of truth, or to allow himſelf to be led by the hand of another, in the broad and beaten path. It may be, that this is the meaning of that old Greek word: " That ſuperſtition followeth in the wake of pride, and " is ſubject to him, as to a father." Ah, knowledge; for how much haſt thou to anſwer!

*   *   *   *   *

Finally, there is nothing conſtant beneath the ſun, either in our own nature, or in the nature which ſurrounds us. Ourſelves, our perceptions, all things mortal, are for ever alterant, chopping and changing about. Hence it comes, that we never can arrive at anything indubitable, either touching them or ourſelves; beholder and beholded being, alike, in a perpetual criſis of metamorphoſe and mutation. We have no acceſs to anything, for all things that be, for ever are in a tranſition ſtate, 'twixt life and death; nor offering, at beſt, but ſome miſerable ſcintillation, ſhadow; ſnatched and uncertain appearance. And if you were to take it into your head to faſten on this or that, it were about as precious a notion as if you would think to grab of ocean in your fift. For the more you would think to gather that which, of its nature, is not to be gathered, the more and the more would it efcape you. So, feeing that all things are interminably occupied in paffing from one ftate into another, reafon, which fancieth, at any moment, to delay a real prefence, difcovers itfelf to be impofed upon; nor is it able to arreft anything permanent or tangible; in as much as all things are either coming into being, and fo, are not yet; or elfe have been, or ever you can fay, Behold! Plato would allow to matter, birth, but not exiftence; and was, farther, of opinion, that Homer had made Ocean the father of the gods, and Thetis mother, to fhow us how all things are in a perpetuity of agitation, tranfmutation, alteration; an opinion, as he tells us, previous to his time, common to all the philofophers, excepting only Parmenides, who refufed to admit of motion, the virtues of which he held in much account. Pythagoras imagined all matter to be reftlefs and flippery; the ftoics, that there was no fuch thing as the paffing moment, and that what we call, Time prefent, is only the foldering of time paft and time coming. Heraclitus infifted that no man ever twice croffed the fame water; Epicharmus, that he who, to-day, is unable to pay the fhot, to-morrow, no longer owes his reckoning; that he who is invited, one day, to a feaft, prefents himfelf, the next, an utter ftranger: they are no longer the fame parties;

and that it was impoffible to find any one mortal thing twice in the like condition. "For, fuch is the inftabi-
"lity and volatility of nature, that now will it diffolve;
"now will it come together again: it is, and it is no
"more. So that nothing of all which begins to be
"ever arrives to all the height of being; in as much
"as this eternal birth is ever occupied on her parturi-
"tion, nor does it for an inftant, come to an head.
"Hence it follows, that from the very hour in which
"we are begotten, all is endlefs change and mutation.
"[1] For even as from a drop is quickened, in the bowels
"of our mother, a lifelefs form; freed from the womb,
"an infant to the breaft to come; anon a lad, then
"a young man; again, one in his prime; too foon in
"his decline; laft fcene of all, inanity and wretched-
"nefs; fo may we fee that every alteration, every fub-
"fequent generation, is at the coft and corruption of
"the precedent. And yet, miferables that we are, we
"ftand fottifhly aghafted at one death, we, who are
"dying daily; we, who have already paffed through fo
"many. For not only, as faid Heraclitus, is the
"extinction of fire the generation of air, of air water;
"but as much is manifefted, as clearly, in ourfelves.
"The flower of our prime withereth and fadeth away,
"as old age creepeth upon us; adolefcence dieth in our
"prime, infancy in adolefcence, the day of our birth in
"the day of our life. Yefterday is dead to this day,

[1] See note C·C, at the end.

" and this day will be engulphed in to-morrow; nor is
" there any one thing which abideth, and which altereth
" not. For, suppofing it to be otherwife; that we are
" always one and the fame; how would it then be,
" that this moment we fhould delight in this object, the
" fucceeding in another: how fhould we then love and
" hate the fame thing, and within an hour; extol and
" defame, things and their oppofites? How is it that
" we have different affections; or that our opinions
" vary upon one and the fame head? For it is not to
" be prefumed, that without fome inward mutation,
" diffimilar affections fhould be evidenced. Now that
" which fuffers mutation is no more the fame, and if it
" is no more the fame, it is no more at all. And fo, as
" the whole man is for ever changing, fo are the
" fucceffive phafes of that man for ever changing;
" ever paffing from one ftate into another ftate. Hence
" of neceffity, it comes, that we are hoaxed and co-
" zened in our apprehenfion of nature and of things,
" confounding that which avows itfelf but in appear-
" ance, with that which really may be; and all this
" from being unable thoroughly to know what actually
" is. What then is that which actually is? That
" which is eternal: which is to fay, which never had
" a beginning, nor ever will know an end; that fuffer-
" eth not, of time, mutation. For time, in itfelf, is
" a thing evanifhing, nor other than a fhadow; of its
" very nature, fleeting and. paffagery; nor fixed, nor

" ftable, nor tied to a place. Before, After, Will be,
" Has been, its very appellatives, carry, on the face
" of them, evidence that no fuch thing can Be, or Is.
" For, were it not monftrous to talk of a thing being
" in Being, which is not yet, or that has already ceafed
" to be! Very now, This inftant, Whilft I fpeak,
" defignations upon which it is apparent that we prin-
" cipally bafe our notions of time; reafon, once brought
" to bear upon them, demolifhes them at a ftroke; re-
" folving the whole into two—time paft and time to
" come; nor admitting of the affumption of a third,
" prefent. Nor is that nature which is meafured in
" any way more favoured than that time which would
" meafure it. For neither is there in her any one
" ftate which continueth, or is eternal: for all things
" are either exiftent, or being ufhered into exiftence,
" or hurried away from exiftence. So that it is infuf-
" ferable to hold of the Deity, who alone Is, that he
" Was, or Will be. For thefe are derogatories, allay-
" ments, abatements; on the very face of them, ad-
" miffive of change and mutation, and confequently,
" but applicable to that which is capable of change and
" of mutation. Wherefore muft we conclude, that
" God alone Is; nor is the exiftence of him to be
" meafured of any time, but of an eternity, eternal, fixed,
" unvanifhing, immutable; that before him nothing was,
" and that after him, nothing will be, or newer or more
" recent: in a word, that he alone is the only *I am*,

"whose eternal *now* is the everlasting *ever*. Nor is there aught, save He alone, but of which it must be said, 'It has been,' or 'It will be;' without beginning and without end."

[1] To this, so pious a conclusion of a pagan man, I will but simply tack this little other, (and it cometh of one of a like condition,) as a wind up to all this long and unconscionable discourse; and which, had I pursued it as far as the matter had led me, peradventure might never have come to a close.—" O, how vile and fallen a thing is man, unexalted above the pitch of his humanity!" A notable saying, truly, and a wholesome wish, yet preposterous withal! For to think to clutch an handfull bigger than the hand, an armfull than the arm; farther to straddle than the legs will stride, were not more monstrous or more ridiculous than for man to say, He would soar above himself or his humanity. He can see but with his eyes, nor can he touch but to what his senses will attain. Yes; he will rise, but it will be when God shall extend to him his divine interposition. He may rise, abandoning and renouncing his own proper endeavours; allowing himself to be raised and supported by an influence pure and heavenly. It is to our Christian faith, and not to this virtue stoic, to aspire to such, so miraculous and divine a metamorphose!

[1] See note D D, at the end.

NOTES

NOTES.

Note A, *page* 2.

IF we would but condefcend to look at the matter difpaffionately, it might, perhaps, a good deal puzzle us to fay, why a fimilitude, is to pafs unchallenged in poetry, which, embodied into a conception in the fifter art of fculpture, is to be pronounced indecorous. The very fame idea is to be found in the book of Job; the fevereft poem which ever was, or probably, ever will be written. See Job, xxxviii. 8.

Note B, *page* 71.

It is a deplorable thing to think, that the following is the only veftige which time has fpared to us, of a fchool or character of literature, apparently of an even more than Pindaric audacity, fire, fublimity and eloquence.

Note C, *page* 77.

St. Denis is a village near Paris, and in the cathedral of which, the ancient monarchs of France were moftly buried. It is here put for France itfelf.

Monjoie St. Denis, was the war cry of the hofts of France, as was *St. George* that of thofe of England.

Note D, page 85.

"Nothing," says M. de St. Pelaye, "can appear more incredible, in our poem, than this vow of the queen of England. Her undertaking to kill herself, with her infant, if she is not allowed to take part in the expedition of the King, is an atrocity which revolts, alike, nature and reason. But the manners of antiquity were ruthless, and such as aroused passions and sentiments which, now-a-days, we should recoil from. In support of this, from many instances which might be cited, I shall give two.

"The pious queen, Margaret, wife to St. Louis, as she was on the point of being brought to bed, at Damietta, learned that the King had just fallen into the hands of the Saracens: which threw her into such an agony, says Joinville, that as soon as ever she would get into her bed, she would start from it afresh, calling out to everyone, *Help; Help!* On this, an old knight, of eighty years of age, and who never for a moment quitted her, would say to her, '*Madame, be under no apprehension; I am with you.*' And as she was on the eve of being delivered, she put everyone out of the room, excepting this old knight; and falling on her knees before him, she told him that she had a favour to crave of him. And when she had made him swear to her to perform it, she said, '*What I have to require of you is this, that should the infidels take this city, you will take my head from my shoulders, sooner than I shall be allowed to fall into their hands.*' To which the old knight replied, '*Madame, it will be a pleasure to me to fulfil your will; for, from the first, I had determined that I would sooner so do, than permit you to fall into their power,*'" &c.

Note E, page 99.

Shakespere, as Burns, was a great *worker up* of kindred and contemporary literature. Nothing almost was too poor or too rich to be turned to account.

"Nymph, in thine orisons be all my sins remembered!"
Hamlet.

Note F, *page* 132.

This tale does not exactly end here; a passage being omitted, which, with great propriety, has been transferred to the notes, in all the more respectable editions of our author. It consists of " a reflection," says an editor, " well worthy of Brantôme, who " would sooner mar this touching and this tragic tale, than lose " an occasion for the display of his miserable facetiousness; and " assuredly much fitter calculated to adorn the pages of his ' Easy " ' Ladies ' than his Incidents of Duelling." Brantôme seems to have had a strong touch of that inherent filthiness and loathsomeness of mind which characterized the famous dean of St. Patrick's. Swift had none of Brantôme's grace, voluptuousness; Brantôme had none of Swift's virtues.

Note G, *page* 135.

Most unquestionably it was the *extraction royal* which carried the day. This great statesman; one of the greatest, if not the greatest that ever lived, was most miserably accessible on the score of family. Lafond, his valet-de-chambre, clearly knew his weak side.

Note H, *page* 187.

Henry and our Elizabeth, were, most assuredly, two of the greatest princes which sat upon their respective thrones, or ever reigned. They had much that was in common; in fact, almost every thing which their relative positions, careers, and sexes would permit to be so. Side by side with this noble speech, I have placed the famous *golden one* of Elizabeth: the last which she ever delivered to her faithful commons.

" Mr. Speaker. We perceive your coming is to present thanks unto us. Know I accept them with no less joy than your loves can have desire to offer such a present, and do more esteem it than any treasure or riches; for those we know how to prize; but loyalty, love and thanks, I account them invaluable; and though God hath raised me high, yet this I account the glory of my crown, that I have reigned with your loves. This makes that I do not so much rejoice that God has made me to be a queen, as to be a queen over so thankful a people, and to be the means under God to conserve you in safety, and preserve you from danger; yea, to be the instrument to deliver you from dishonour, from shame and from infamy, to keep you from out of servitude, and from slavery under our enemies, and cruel tyranny, and vile oppression intended against us; for the better withstanding whereof, we take very acceptable their intended helps, and chiefly in that it manifesteth your loves and largeness of hearts to your sovereign. Of myself I must say this, I never was any greedy, scraping grasper, nor a strict fast-holding prince, nor yet a waster; my heart was never set upon any worldly goods, but only for my subjects' good. What you do bestow on me I will not hoard up, but receive it to bestow on you again; yea, mine own properties I account yours, to be expended for your good, and your eyes shall see the bestowing of it for your welfare.

Mr. Speaker, I would wish you and the rest to stand up, for I fear I shall yet trouble you with longer speech.

Mr. Speaker, you give me thanks, but I am more to thank you, and I charge you thank them of the Lower House from me; for had I not received knowledge from you, I might a' fallen into the lapse of an error, only for want of true information.

Since I was queen, yet did I never put my pen to any grant but upon pretext and semblance made me, that it was for the good and avail of my subjects generally, though a private profit to some of my ancient servants, who have deserved well; but that my grants shall be made grievances to my people, and oppressions, to be privileged under colour of our patents, our princely dignity shall not suffer it.

When I heard it, I could give no rest unto my thoughts until I had reformed it, and those varlets, lewd persons, abusers of my bounty, shall know I will not suffer it. And, Mr. Speaker, tell the House from me, I take it exceeding grateful, that the knowledge of these things are come unto me from them. And though amongst them the principal members are such as are not touched in private, and therefore need not speak from any feeling of the grief, yet we have heard that other gentlemen also of the House, who stand as free, have spoken as freely in it; which gives us to know, that no respects or interests have moved them other than the minds they bear to suffer no diminution of our honour and our subjects' love unto us. The zeal of which affection tending to ease my people, and knit their hearts unto us, I embrace with a princely care far above all earthly treasures. I esteem my people's love, more than which I desire not to merit: and God, that gave me here to sit, and placed me over you, knows, that I never respected myself, but as your good was conserved in me; yet what dangers, what practices, and what perils I have passed, some, if not all of you, know; but none of these things do move me, or ever made me fear, but it is God that hath delivered me.

And in my governing this land, I have ever set the last judgment-day before mine eyes, and so to rule as I shall be judged and answer before a higher Judge, to whose judgment-seat I do appeal: in that never thought was cherished in my heart that tended not to my people's good.

And if my princely bounty have been abused, and my grants turned to the hurt of my people, contrary to my will and meaning, or if any in authority under me have neglected, or converted what I have committed unto them, I hope God will not lay their culps to my charge.

To be a king, and wear a crown, is a thing more glorious to them that see it than it is pleasant to them that bear it: for myself, I never was so enticed with the glorious name of a king, or the royal authority of a queen, as delighted that God had made me his instrument to maintain his truth and glory, and to defend this kingdom from dishonour, damage, tyranny and oppression. But should I ascribe any of these things to myself or my sexly weakness, I were not worthy to live, and of all most unworthy of the mercies I have received at God's hands; but to God only and wholly all is given and ascribed.

The cares and troubles of a crown I cannot more fitly resemble than to the drugs of a learned physician, perfumed with some aromatical savour, or to bitter pills gilded over, by which they are rendered more acceptable or less offensive, which indeed are bitter and unpleasant to take; and for my own part, were it not for conscience sake, to discharge the duty that God hath laid upon me, and to maintain his glory, and keep you in safety, in my own difpofition I fhould be willing to refign the place I hold to any other, and glad to be freed of the glory with the labour, for it is not my defire to live nor to reign longer than my life and reign fhall be for your good. And though you have had, and may have, many mightier and wifer princes fitting in this feat, yet you never had, nor fhall have any that will love you better.

Thus, Mr. Speaker, I commend me to your loyal loves, and yours to my beft care and your farther counfels; and I pray you, Mr. Controuler and Mr. Secretary, and you of my council, that before thefe gentlemen depart to their counties, you bring them all to kifs my hand."—*Ld. Somers' Tracts.*

Note I, *page* 199.

It is hardly neceffary to recall, that Henry had been brought up in the proteftant, or Huguenot faith; which, however, from political confiderations, he was induced to abandon.

Note J, *page* 226.

In the paraphrafe of Chaucer, one or two beautiful verfes occur, about this part:

> " O ftormy peple, unfad and ever untrewe,
> And undifcrete, and changing as a fane;
> Delighting ever in rombel that is newe;
> For like the mone waxen ye and wane!
> Ay full of clapping, dere ynough a jane;
> Your dome is fals, your conftance evil preveth,
> A ful gret fool is he that in ye leveth!"

> " O ftormy people; unfad and ever untrue;
> And indifcreet, and changing as the fane *;
> Delighting ever in rumour that is new:
> E'en as the moon, ye waxen and ye wane!
> Aye full of clack; to win ye were a pain:
> Your judgment's falfe; your conftancy the wind;
> As he who trufts you to his coft will find!"

* Weathercock.

Note **K**, *page* 243.

How curious is it to contraſt the account of plain, honeſt Pitſcottie, with that of this ſplendid, blazeed, voluptuous, worthleſs *roué* of a Frenchman!

He ſays, " In the meantyme the queine maid her entres in " Edinburgh as the lyk was not ſeine a befoir, ſhoe was ſo gorge- " ouſlie and magnificientlie receaved ; " &c.

Note **L**, *page* 267.

For the credit of this reſpectable young lady's mamma, it may be as well to ſtate, what may not, poſſibly, be known to all ; that *Mademoiſelle* was originally the appellative of a married woman whoſe huſband's rank was beneath that of a noble, yet above that of a burgeſs ; as well as that of a maid.

Note **M**, *page* 285.

The family of *Landry* was one of great antiquity. A very curious anecdote of one of them, who lived in the ſixth century, occurs in " A Mirrour or Looking-Glaſſe both for *Saints*, and *Sinners*, &c. &c. By *Sa. Clark*, Paſtor in *Bennet Fink*. The Second Edition. London. 1654."

" In *France* there was one *Fredegundis*, a famous * * * * * who for her beauty was entertained by *Chilperic* King of *France*, whom ſhe cauſed to baniſh his Queen *Andovera*, and his other wife called *Galſuinda* ſhe cauſed to be murthered, that ſhe might enjoy the King alone: yet neither was ſhe faithful to him, but proſtituted her body to *Landric*, Maſter of the King's horſe. On a time the King being to go a hunting, went to bid his wife farewell, who was combing her haire : The King went ſoftly behinde her, and with his wand in ſport ſtruck her behinde : She thinking it had been her *Landric*, ſaid : *What doeſt thou do, my* Landric ? *It's the part of a good Knight to charge a Lady before, and not behinde :* The King by this means finding her falſhood, went his wayes on hunting, and ſhe finding herſelf diſcovered, ſent for *Landric :* told him what was happened, and therefore perſwaded him to kill the King for his, and her ſafety: which he undertook, and effected that night as the King came late from hunting."—*French Hiſt.*

Note **N**, *page* 287.

The extraordinary temperance which prevailed, during at leaſt a conſiderable portion of the middle ages, may, poſſibly, have been a good deal owing to the actual ſcarcity of proviſions, as the earlier nakedneſs to want of manufactures. Holinſhed, who lived in Elizabeth's time, in his moſt curious chronicles, tells us, " how
" theſe od repaſts, thanked be God, are verie well left, and ech
" one, in manner, (except, here and there, ſome young hungrie
" ſtomach, that cannot faſt till dinner-time,) contenteth himſelf
" with dinner and ſupper onelie. The Normans, miſliking the
" gormandiſe of *Canutus*, ordeired after their arrivall, that no
" table ſhould be covered above once in a daie, which *Huntingdon*
" imputeth to their avarice: but in the end, either waxing wearie
" of their oune frugalitie, or ſuffering the cockle of old cuſtom to
" overgrow the good corne of their new conſtitution, they fell to
" ſuch libertie, that in often feeding, they ſurmounted *Canutus*,
" ſurnamed the hardie.* * * For my part, I am perſuaded,
" that the purpoſe of the Normans, at the firſt, was to reduce the
" ancient Roman order, or Daniſh cuſtom, in feeding once in a
" day, as I have read and noted.* * * With us, the nobilitie,
" gentrie and ſtudents, doo ordinarilie go to dinner at eleven
" before noone, and to ſupper at five, or betweene five and ſix at
" afternoon. The merchants dine and ſup ſeldome before twelve
" at noone, and ſix at night, eſpeciallie in London. The huſband-
" men dine at high noone, as they call it, and ſup at ſeven or
" eight: but out of the tearme in our univerſities, the ſcholars
" dine at ten. As to the pooreſt ſort, they generallie dine and
" ſup when they may, ſo that to talk of their order or repaſt, it
" were but a needleſſe matter."

Note **O**, *page* 290.

In an admirable and contemporary, though ſomewhat careleſs tranſlation, preſerved, in manuſcript, in the Britiſh Muſeum, the elements are rendered, " her favioure." They were, for the moft part, I believe, thus called, or fimply, *The Lord*. The paffage ftands thus; *Sy cuidoit tranfir de la mort, et fe fift apporter beau fire Dieux*. *Beau fire Dieux*, is, literally, Fair Sir God. *Beau*, fair, was an honorary, I fancy, feldom or never ufed, except to, or by the royal family. *Beau Sire roi*, Fair Sir King; *Beau fils*, Fair fon; *Bel oncle, Beau neveu*, Fair uncle; Fair nephew; are everywhere met with.

In fo extraordinary a manner had the principles of chivalry become engrafted upon thofe of religion, that it is no uncommon thing to find apoftles and faints figuring in the ranks of the nobility. Froiffart, having occafion to fpeak of the fhrine of St. James of Compoftello, mentions it as that of "the *baron* " St. James!" As much will be feen prefently in de Commines.

Note P, page 300.

It had been mutually agreed, between the French king, Philip Auguftus, and Richard, that neither fhould moleft the other's dominions, during the continuance of their common endeavour for the recovery of the holy fepulchre.

Note Q, page 300.

The infatuation of the times is fomething almoft beyond conception. One favage of a fellow coolly tells the barons, "*That*
" *hell will be the portion of the man who refufes to draw his*
" *fword in the caufe of Chrift* ;" and that if they fall, all that they have to do is to tell God, "*That he did no more, in dying for them,*
" *than they did in dying for him! !*" Another crackbrained enthufiaft tells them "that he can only confent to look on him as a true
" knight, who will go of his own free will, and without grudging,
" *to the fuccour of God, who is in fuch extremity* ;" continuing,
" Do you think, fcoundrel barons, *that you can expect God to ftand*
" *by you, if you refufe to ftand by him* ? Do you know, that it
" was for you that he died upon the crofs? I will fay no more
" than this, If you do not, this day, affume the crofs; you forfeit,
" for ever, the benefit of his fufferings!"

Note **R,** *page* 310.

As I have not been able to examine, with any attention, this famous and interminable romance, I am obliged to risk one or two passages; which, confcientiously to give, would require the perufal of the whole affair.

Fundateur du franc palais, which I have here rendered, "founder of the open hall," I fear, is not the thing. A legift could probably fuggeft fomething much more to the point. There is no Englifh tranflation, nor do I believe that there are above half a dozen copies in exiftence; which is very fad. The author was almoft certainly an Englifhman: the prevalence of Englifh words attefts as much. It belongs to the beginning of the 16th century.

I will take this occafion of ftating fome few rules which I laid down to myfelf in making thefe tranflations. 1ft. To be as fparing as poffible of the introduction of obfolete or unufual words. Indeed, I can only recall one, *ingyne,* (wit), in the whole of them. Wifhing to avoid the charge of affectation, on the one part; I fear that I have laid myfelf open to that of negligence upon the other. For it is clear, that if the old-fafhioned mortals, heavy weights and flow coaches, like myfelf; men who find themfelves completely diftanced in the race of life, in thefe faft times of periodicals and newfpapers, will not be at the pains to pick up the good old Saxon words which are being daily voted too lumberfome to be carried any farther; in another generation or two, they will have been completely trodden under foot, and be no longer to be recognized. In no place could they appear to fo much advantage, or tafte, as in fuch a work as this; or would the public be more readily reconciled to them. It were like putting old embroidery upon an old garment.

Another rule was, as much as poffible to employ words at their *actual* fignification; yet occafionally to attempt to *recover cafte* for a good old word which now has loft it.

As my chief aim has been to reproduce the *fpirit* of thefe old worthies, I have, fometimes on purpofe, other times through downright careleffnefs, deliberately broken the fentences in two; commencing the fecond with a *relative*. It is occafionally very hard to avoid this; such is the slovenliness and construction of these writings.

The general reader it may be necessary to inform, that he is not to look for any sort of method, consistency or accuracy in these old worthies. I mention this, as I do not wish to have their garrulity, iterations, anachronisms, ramblings, placed to my account. Even Sully, at times, is anything but clear in his statements.

Finally, I have endeavoured, as much as possible, to steer clear of all that quaintness, mannerism, which so sadly pervaded so much of the contemporary English literature; an end, none of the easiest, in such a case, to effect. For, a man who has muddled away so much of his life as I have, among old books, will, I am afraid, consciously or unconsciously, be betrayed into some sort of affectation, confusion, nonsense, conceit, or another.

Note **S**, *page* 323.

It has often been observed, that the religion of a nation, or its sacred literature, is a very false standard whereby to gauge the national intelligence. To judge of the literary pretensions of what we call, *The darken ages*, we must look elsewhere than to the "mysteries" and "moralities." The church of Rome is as clearly answerable for them as for the Crusades. *All* ages both *are*, and *become* darken ages. Could we but *get back to them*, I much question if we should not find as much light to have been then as now. This piece, which is merely given as a literary curiosity, is anterior to the "mysteries;" yet, I am sure, such miserable slang, banter may be heard, any day, from the clowns, at our lower theatres or circuses. M. Le Grand has given us the pastoral of the "Shepherd and the Shepherdess," which is of the same epoch, yet clearly *must* have been written early in the decay and decline of an highly polished and probably nervous, literature. It evidences all the exquisite moral purity, delicacy, tenderness, to which, let me add, *namby pamby*, of a Rowe, a Shenstone. There is nothing either natural, or pastoral, or primitive about it.

I think we greatly exaggerate the distraction of the middle ages, and that they were much more favourable to literary culture than we at all imagine. Literature, affuredly, there muft have been, and of an high order, all through. I much queftion if Atilla, and all his Huns, ever played a greater amount of mifchief with the world, than the firft Napoleon did; yet what a very *pop gun* was the whole affair, once over? Diftance lends as well exaggeration, as "enchantment" to the fcene. Some of the greateft names in Englifh literature, Clarendon, Cowley, Taylor, Milton, Dryden, Walton, Ufher, flourifhed in the moft diftracted times that this country ever knew. In fact, in many refpects, they are even favourable to literary purfuit.

The following piece, *The Crufades*, M. Le Grand fuppofes to have been written at the inftigation of the queen and minifters of St. Louis, to diffuade him from the vifionary attempt which he was meditating toward the recovery of the Holy Land. I do not fee how, even at this day, anything much more to the purpofe could have been elicited. It is at once farcaftic, courteous, artful, fuggeftive.

Note T, page 360.

According to tradition, by the orders of this inhuman tyrant, the children of the Duke de Nemours were placed, in their fhirts, under the fcaffold where their father was beheaded, fo that they might be covered with his blood.

Note U, page 381.

It is to the infpiration of this moft magnificent chapter, and to which I am afhamed to fay, I have done fo poor a juftice, that we are indebted for one of the moft gorgeous paffages in Englifh literature—the opening pages of the "Holy Dying."

Note V, page 381.

As the majority of the Latin quotations are clearly of the nature of notes or references; the fubftance being embodied into the text; and as they fadly allay the heat and vehemence with which thefe magnificent pages fhould be read, I have moftly fuppreffed them. Of courfe, in a regular tranflation, this could not be: they fhould then appear as notes. They are chiefly from

Lucretius, Manilius, and the more solemn, weightier, sublimer of the ancient poets, fathers, and philosophers.

Note W, page 390.

"*Les plus mortes morts sont les plus saines:*" *Most dead is best dead.* I cannot at all agree with the interpretation placed by Mr. Hazlitt, in common with the French commentators, on this passage. "Death," says Mr. Hazlitt, "is here considered as the introduction and actual passage to a state of insensibility which puts a period to our life. The more silently and rapidly we arrive to that state the less ought the passage to terrify us. This comes up very near to the import of that bold and enigmatical expression of Montaigne, viz. 'That the deadest deaths are the best.'" I would rather conceive his meaning to be this; That that death is roundest, fullest, *which takes most with it*; which closes up as well the legitimate offices of life, as life itself.

Note X, page 397.

Much of the following, as to manner, may have been suggested by that beautiful chapter in "Boethius on Consolation," wherein "*Fortune showeth, that shee hath taken nothing from Boethius, that was his.*"

"But I would urge thee a little with Fortune's owne speeches. Wherefore consider thou, if shee asketh not reason. For what cause, O man, chargest thou mee with daily complaints? What injurie have I done thee? What goods of thine have I taken from thee? Contend with me before any Judge, about the possession of riches and dignities: and if thou canst show, that the propriety of any of these things belong to any mortal wight, I will foorthwith willingly graunt, that those things which thou demandest, were thine. When nature produced thee out of thy mother's wombe, I received thee naked and poore in all respects, cheerished thee with my wealth, and (which maketh thee now to fall out with me (being forward to favour thee, I had most tender care for thy education, and adorned thee with aboundance and splendour of all things, which are in my power. Now it pleaseth mee to withdraw my hand, yeeld thankes, as one that hath had the ufe of that which was not his owne. Thou haſt no juſt caufe to complaine, as though thou hadſt loſt that which was fully thine owne. Wherefore lamenteſt thou? I have offered thee no violence. Riches, honours, and the reſt of that fort belong to mee. They acknowledge mee for their Miſtreſſe, and themfelves for my fervants; they come with me, and when I goe away, they likewife depart. I may boldly affirme, if thofe things which thou complaineſt to be taken from thee, had beene thine owne, thou ſhouldeſt never have loſt them. Muſt I onely be forbidden to ufe my right? It is lawful for the heaven to bring foorth faire dayes, and to hide them againe in darkefome nights. It is lawfull for the yeere fometime to compaſſe the face of the earth with flowers and fruites, and fometime to cover it with clouds and cold. The·Sea hath right fometime to faune with calmes, and fometime to frowne with ſtormes and waves. And ſhall the unfatiable defire of men tie me to conſtancie, fo contrarie to my cuſtome? This is my force, this is the fport which I continually ufe. I turn about my wheele with fpeed, and take a pleafure to turne things upfide doune; Afcend, if thou wilt, but with this condition, that thou thinkeſt it not an injurie to defcend, when the courfe of my fport fo requireth. Diddeſt thou not know my faſhion? Wert thou ignorant how *Crœfus* King of the *Lydians*, not long before a terrour to *Cyrus*, within a while after came to fuch miferie, that he would have beene burnt, had he not beene faved by a ſhower fent from heaven? Haſt thou forgotten how Paul (Paulus) pyoufly bewailed the calamities of King Perfus his prifoner? What other thing doeth the outcrie of Tragedie's lament, but that fortune, having no refpect, overturneth happie ſtates? Diddeſt thou not learne in thy youthe, that there lay two barrels, th' one of good things, and the other of bad, at *Jupiter's* threſhold? But what if thou haſt taſted more abundantly of the good? What if I be not wholly gone from thee? What if this mutabilitie of mine be a juſt caufe for thee to hope for better? Notwithſtanding lofe not thy courage, and living in a Kingdome which is common to all men, defire not to be governed by peculiar Laws, proper onely to thyfelfe."

     BOETHIUS—*Philofophicall Comfort.* (*Ed.* 1609.)

Note Y, *page* 403.

Montaigne was not the only one of the leading catholic minds who feemed clearly to have forefeen, and foretold the great French revolution. *Beyond it*, they do not appear to have looked. Though, indeed, it is queftionable whether France and the world have not as much to thank Montaigne himfelf, as Luther, for that cataftrophe; if, *in the long run*, it was one, which remains yet to be feen.

Note Z, *page* 408.

No one who has ever waded through that moft tedious of all hiftories, *The hiftory of the World*, by Raleigh; but redeemed by fome of the nobleft paffages in Englifh literature, can have forgotten the beautiful vindication of the *heavenly influences*. But, to vindicate the "influence" of *Montaigne*, would be to write the hiftory of modern literature. No man, probably, excepting, perhaps, Ariftotle, ever more powerfully, filently, unpretendingly, wielded, attracted, or directed the minds of men. That Raleigh had this paffage of Montaigne's in his eye, when penning it, I think is evident. It is curious to obferve, how much more paffionately Montaigne abandons and *lends himself* (for, in his *harder* moments, he muft have feen the matter as Raleigh did) to fo enchanting, fo poetic an illufion, than did the other; how much more touchingly he pleads for it.

Note AA, *page* 413.

I have often thought, that what Montaigne fays of Plato, "that he was but a fort of loofe, or unripped poet," might, with no lefs propriety, be faid of our great Bacon; the whole key to whofe character might be given in two words — *A legal head; a poetical, a fanguine temperament.* How he could ever come to attach the importance that he did to his writings, I cannot diftinctly underftand; or yet again, how he could fancy that his philofophy had never occurred to any other man than himfelf. In fact, the whole pith and marrow of what we call, *The Baconian philofophy*, is concentrated in the two following paffages. And how deeply

Bacon was indebted to Montaigne, thofe fkilled in *mental chemiftry* will have little difficulty in perceiving. Methinks, there was much good fenfe in honeft Sir Thomas Bodley's verdict on the Inftauration; nor do I believe, had Bacon never been fo much as born, that it would have retarded the opening of the Liverpool and Manchefter railway by four and twenty hours. *The lofs had been to letters, not to phyfics or fcience.* It is Manchefter and Birmingham, not Oxford and Cambridge, that have called into being the nineteenth century; it is men who knew little of, and cared lefs for, either Bacon or his philofophy. It may be faid, that he gave the deathblow to *Ariftotling* and dogmatifm. This is a miftake. It would have been given without him. What he fhowed the *folly* of; thefe rough, hardheaded men fhowed the *impracticability* of. Why, fimply to *regifter*, not to fay, *claffify* the inventions and difcoveries of the laft hundred years, would require the intelligence of a dozen Ariftotles, or the lifetimes of as many Methufelahs. Let *fcience* once get to the end of its tether, as *contemplation* had of its, in the time of Ariftotle, and Ariftotles will be as plenty as blackberries; whilft in ethics, divinity, metaphyfics, Ariftotles, or their like, are as rampant among us, at this day, as ever they were in thofe of Bacon.

The beauty, richnefs, grace, fublimity of Bacon's mind and temperament, it would be literally impoffible to overrate. His perceptive powers were prodigious; yet, for all that, I cannot allow his mind to have been of anything like the *originality* which he took it to be. He could fee, and take in, everything that was before him; but what was *not* before him, fo to fpeak, he could not fee. In a word, he was not an inventor in philofophy, in the fame fenfe that Galileo, Newton, Archimedes were inventors in phyfics.

Note BB, *page* 427.

Bacon may blefs his ftars that he has efcaped the honour of figuring in this catalogue of *infufferables*. How Montaigne would have chuckled, could he but have feen " *The greateft birth of time,*" or the letter addreffed by that promifing young gentleman to his uncle, Burleigh, wherein he tells him, "that he has taken all knowledge to be his providence," (province!) a moſt unaccountable piece of preſumption, or rather naïveté, on the part of a man of ſo much cloſeneſs and warineſs, and which muſt have infinitely difguſted, and injured him with the Cecils. Surely, a very little conſideration might have taught him, that the very *want* of thoſe almoſt ſuperhuman powers of perception, the poſſeſſion of which enabled him to perceive by how much he towered above the reſt of mankind, muſt have prevented them, no leſs, from ſeeing the ſame. Had Burleigh, or had any other man, ſeen all that there was in Bacon, then would he have ſeen *all that Bacon ſaw*; in which caſe we ſhould have had *two* " Inſtaurations;" *two* prophets of the 16th century.

I know not whether is to me more bewitching; the goodnatured, half unconſcious, ſelfcomplacency and egotiſm of a Bacon, a Hobbes, a Montaigne; or the downright, brutal, ſavage vindictiveneſs and predominance of a Milton. All, in their way, are equally in character, and to be admired. All that arrogance, inſolence, defiance, which is ſo graceful in the mouth of an haughty, a tempeſtuous, an earneſt, and a burning ſpirit, would come with a very poor figure from a man of Bacon's conſtitutional timidity, dignity and ſublimity of temperament.

Note CC, *page* 435.

We have here Shakeſpere's " ſeven ages of man."

Note DD, *page* 438.

Plutarch.

www.ingramcontent.com/pod-product-compliance
Lightning Source LLC
Chambersburg PA
CBHW031954300426
44117CB00008B/761